PostgreSQL 13 Cook

Over 120 recipes to build high-performance and fault-tolerant
PostgreSQL database solutions

Vallarapu Naga Avinash Kumar

PostgreSQL 13 Cookbook

Group Product Manager: Kunal Parikh
Publishing Product Manager: Mrinmayee Kawalkar
Senior Editor: Roshan Kumar
Content Development Editor: Joseph Sunil
Technical Editor: Arjun Varma
Copy Editor: Safis Editing
Project Coordinator: Aishwarya Mohan
Proofreader: Safis Editing
Indexer: Tejal Soni
Production Designer: Aparna Bhagat

First published: February 2021

Production reference: 1250221

Published by Packt Publishing Ltd.
Livery Place
35 Livery Street
Birmingham
B3 2PB, UK.

ISBN 978-1-83864-813-8

www.packt.com

Contributors

About the author

Vallarapu Naga Avinash Kumar (Avi) is the CEO and co-founder of MigOps Inc, a company focused on migrations to open source databases such as PostgreSQL. Before co-founding MigOps, Avi worked as a PostgreSQL tech lead for global services at Percona, as a database architect at OpenSCG for 2 years, and as a DBA lead at Dell for 10 years in database technologies such as PostgreSQL, Oracle, MySQL, and MongoDB. He has given several talks and training on PostgreSQL. He has good experience in performing architectural health checks, performance tuning, and migrations to PostgreSQL environments. He has also co-authored a book – *Beginning PostgreSQL on the Cloud* – which gives an introduction to building PostgreSQL on the AWS, Microsoft Azure, Google Cloud, and Rackspace cloud platforms. He has been a speaker at several PostgreSQL conferences in North America, Europe, and Asia for many years and continues to blog about PostgreSQL.

About the reviewers

Marcelo Diaz is a software engineer with more than 15 years of experience, and with a special focus on PostgreSQL. He is passionate about open source software and has promoted its application in critical and high-demand environments where he has worked as a software developer and consultant for both private and public companies. He currently works very happily at Cybertec and as a technical reviewer for Packt Publishing. He enjoys spending his leisure time with his daughter, Malvina, and his wife, Romina. He also likes playing football.

Sandeep Purbiya has a bachelor's degree in the field of computer science from Shivaji University, India. He has over two decades of experience in software product design, development, and delivery. He has worked with start-ups as well as large software product organizations. He is a full stack developer and has designed and developed applications using Java, JDBC, JavaScript, microservices, and databases such as Oracle, MySQL, MSSQL, and Postgres. In his free time, he likes to read about new tools and technologies, build prototypes to gain knowledge, and experience and enjoy life with family and friends.

Table of Contents

Preface

PostgreSQL has become the most advanced open source database on the market. This book follows a step-by-step approach to guide you effectively in deploying PostgreSQL in production environments.

The book starts with an introduction to PostgreSQL and its architecture. You'll cover common and not-so-common challenges faced while designing and managing a database. Next, the book focuses on backup and recovery strategies to ensure your database is steady and achieves optimal performance. Throughout the book, we'll address key challenges such as maintaining reliability, data integrity, a fault-tolerant environment, a robust feature set, extensibility, consistency, and authentication. Moving ahead, you'll learn how to manage a PostgreSQL cluster and explore replication features for high availability. Later chapters will assist you in building a secure PostgreSQL server, along with covering recipes for encrypting data in motion and data at rest. Finally, you'll not only discover how to tune your database for optimal performance but also understand ways to monitor and manage maintenance activities, before learning how to perform PostgreSQL upgrades during downtime.

By the end of this book, you'll be well-versed in the essential PostgreSQL 13 features that are needed to build enterprise relational databases.

Who this book is for

This PostgreSQL book is for database architects, database developers, and administrators, or anyone who wants to become well-versed in PostgreSQL 13 features in order to plan, manage, and design efficient database solutions. Prior experience with the PostgreSQL database and SQL language is expected.

What this book covers

Chapter 1, *Cluster Management Fundamentals*, starts by showing how to install PostgreSQL 13 and initializing a data directory. We will then discuss pg_ctl and how it can be used to start and stop a PostgreSQL cluster.

Chapter 2, *Cluster Management Techniques*, helps you get familiar with some of the important routine tasks in PostgreSQL.

Chapter 3, *Backup and Recovery*, shows you several methods available to back up and restore a PostgreSQL database.

Chapter 4, *Advanced Replication Techniques*, teaches you how to configure both streaming and logical replication, and you'll learn about some more crucial tasks in a production database environment.

Chapter 5, *High Availability and Automatic Failover*, discusses one of the most heavily adopted open source high-availability tools available, called Patroni. It can be used to set up automatic failover. We shall learn how it can be configured and will also discuss the advantages and disadvantages of using it for high availability.

Chapter 6, *Connection Pooling and Load Balancing*, discusses pgBouncer, which is a widely implemented, lightweight external pooler.

Chapter 7, *Securing through Authentication*, teaches you how to secure PostgreSQL encryption through authentication, authorization, and auditing. You will also see how to encrypt connections over the wire and also at rest using SSL. We will also look at some extensions for performing auditing in PostgreSQL

Chapter 8, *Logging and Analyzing PostgreSQL Servers*, has been designed to let admins know of the available options in PostgreSQL to enable the logging of certain important activities and to help admins/developers get familiar with some views, extensions, and tools to analyze live and historic activity in Postgres catalogs and log files.

Chapter 9, *Critical Services Monitoring*, shows how we can set up the monitoring of servers using Grafana and Prometheus.

Chapter 10, *Extensions and Performance Tuning*, shows us what extensions are and examines some of the most commonly used extensions for routine maintenance activities. We will also discuss some of the extensions that are helpful in many of the more important activities performed by an administrator or developer.

Chapter 11, *Upgrades and Patches*, shows us the various upgrade paths for PostgreSQL and how to implement them.

To get the most out of this book

You will need a virtual machine with either the CentOS/Red Hat or Debian/Ubuntu families of operating systems installed on it. This server must be able to connect to the internet to download the packages required to install PostgreSQL 13.

Software/hardware covered in the book	OS requirements
PostgreSQL 13	Linux

If you are using the digital version of this book, we advise you to type the code yourself or access the code via the GitHub repository (link available in the next section). Doing so will help you avoid any potential errors related to the copying and pasting of code.

Download the color images

We also provide a PDF file that has color images of the screenshots/diagrams used in this book. You can download it here: `https://static.packt-cdn.com/downloads/9781838648138_ColorImages.pdf`

Conventions used

There are a number of text conventions used throughout this book.

`CodeInText`: Indicates code words in text, database table names, folder names, filenames, file extensions, pathnames, dummy URLs, user input, and Twitter handles. Here is an example: "So, it is always recommended to add the directory to `PATH` for ease."

A block of code is set as follows:

```
# yum install -y postgresql13-server

-- To need contrib for the extensions, install postgresql13-contrib as well
# yum install -y postgresql13-server postgresql13-contrib
```

Bold: Indicates a new term, an important word, or words that you see onscreen. For example, words in menus or dialog boxes appear in the text like this. Here is an example: "**PGDG** stands for the **PostgreSQL Global Development Group**."

Warnings or important notes appear like this.

 Tips and tricks appear like this.

Sections

In this book, you will find several headings that appear frequently (*Getting ready, How to do it..., How it works..., There's more...,* and *See also*).

To give clear instructions on how to complete a recipe, use these sections as follows:

Getting ready

This section tells you what to expect in the recipe and describes how to set up any software or any preliminary settings required for the recipe.

How to do it...

This section contains the steps required to follow the recipe.

How it works...

This section usually consists of a detailed explanation of what happened in the previous section.

There's more...

This section consists of additional information about the recipe in order to make you more knowledgeable about the recipe.

See also

This section provides helpful links to other useful information for the recipe.

Get in touch

Feedback from our readers is always welcome.

General feedback: If you have questions about any aspect of this book, mention the book title in the subject of your message and email us at customercare@packtpub.com.

Errata: Although we have taken every care to ensure the accuracy of our content, mistakes do happen. If you have found a mistake in this book, we would be grateful if you would report this to us. Please visit www.packtpub.com/support/errata, selecting your book, clicking on the Errata Submission Form link, and entering the details.

Piracy: If you come across any illegal copies of our works in any form on the Internet, we would be grateful if you would provide us with the location address or website name. Please contact us at copyright@packt.com with a link to the material.

If you are interested in becoming an author: If there is a topic that you have expertise in and you are interested in either writing or contributing to a book, please visit authors.packtpub.com.

Reviews

Please leave a review. Once you have read and used this book, why not leave a review on the site that you purchased it from? Potential readers can then see and use your unbiased opinion to make purchase decisions, we at Packt can understand what you think about our products, and our authors can see your feedback on their book. Thank you!

For more information about Packt, please visit packt.com.

1
Cluster Management Fundamentals

PostgreSQL is one of the most advanced and widely used open-source databases that is growing in popularity every year. While it is a relational database similar to Oracle, MySQL, or SQL Server databases, its JSON features make it stand out from some of the most widely used NoSQL databases. While it makes PostgreSQL unique in the database world, several of its techniques work slightly differently from those of other relational databases, such as MVCC implementation.

In this chapter, we shall start by learning how to install PostgreSQL 13 and initializing a data directory. We will then discuss `pg_ctl` and how it can be used to start and stop a PostgreSQL cluster.

We will then move on to discussing various shutdown modes available in PostgreSQL. After getting familiar with start and shutdown, we will discuss all the directories, sub-directories, and configuration files inside a data directory. After discussing the data directory in detail, we will look at the steps involved in modifying the default location of WAL segments that are stored in a data directory by default.

We will then discuss how `psql` can be helpful for performing a lot of activities using several shortcuts. We will also get familiar with some of the catalogs that are helpful in daily admin life.

The performance of a database may be dependent on its SQL traffic. At the same time, it is also dependent on the resources that have been allocated to the database through several configuration parameters. For example, the total number of concurrent connections to a PostgreSQL cluster can be configured through the `max_connections` parameter. The default value set to this parameter, such as 100, may not be appropriate for all the millions of applications connecting to PostgreSQL databases today. So, we need to modify this parameter, depending on the estimated concurrent traffic.

Sometimes, it will be challenging for beginners or admins to locate the configuration file of Postgres. Due to this, we will discuss how a Postgres configuration file can be located and how to modify a parameter, and then discuss the community-recommended best practices for modifying one.

PostgreSQL is a database that satisfies ACID properties. To ensure durability, PostgreSQL writes all its transactions to a WAL segment on disk, to ensure that a committed transaction is safe if a crash occurs. These WAL segments also serve the purpose of replication and recovery. However, a WAL segment is recycled upon a certain interval. So, it is important to archive a WAL segment to a safe location where it is safely stored for a longer duration. To achieve this, we will end this chapter with a recipe that explains how to archive WAL segments to ensure their durability.

The following recipes will be covered in this chapter:

- Installing PostgreSQL 13 using RPMs on CentOS
- Initializing a PostgreSQL cluster using initdb
- Starting a PostgreSQL cluster using pg_ctl
- Shutting down a PostgreSQL cluster using different shutdown modes
- Identifying a PostgreSQL data directory and its contents
- Moving pg_wal to another location
- Running the psql client and some psql shortcuts
- Locating the PostgreSQL configuration file
- Modifying the location of a postgresql.conf file
- Modifying the postgresql.auto.conf file in PostgreSQL
- Enabling archiving in PostgreSQL

Let's get started!

Technical requirements

To complete the recipes in this chapter, you will need a virtual machine with either the CentOS/Red Hat family or a Debian/Ubuntu operating system installed on it. This server must be able to connect to the internet to download the packages required to install PostgreSQL. If you have already got a server with PostgreSQL 13 installed, then all the commands that will be discussed in this chapter should work for you.

Installing PostgreSQL 13 using RPMs on CentOS

Since we already expect you to know how to install PostgreSQL, I am going to talk about how to install it (in brief) before proceeding to the next recipes. PostgreSQL can be installed using both sources and packages. This recipe will show a few simple steps on how to install Postgres on CentOS.

Getting ready

To install PostgreSQL on CentOS, it is important that you have root access or sudo access to perform the installation using YUM. Additionally, the server should be able to connect to the PGDG repository over the internet and download the necessary packages and dependencies.

How to do it...

Follow these steps to complete this recipe:

1. Go to https://postgresql.org/download and click on the operating system that you'll be downloading the PostgreSQL packages for, such as Linux for CentOS or Ubuntu/Debian distributions:

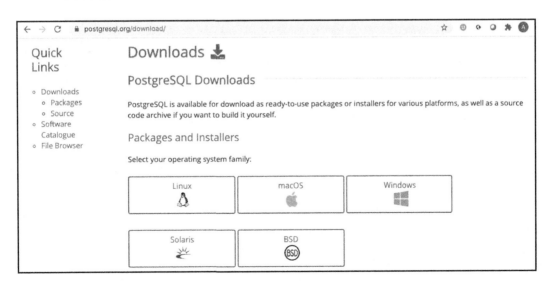

3. Click on the appropriate distribution the packages are needed for.
4. After clicking on the appropriate distribution, we'll land on the page that contains dropdowns, where we can choose the OS version and the PostgreSQL version. Once all the fields have been selected, we should see the steps to set up the PGDG repository and install the PostgreSQL server:

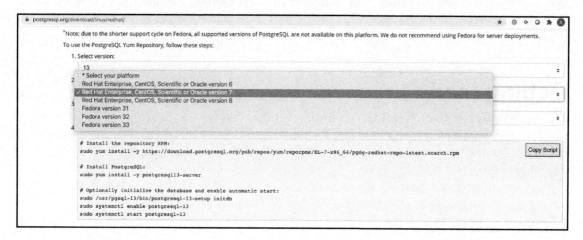

The following code block shows the line needed to download the files:

```
# yum install https://download.postgresql.org/pub/repos/yum/
reporpms/EL-7-x86_64/pgdg-redhat-repo-latest.noarch.rpm
```

4. Use the following code to install the PostgreSQL server:

```
# yum install -y postgresql13-server

-- To need contrib for the extensions, install postgresql13-contrib
as well
# yum install -y postgresql13-server postgresql13-contrib
```

5. Set a PATH for all Postgres binaries so that a full path doesn't need to be specified each time we install a new server:

```
# su - postgres
$ echo "PATH=/usr/pgsql-13/bin:$PATH" >> ~/.bash_profile
$ source .bash_profile
```

How it works...

PostgreSQL 13 can be installed on CentOS using `rpms`, which is provided by the PostgreSQL community through the PGDG repository. **PGDG** stands for the **PostgreSQL Global Development Group**. The packages can be downloaded from the URL mentioned in *Step 1*. From here, we can choose the version we wish to install so that the corresponding packages can be downloaded.

Following that, click on the distribution that suits your environment, as shown in *Step 2*. There is only one rpm per distribution. You may download this rpm and install it on your server.

Assuming you're using CentOS 7 as your operating system, for installing PostgreSQL 13, you may use the simple command provided in *Step 3*. This is a generic rpm that allows you to install not only PostgreSQL 13 but also other versions of it. Once this rpm has been installed, we can install PostgreSQL packages. For simplicity, I listed the minimal PostgreSQL packages needed to configure a PostgreSQL server for a production environment in *Step 4*. However, you may install the other packages as needed.

Upon completing the installation, you should see that a Postgres user is automatically created, as shown in *Step 5*. All the utilities needed to manage PostgreSQL are stored inside the bin directory (`/usr/pgsql-13/bin`) by default. So, it is always recommended to add the directory to `PATH` for ease.

Initializing a PostgreSQL cluster using initdb

Now that we've installed Postgres, we need to choose a directory where the data directory can be created. This data directory will be used to store the databases and the underlying objects we create. To create a data directory, we must use `initdb`. In this recipe, we shall see the steps involved in initializing a PostgreSQL cluster using `initdb`.

Getting ready

The `postgresql13-server` package must be installed on the database server for us to use `initdb`. Follow the previous recipe to perform the installation. `$PGDATA` is the environment variable used by Postgres to identify its data directory. This variable can be optionally set in `.bash_profile` of the Postgres home directory to avoid passing the data directory location to `initdb`.

How to do it...

In this recipe, we will be using the default data directory for PostgreSQL 13 on CentOS/RedHat and using `initdb` to initialize the data directory. Let's get started:

1. Set the location of the data directory to `PGDATA`:

```
$ sudo su - postgres
$ echo $PGDATA
/var/lib/pgsql/13/data

-- If PGDATA is not set, set it using the following commands.
$ export PGDATA=/var/lib/pgsql/13/data
or
$ echo "PGDATA=/var/lib/pgsql/13/data" >> ~/.bash_profile
$ source ~/.bash_profile
```

2. Use `initdb` to initialize a data directory:

```
$ initdb
```

How it works...

Upon installing Postgres using RPMs on CentOS, you should see the default data directory set to `/var/lib/pgsql/13/data` in the `.bash_profile` file. This can be verified using the command specified in *Step 1*. If required, the path can be modified to set the data directory to an appropriate location.

Once the path has been set, you can simply run `initdb`, as shown in *Step 2*. It creates the data directory in the directory specified to the `PGDATA` environment variable.

Once you are done with `initdb`, you should see that it has created several directories and sub-directories, along with some configuration files. This will be further understood in the later portions of this chapter.

Starting a PostgreSQL cluster using pg_ctl

In this recipe, we are going to discuss how to start a PostgreSQL cluster. After using `initdb` to initialize a data directory, you will see a message that provides a command we can use to start using PostgreSQL; that is, `pg_ctl`. `pg_ctl` is a utility used to manage the start, stop, and promotion/failover of PostgreSQL. In this recipe, we will learn how a PostgreSQL cluster can be started using `pg_ctl`.

Getting ready

To use `pg_ctl` to start PostgreSQL, we must have an already existing or a newly initialized data directory. Please take a look at the previous recipe to see the steps involved in initialization.

If there is an already existing PostgreSQL cluster running on port 5432 (default), we must set the port to a different value in `postgresql.conf` or the `postgresql.auto.conf` file corresponding to the new data directory.

Make sure to set the PATH variable to the following (can be added to `.bash_profile`) so that you can use the `pg_ctl` utility without adding its full path:

```
export PATH=/usr/pgsql-13/bin:$PATH
```

How to do it...

The following steps assume that the `PGDATA` environment variable has been already set with the data directory location of the PostgreSQL cluster:

1. Start PostgreSQL using `pg_ctl`:

    ```
    $ pg_ctl -D $PGDATA start
    ```

2. Check its status:

    ```
    $ pg_ctl -D $PGDATA status
    ```

How it works...

`pg_ctl` can be used to perform several actions, as shown in the following log. We could specify the data directory corresponding to the cluster that we wish to act on by using commands such as `start` or `stop`, or `status` or `promote`:

```
$ pg_ctl -D <data_directory> <start | stop | status | promote>
```

We could start a PostgreSQL cluster using a simple start, as shown in *Step 1*. There are no multiple startup modes, as seen in some of the RDBMSes. Once started, we can check the status using the command provided in *Step 2*.

However, it is important to know the difference between a cluster and a database in PostgreSQL. Let's take a look.

Clusters in PostgreSQL

A cluster in the database world may be x number of servers (in replication), where x can be 2 or more. But in Postgres, a cluster may sound slightly different. A cluster in PostgreSQL is a database server that's started using one data directory and one port on just one host. This is because you can have more than one database in a single Postgres server. However, when one or more such servers (running on multiple ports or hosts) are connected through replication, this is known as a replication cluster.

Databases in PostgreSQL

A database in PostgreSQL is similar to a database in Oracle, but not MySQL. What this means is that a database can have more than one schema, and each schema can have several tables, indexes, and other database objects. One more interesting fact is that there can be database objects sharing the same name in multiple schemas of a single database.

There's more...

The same `pg_ctl` utility could also be used to promote a standby server as a primary server.

A standby in PostgreSQL can only accept READS, not WRITES. To promote a standby during a failover, we just use a simple promotion command on the standby that needs to be promoted to a Master/Primary:

```
$ pg_ctl -D $PGDATA promote
```

Shutting down a PostgreSQL cluster using different shutdown modes

In the previous recipe, you saw that there is just one straightforward command for starting a PostgreSQL cluster. In some relational databases, there are multiple shutdown modes for different situations. Similarly, there are three modes in which a shutdown can be performed, as follows:

- Smart mode
- Fast mode
- Immediate mode

We shall discuss the steps involved in performing a shutdown using these three modes in PostgreSQL.

Getting ready

To shut down Postgres using a specific model, you can use the −m flag. You shall see this flag being passed to pg_ctl in the steps discussed in this recipe.

Make sure to set the PATH variable to the following (can be added to .bash_profile) in order to use the pg_ctl utility without adding its full path:

```
export PATH=/usr/pgsql-13/bin:$PATH
```

How to do it...

There are three modes that can be used for performing shutdowns. We will explore all of them here:

- **Smart mode**: The following two commands can be used to perform a shutdown using smart mode. As the default mode is smart, just a stop should work. We do not need to explicitly mention that the mode is smart:

```
$ pg_ctl -D $PGDATA stop
Or
$ pg_ctl -D $PGDATA stop -ms
```

- **Fast mode**: We must use −mf instead of "" to stop PostgreSQL using fast mode, as shown in the following command:

```
$ pg_ctl -D $PGDATA stop -mf
```

- **Immediate mode**: To stop a PostgreSQL server using immediate mode, we must use −mi, as shown in the following command:

```
$ pg_ctl -D $PGDATA stop -mi
```

How it works...

Here, we have seen how the three shutdown modes can be used in PostgreSQL. Let's take a look at them in more detail:

- **Smart mode** (−ms): This is the default mode used to shut down a PostgreSQL server. When this mode is used, Postgres waits for all the connections to exit before shutting it down completely. It does not allow new connections but waits for existing connections. Once all the connections have exited, the postmaster sends a SIGUSR2 signal to the checkpointer backend process to execute a shutdown checkpoint and then shuts down Postgres completely. This way, all the committed data has been written to disk (datafiles), and Postgres does not need to perform any crash recovery upon restart.
- **Fast mode** (−mf): This may be one of the modes that's heavily used on production database servers. When we shut down PostgreSQL using fast mode, it terminates all the open transactions by sending SIGTERM and does not allow new connections any more. However, upon terminating all the connections, it performs a CHECKPOINT, similar to smart mode, to avoid crash recovery upon restart. This is a mode that is recommended on busy systems, provided that you know the fact that it terminates any existing connections.
- **Immediate mode** (−mi): An immediate shutdown mode does an abnormal or a forced shutdown that requires crash recovery upon restart. Postgres sends SIQUIT to all processes in order to exit immediately. As it does not perform a clean CHECKPOINT before the shutdown, all the transaction logs (WALs) since the last checkpoint are important upon restart. This is because, upon restart, Postgres reads the WALs from the last checkpoint until the latest committed transaction to apply changes to disk (datafiles). This is a mode that's preferred in emergencies because it is quick.

There's more...

Some of us may try to terminate the postmaster process using kill on Linux. While that works, it may be dangerous. If you need to terminate a PostgreSQL server abruptly, use the immediate mode instead. This is to ensure that we do not cause any issues, such as corruption.

Identifying a PostgreSQL data directory and its contents

In the previous recipes, we discussed how a data directory can be initialized using `initdb` and how a PostgreSQL cluster can be started using `pg_ctl`. A data directory in PostgreSQL is a directory that contains several directories and sub-directories for storing data. It contains several configuration files and sub-directories that play a crucial role in running a Postgres database. The location of the data directory and some of its configuration files may change, depending on the OS distribution. For example, on Ubuntu or Debian, the configuration files are visible in a different location under `/etc`.

In this recipe, we are going to talk about the data directory and its contents in detail.

Getting ready

The following recipe involves running some Linux-level commands to identify the data directory. We require access to the OS to run these commands. As long as we can ssh to the database server as root or the Postgres user, we should be able to use the commands discussed in this recipe.

How to do it...

Let's learn how to identify the location of the data directory in the simplest way possible:

1. Use `ps` to identify a running PostgreSQL cluster:

```
$ ps -eaf | grep /post
```

Output :
```
$ ps -eaf | grep /post
postgres  1504 1  0 Nov1 ?     00:00:00 /usr/pgsql-13/bin/postgres
-D /var/lib/pgsql/13/data
```

2. Use `locate` to search for specific configuration files:

```
# yum install locate
# updatedb
# locate postgresql.auto.conf
/var/lib/pgsql/13/data/postgresql.auto.conf
```

How it works...

The simplest way to find the data directory for running a PostgreSQL cluster is by running the command shown in *Step 1* in a Linux OS. As shown in the output, the location beside -D is the data directory. If it is not a running PostgreSQL cluster, you may be able to identify the data directory by searching for the content you see in a data directory.

For example, when searching for files such as `postgresql.auto.conf` or `PG_VERSION`, you may find it easier to identify what might be in your data directory. As shown in *Step 2*, we tried to locate the `postgresql.auto.conf` file in order to search the `data_directory` location. This is because a `postgresql.auto.conf` cannot be stored in a different location other than the data directory.

Let's understand the following contents of a data directory in detail:

1. `base ($PGDATA/base)`: When we create a database in PostgreSQL, the directories specific to each database, along with the objects created in them, are stored inside the base directory.
2. `current_logfiles`: This is a file that contains the current log file Postgres is writing to. This information is very useful for scripting purposes. An example of this is an automated script that could parse the current log file for any errors and start sending alerts if any errors are found.
3. `global`: This directory contains several files that store the details of cluster-wide users, roles, databases, tablespaces, and toast tables in the database cluster.
4. `log`: This is the default directory for storing the log files of PostgreSQL. This location can be changed by modifying the `log_directory` parameter. Modifying this parameter does not require a restart.
5. `pg_commit_ts`: This is the directory that contains data about the transaction's committed timestamps.
6. `pg_dynshmem`: This directory contains the files used by the dynamic shared memory subsystem.
7. `pg_logical`: This directory contains the status data of logical decoding when logical replication is implemented.

8. `pg_multixact`: This directory contains multi-transaction status data.

9. `pg_notify`: This directory contains LISTEN/NOTIFY status data.

10. `pg_replsot`: This directory contains replication slot data.

11. `pg_serial`: This contains information about committed serializable transactions.

12. `pg_snapshots`: This contains exported snapshots.

13. `pg_stat`: This contains files for the statistics subsystem.

14. `pg_stat_tmp`: This contains the temporary files for the statistics subsystem.

15. `pg_subtrans`: This contains the subtransaction status data.

16. `pg_tblspc`: This contains symbolic links to the actual tablespace directories.

17. `pg_twophase`: This contains the state files for the prepared transactions.

18. `pg_wal`: This contains the transaction logs (write-ahead logs) of the PostgreSQL cluster, which are used for durability.

19. `pg_xact`: This contains the transaction's commit status data.

20. `pg_hba.conf`: This is the host-based authentication file that contains crucial data needed for client authentication. This file acts as a firewall to allow/restrict connections from remote hosts to the database server.

21. `pg_ident.conf`: PostgreSQL provides Ident-based authentication. It uses the client's operating system username as the allowed database username with an operating system username mapping.

22. `PG_VERSION`: This file contains the major version number of PostgreSQL that the data directory has been initialized with.

23. `postgresql.conf`: This file is the main configuration file used by PostgreSQL. The location may default to the data directory in RedHat/CentOS distributions but changes to `/etc/postgresql/13/main` in Ubuntu/Debian distributions. This file contains all the parameters used to change PostgreSQL's behavior.

24. `postgresql.auto.conf`: This file contains the parameters that have been modified using ALTER SYSTEM in PostgreSQL. When PostgreSQL is started, this is the last configuration read by PostgreSQL. So, if a parameter has two different values in the `postgresql.conf` and `postgresql.auto.conf` files, the value that's set in the `postgresql.auto.conf` file is considered by PostgreSQL.

25. `postmaster.opts`: This file contains the command that's used to start the PostgreSQL cluster.

26. `postmaster.pid`: This file contains data such as the process ID of the postmaster process, the data directory's location, port numbers, and the connection's acceptance state of the cluster.

There's more...

You can also have multiple PostgreSQL instances running on one server. To do that, you must have two different data directories as the first criteria. The next important criterion is that the port number using these instances must be different. For example, consider that you have the following two data directories:

- **Data directory 1:** `/var/lib/pgsql/13/data_1`
- **Data directory 2:** `/var/lib/pgsql/13/data_2`

Now, you must make sure that the port number in the configuration files of the two data directories are different:

```
$ echo "port = 5432" >> /var/lib/pgsql/13/data_1/postgresql.auto.conf
$ echo "port = 5433" >> /var/lib/pgsql/13/data_2/postgresql.auto.conf
```

Since `postgresql.auto.conf` is the last file you read when you started Postgres, the changes that are made to this file take precedence over any other configuration file.

Moving pg_wal to another location

Every committed transaction is WAL logged to ensure durability. This ensures that your PostgreSQL instance can perform crash recovery and avoid losing any of its committed transactions. PostgreSQL writes the entire content of each disk page to WAL. along with row-level changes. when `full_page_writes` is set to ON. This is important for safe crash recovery. However, this could write more data into WALs.

Writing WALs to the same disk as the data directory that contains tables/indexes may add I/O bottlenecks to a busy transactional database. Thus, it is always recommended to move the WAL's directory to a new disk, if you have observed I/O waits in your server due to huge WAL generation (due to a lot of DMLs).

In this recipe, we will learn how to move the `pg_wal` directory that stores WAL segments to a different disk or a faster disk.

Getting ready

To move the WALs to a different directory, we must restart our PostgreSQL server. This may cause downtime, so it needs to be planned appropriately. Also, make sure that you plan for enough storage in the new pg_wal directory for storing all the WAL segments pending to be applied by a standby when replication slots are enabled. We must do this because, when replication slots are used, a WAL segment that has not been acknowledged as applied by standby will not be removed from the pg_wal directory of the master. This may accumulate several GBs or WAL segments if this goes unnoticed for a longer duration.

How to do it...

The following steps can be used to move pg_wal to a new location:

1. Create a new directory on a new disk and assign ownership to Postgres:

   ```
   # mkdir -p /wals
   # chown postgres:postgres /wals
   ```

2. Stop your PostgreSQL cluster, if it is already running:

   ```
   $ pg_ctl -D $PGDATA stop -mf
   ```

3. If you would like to avoid more downtime due to the huge number of WALs, skip *Step 2* and proceed to *Step 3b*. Otherwise, proceed to *Step 3a*:

   - Move all the existing WALs and the archive_status directory inside pg_wal to the new directory on another disk. Make sure that pg_wal is empty and everything is moved to a new directory:

     ```
     $ mv $PGDATA/pg_wal/* /wals
     ```

   - Use rsync to avoid a huge downtime while copying a huge number of WAL segments to a different disk:

     ```
     $ rsync -avzh $PGDATA/pg_wal/ /wals
     $ pg_ctl -D $PGDATA stop -mf
     $ rsync -avzh $PGDATA/pg_wal/ /wals
     ```

4. Create a `symlink` after removing the old WAL directory:

    ```
    $ rmdir $PGDATA/pg_wal
    $ ln -s /wals pg_wal

    $ ls -alrth pg_wal
    lrwxrwxrwx. 1 postgres postgres 5 Nov 10 00:16 pg_wal -> /wals
    ```

5. Start your PostgreSQL cluster now:

    ```
    $ pg_ctl -D $PGDATA start
    ```

With that, you have successfully moved your WALs directory to another location.

How it works...

To move `pg_wal`, we must add a new disk to the server and create the new directory that the WAL segments will be stored in. We also need to make sure that we give appropriate permissions to the directory, as shown in *Step 1*. As this requires you to shut down the Postgres server to move the WAL directory, we could use a command similar to the one shown in *Step 2* to shut down Postgres.

If you have a huge number of WAL segments, you can avoid more downtime by skipping this step and moving on to *Step 3b*. If not, you may use *Step 3a*, which simply moves all the content of the existing `pg_wal` directory to the new directory.

If you wish to avoid the huge downtime and wish to skip *Steps 2* and *3a*, you could simply use *Step 3b*, which uses `rsync` to copy all the existing WAL segments from `pg_wal` to the new WAL directory. Once done, we can simply shut down Postgres and use `rsync` again to copy the newly generated WAL segments. After moving all the WAL segments, remove the old WALs directory, and create a symbolic link to the new directory, as shown in *step 4*.

As we have seen, `pg_wal` is not removed from the data directory permanently. Instead, a symbolic link is created to the new directory that we are moving WALs to. Once the symlink has been created, we can start PostgreSQL, as shown in *Step 5*, which starts writing the newly generated WAL segments to the new WAL directory.

If you have a high availability cluster with 1 master and 1 or more standbys, you can perform these steps in a rolling fashion or all at once. Having different locations in each of the servers of a replication cluster is always possible. Thus, you can stop all the servers and perform these steps or perform them on one server after another.

Running the psql client and some psql shortcuts

After creating a cluster and starting Postgres, the next step is to connect to and start creating databases and other objects. You may want to connect to Postgres as a client, create a database or create few tables, run some queries, and so on. To achieve this, we have a utility called psql. This utility acts as a client. psql is a client that can be used to interact with a PostgreSQL cluster and perform several actions. In the recipe, we shall discuss how psql and some of its shortcuts can be helpful for routine activities.

Getting ready

psql is a client that can be used to connect to the PostgreSQL server both locally and remotely (from another server). If psql is not executed as a Postgres user (defaults to Postgres when used on the database server as a Postgres OS user), then the appropriate database user should be used to connect to the PostgreSQL server to run the psql commands in this recipe.

How to do it...

Let's learn how to use some of the psql shortcuts that are available for use in everyday admin life:

1. Use the following code to install the Postgres client using psql:

```
On Ubuntu/Debian
# apt install postgresql-client

On RedHat/CentOS
# yum install postgresql13
```

2. Use the psql binary in the path to connect to the PostgreSQL server:

```
$ /usr/pgsql-13/bin/psql
psql (13.1)
Type "help" for help.
postgres=#
```

To connect to a remote server, we need to pass the IP or the hostname of the server, as shown in the following command:

```
$ psql -h Server_A_IP -p 5432 -d postgres -U postgres
```

3. Now, use `-c` to run a SQL server using `psql`:

```
$ psql -d percona -c "select * from foo.employee" > results.out
```

4. To get the list of databases in the server, we can use the `\l` shortcut or `$ psql -l`:

```
$ psql
psql (13.1)
Type "help" for help.
postgres=# \l
                                      List of databases
    Name    |  Owner   | Encoding |  Collate    | Ctype       | Access
privileges
-----------+----------+----------+-------------+-------------+-----
-------------------
 percona    | postgres | UTF8     | en_US.UTF-8 | en_US.UTF-8 |
=Tc/postgres           +
            |          | |        |             | | postgres=CTc/postgres+
            |          | |        |             | | user1=C/postgres
 postgres   | postgres | UTF8     | en_US.UTF-8 | en_US.UTF-8 |
 template0  | postgres | UTF8     | en_US.UTF-8 | en_US.UTF-8 |
=c/postgres            +
            |          | |        |             | | postgres=CTc/postgres
 template1  | postgres | UTF8     | en_US.UTF-8 | en_US.UTF-8 |
=c/postgres            +
            |          | |        |             | | postgres=CTc/postgres
 testing    | postgres | UTF8     | en_US.UTF-8 | en_US.UTF-8 |
(5 rows)
```

5. Use `\l+` to get the size of all the databases in the cluster:

```
$ psql
psql (13.1)
Type "help" for help.

postgres=# \l+
List of databases
    Name    |  Owner   | Encoding |  Collate    | Ctype       | Access
privileges |  Size  | Tablespace |                 Description
-----------+----------+----------+-------------+-------------+-----
-------------------+--
------+-----------+------------------------------------------------
```

```
 percona   | postgres | UTF8     | en_US.UTF-8 | en_US.UTF-8 |
=Tc/postgres          +| 7957 kB | pg_default |
             |            | |                | | postgres=CTc/postgres+|
| |
             |            | |                | | user1=C/postgres       | |
|
 postgres  | postgres | UTF8     | en_US.UTF-8 | en_US.UTF-8 |
| 7949 kB | pg_default | default administrative connection database
 template0 | postgres | UTF8     | en_US.UTF-8 | en_US.UTF-8 |
=c/postgres          +| 7809 kB | pg_default | unmodifiable empty
database
             |            | |                | | postgres=CTc/postgres |
| |
 template1 | postgres | UTF8     | en_US.UTF-8 | en_US.UTF-8 |
=c/postgres          +| 7809 kB | pg_default | default
template for new databases
             |            | |                | | postgres=CTc/postgres |
| |
 testing   | postgres | UTF8     | en_US.UTF-8 | en_US.UTF-8 |
| 7949 kB | pg_default |
(5 rows)
```

6. To switch to another database in the cluster, we can use the \c shortcut, as shown in the following log:

```
$ psql
psql (13.1)
Type "help" for help.
postgres=# select current_database();
 current_database
------------------
 postgres
(1 row)

postgres=# \c percona
You are now connected to database "percona" as user "postgres".
percona=#
percona=# select current_database();
 current_database
------------------
 percona
(1 row)
```

7. To get the list of schemas in a database, we can use \dn:

```
percona=# \dn
  List of schemas
  Name  | Owner
```

```
--------+----------
 foo    | user2
 foo1   | user2
 public | postgres
(3 rows)


percona=# \dn+
                        List of schemas
  Name  | Owner    | Access privileges     | Description
--------+----------+-----------------------+-------------------------
 foo    | user2    |                       |
 foo1   | user2    |                       |
 public | postgres | postgres=UC/postgres+ | standard public schema
        |          | =UC/postgres          |
(3 rows)
```

8. To obtain the list of tables in a database, we can use \dt, as shown in the following code:

```
percona=# \dt
               List of relations
 Schema |       Name       | Type  | Owner
--------+------------------+-------+----------
 public | pgbench_accounts | table | postgres
 public | pgbench_branches | table | postgres
 public | pgbench_history  | table | postgres
 public | pgbench_tellers  | table | postgres
(4 rows)


percona=# show search_path ;
   search_path
-----------------
 "$user", public
(1 row)


percona=#
percona=# \dt foo.*
          List of relations
 Schema |   Name   | Type  | Owner
--------+----------+-------+----------
 foo    | dept     | table | postgres
 foo    | employee | table | postgres
(2 rows)


percona=# \dt+ foo.*
                       List of relations
 Schema |   Name   | Type  | Owner   | Size    | Description
--------+----------+-------+---------+---------+-------------\
```

```
foo     | dept     | table | postgres | 3568 kB |
foo     | employee | table | postgres | 3458 MB |
(2 rows)
```

9. Now, we need to describe a table to get the list of columns and their data types, indexes, constraints, and triggers:

```
percona=# \d foo.employee
                          Table "foo.employee"
 Column  | Type    | Collation | Nullable |          Default
---------+---------+-----------+----------+------------------------
 id      | integer |           | not null |
nextval('emp_id_sequence'::regclass)
 dept    | integer |           |    |
 id2     | integer |           |    |
 id3     | integer |           |    |
 id4     | integer |           |    |
 id5     | integer |           |    |
 id6     | integer |           |    |
 id7     | integer |           |    |
 details | text    | |         |
 zipcode | integer |           |    |
Indexes:
    "employee_pkey" PRIMARY KEY, btree (id)
    "idx_btree_dept_id2" btree (dept, id2)
Foreign-key constraints:
    "fk_emp_dept_id" FOREIGN KEY (id5) REFERENCES foo.dept(id)
Triggers:
    audit_id5 BEFORE UPDATE ON foo.employee FOR EACH ROW EXECUTE
PROCEDURE foo.audit_id5_mod()
```

How it works...

You can connect to both local and remote database hosts using psql. Let's say that your database server is running on Server A and you wish to connect to Server A from Server B. You would need to have the psql client on Server B to connect to Server A. The simple steps to install only the client but not all the Postgres packages are listed in *Step 1* for Ubuntu/Debian and RedHat/CentOS.

Once the client has been installed, you should use the appropriate hostname, port number, database name, and username to connect to the remote server, as shown in *Step 2*.

So far, we have seen that psql is a client that helps us connect to a database. However, psql is very user-friendly. It has several shortcuts to make user's lives easy.

Running a SQL server using psql

In *Step 3*, we saw that we can run a SQL server through `psql` using the `-c` flag, where the results are printed to the Terminal. If you do not want to print the result but send the output to a file, you can simply direct it to a file.

Getting a list of databases

When you connect to a Postgres server, the first thing we wish to see is the database's information. To get the list of databases, you can just run a simple `\l` command. Some sample output is provided in the log in *Step 4*.

Finding the database's size

Adding a + sign after `\l` gives us much more detailed information, such as the database's size, tablespaces details, and the description, as shown in the log in *Step 5*.

Connecting to a database

To connect to a specific database, we could use the `\c` option, as shown in *Step 6*. This can be used to switch between multiple databases so that you can query the information of the objects that were created in that specific database.

Getting the list of schemas in a database

We can have many schemas in each database. To get the list of schemas in a database, we can use `\dn`. Using `\dn+` gives us some additional information, such as the privileges and description that was passed while creating that schema, as shown in *Step 7*.

Getting the list of tables

You can get the list of tables in a database using `\dt`. However, it only lists the tables that are in the first schema listed in `search_path`. To select the list of tables for a specific schema, pass the schema name to `\dt`. Adding a + sign to it provides us with more details, such as the table size and description. In the log shown in *Step 8*, you should see that the tables in the public schema are listed when no schema is passed to `\dt`. If you looked at the log carefully, then you'll be able to see that `\dt+` also shows the size of each table.

Describing a table

In some of the databases, we can use `desc` or `describe` to print the columns and their data types and the list of indexes and triggers of a table. In PostgreSQL, a simple `\d` or `\d+` prints that information, as visible in the log shown in *Step 9*.

There's more...

There is a big list of shortcuts that are handy for PostgreSQL users. All of them can easily be found using `\?`, as shown in the following code:

```
$ psql
psql (13.1 )
Type "help" for help.

postgres=# \?
General
  \copyright             show PostgreSQL usage and distribution terms
  \crosstabview [COLUMNS] execute query and display results in crosstab
  \errverbose            show most recent error message at maximum
verbosity
  \g [FILE] or ;         execute query (and send results to file or |pipe)
  \gdesc                 describe result of query, without executing it
  \gexec                 execute query, then execute each value in its
result
  \gset [PREFIX]         execute query and store results in psql variables
  \gx [FILE]             as \g, but forces expanded output mode
  \q                     quit psql
  \watch [SEC]           execute query every SEC seconds

Help
  \? [commands]          show help on backslash commands
```

SQLs behind the shortcuts

The shortcuts we have discussed so far should make it easy for users to complete routine tasks. If you would like to know the SQL behind a shortcut, you can connect to `psql` using `-E`. As shown in the following log, you can see the SQL that ran in the background to list the schemas in a database:

```
$ psql -d percona -E
psql (13.1)
Type "help" for help.
```

```
pg13=# \dn
********* QUERY **********
SELECT n.nspname AS "Name",
  pg_catalog.pg_get_userbyid(n.nspowner) AS "Owner"
FROM pg_catalog.pg_namespace n
WHERE n.nspname !~ '^pg_' AND n.nspname <> 'information_schema'
ORDER BY 1;
**************************
  List of schemas
  Name   | Owner
--------+----------
 foo    | user2
 foo1   | user2
 public | postgres
(3 rows)
```

Locating the Postgres configuration file

A Postgres configuration file can exist in any location. It defaults to the data directory in the CentOS or RedHat family of operating systems and
defaults to `/etc/postgresql/${pg_major_version}/main` in Debian/Ubuntu operating systems, where `pg_major_version` is the major version of PostgreSQL that is installed. For PostgreSQL 12, it looks
like `/etc/postgresql/12/main/postgresql.conf`. However, it is easier to modify the default location and store it in a different location. In this recipe, we will discuss how to locate the `postgresql.conf` configuration files that's created for a specific PostgreSQL instance.

Getting ready

To locate the configuration file, we must either have an already running PostgreSQL server or an existing data directory, using which PostgreSQL would have been initialized or started/running already.

How to do it...

Follow these steps to complete this recipe:

1. Search for the value set of the `config_file` parameter:

```
$ psql -c "show config_file"
config_file
------------------------------------------
/var/lib/pgsql/13/data/postgresql.conf
(1 row)
```

2. Use `ps` in Linux to view the configuration file that the PostgreSQL cluster is started with:

```
$ ps aux | grep /postgres
 postgres 3356 0.0 3.4 392980 17188 ? Ss 23:21 0:00
/usr/pgsql-12/bin/postgres -D /var/lib/pgsql/13/data --config-
file=/etc/postgresql/13/main/postgresql.conf
```

How it works...

If you have a running PostgreSQL server, you can connect to it using `psql` and find the default or modified location of this configuration file using the `show` command, as shown in *Step 1*.

If the location of the configuration is modified (to something different than the data directory), the full path to the new configuration file will be used while starting PostgreSQL. So, a simple `ps` in Linux can be used to obtain the location, as shown in *Step 2*.

There's more...

A `postgresql.conf` file may sometimes have zero modifications. However, there are some more configuration files that can include a list of modified parameters.

include_dir

You can specify a location to the `include_dir` parameter. When PostgreSQL starts, it reads all the parameter settings in the files inside this directory that end with `.conf`. The only way to identify the location that's been set to `include_dir` is by reading it from the `postgresql.conf` file:

```
$ grep "include_dir" /etc/postgresql/13/main/postgresql.conf
 include_dir = '/etc/postgresql/13/main/conf.d' # include files ending in
'.conf'
```

`include_dir` is useful when an automated script or a DevOps tool is being used to set up a PostgreSQL server with settings appropriate to a specific environment. In the following example, we can see some `.conf` files specific to timezone and memory:

```
$ ls /etc/postgresql/13/main/conf.d
 memory.conf timezone.conf

$ cat /etc/postgresql/13/main/conf.d/memory.conf
 shared_buffers = '2GB'
 work_mem = '8MB'
 maintenance_work_mem = '256MB'
 effective_cache_size = '6GB'
```

include

Similar to `include_dir`, there exists another parameter called `include`. This is the configuration file that needs to be read by PostgreSQL when it is started. The only way to know what the location of this file is by reading it from the original `postgresql.conf` file:

```
$ grep "include" /etc/postgresql/13/main/postgresql.conf
 ...
 include = '/etc/postgresql/13/main/conf.d/mypgconfig.conf' # include file
```

Please note that a parameter that has been set to different values in multiple configuration files would be assigned a value that was set in the last configuration file read by PostgreSQL in sequence.

Some more configuration files ending in `.conf` can be located by querying the `pg_settings` view:

```
postgres=# select name , setting from pg_settings where setting ilike
'%.conf';
 name | setting
 -------------+-------------------------------------------
```

```
config_file | /etc/postgresql/13/main/postgresql.conf
hba_file | /var/lib/pgsql/13/data/pg_hba.conf
ident_file | /var/lib/pgsql/13/data/pg_ident.conf
(3 rows)
```

Modifying the location of a postgresql.conf file in PostgreSQL

As we discussed in the previous recipes, the location of a configuration file defaults to different locations, depending on the OS distribution that PostgreSQL was installed on. However, you may wish to modify this location for various reasons, such as maintaining a standard location, as decided by your organization, or to put all the configuration files and scripts in a directory that is frequently backed up. In this recipe, we shall discuss the steps involved in modifying the default location of a postgresql.conf file.

Getting ready

To modify the default location of a postgresql.conf file, it is important to have a safe location that can be accessed by a Postgres user. It is also important to periodically back up this configuration file if it is not part of the data directory. If the configuration files are not backed up along with the data directory, we may have to start with an untuned PostgreSQL server when we need to perform restore and recover a PostgreSQL server from backups. Before we modify the default location of the postgresql.conf file, we must make sure that PostgreSQL has been stopped.

How to do it...

Follow these steps to complete this recipe:

1. If the PostgreSQL cluster is running, we can run the following command to stop the cluster:

   ```
   $ pg_ctl -D $PGDATA stop -mf
   ```

2. Create the directory and assign ownership and access to only the Postgres user using the following commands:

```
$ sudo mkdir -p /pgconfigs
$ sudo chown postgres:postgres /pgconfigs
$ sudo chmod -R 700 /pgconfigs
```

3. Now, move the original configuration file to a new location:

```
$ mv $PGDATA/postgresql.conf /pgconfigs/postgresql.conf
```

4. Start the PostgreSQL server that was stopped earlier using the new configuration file:

```
$ pg_ctl -D $PGDATA -o '--config-file=/pgconfigs/postgresql.conf'
start
```

5. Validate the location of the configuration file using the following show command:

```
$ psql -c "show config_file"
 config_file
----------------------------
 /pgconfigs/postgresql.conf
(1 row)
```

How it works...

Modifying the `postgresql.conf` file's location is very easy and straightforward to do. To modify the location of the configuration file, we must shut down the PostgreSQL server, as shown in *Step 1*. Once the PostgreSQL cluster is stopped, we must create the directory that the configuration file must be stored in as shown in *Step 2*. We must also ensure that we give appropriate ownership and privileges to Postgres users on that directory and file, also shown in *Step 2*. You may replace `/pgconfigs` in Step 2 with an appropriate directory name.

Now, we can simply move or copy the file to the new location, as shown in *Step 3*. Since the location of the configuration file has now changed from its default location, we must start PostgreSQL using an additional flag that reads the specified configuration file, as shown in *Step 4*.

Once we have started PostgreSQL, we can validate it using the show command, as shown in *Step 5*.

Modifying the postgresql.auto.conf file in PostgreSQL

Similar to the `postgresql.conf` file, there's another configuration file named `postgresql.auto.conf` whose location always defaults to the PostgreSQL data directory, regardless of the operating system. Its location cannot be modified.

Why do we need another configuration file; that is, `postgresql.auto.conf`*?*

When we open a `postgresql.conf` file and see its contents, we see a big list of parameters. Usually, most of them are commented, which means that the default values are automatically assigned to those parameters. You could always uncomment and edit the values to modify a specific parameter. However, does it not become difficult to track the changes you have made over a certain period of time?

In Oracle-like databases, you can simply run an `ALTER SYSTEM` command to modify a server parameter that may be automatically applied to the `spfile` (server parameter) file. You can also specify that these changes need to be persistent. This means that the newly modified values must be in effect even upon a server restart. In PostgreSQL, you can manually edit the configuration files to make persistent changes to parameters. Additionally, you can also run `ALTER SYSTEM` to modify a parameter value and make it a persistent change.

When you run an `ALTER SYSTEM ...` command, the change is automatically written by PostgreSQL to the `postgresql.auto.conf` file but not the `postgresql.conf` file. Interesting, isn't it? This way, after a few months or years, you can see the parameters you have modified and see whether the workload has changed and if you need to modify them again.

Getting ready

This configuration file only exists in PostgreSQL versions 9.4 and above. So, if we are using an older version such as 9.3 or earlier, this file does not exist. This file can be modified manually. However, the most widely suggested method is to not modify this file directly but rather use `ALTER SYSTEM` to do that. To use ALTER SYSTEM, we must have superuser access to the PostgreSQL server.

How to do it...

Follow these steps to complete this recipe:

1. Run ALTER SYSTEM to modify the work_mem setting, as shown in the following code:

   ```
   $ psql -c "ALTER SYSTEM SET work_mem TO '8MB'"
   ```

2. Following this, we can run either reload or SIGHUP:

   ```
   $ pg_ctl -D $PGDATA reload
    or
   $ psql -c "select pg_reload_conf()"
    or
   $ kill -HUP <pid_of_postmaster>
   ```

3. Validate the work_mem parameter change using the following show command:

   ```
   $ psql -c "show work_mem"
   ```

How it works...

Consider changing the value of work_mem from its default value of 4 MB to 8 MB. For this purpose, we can simply run an ALTER SYSTEM command, as shown in *Step 1*. Once this command is run, the change to work_mem is written to the postgresql.auto.conf file. However, to get this change into effect, we need to either run a reload or SIGHUP, as shown in *Steps 2* and *3*.

In *Step 2*, we can see that the last approach is to perform a SIGHUP using kill -HUP, which requires the PID of the postmaster.

You can get the PID of the postmaster from the postmaster.pid file in the data directory:

```
$ cat $PGDATA/postmaster.pid | head -1
 1209
```

Not all the parameters can be modified without a restart. Some parameters, such as shared_buffers, listen_addresses, archive_mode, and so on, require you to restart Postgres to get the changes into effect.

To find out whether the parameter you have modified requires a restart, you can use the following approach. Let's modify the `shared_buffers` parameter and see if it requires a restart:

1. Execute `ALTER SYSTEM`:

   ```
   $ psql -c "ALTER SYSTEM SET shared_buffers TO '512MB'"
   ```

2. Reload the configuration:

   ```
   $ pg_ctl -D $PGDATA reload
   ```

3. Query the view using `pg_settings` to see whether the change is pending for a restart:

   ```
   $ psql -c "select name, setting, pending_restart from pg_settings
   where name = 'shared_buffers'"
    name | setting | pending_restart
   ----------------+---------+-----------------
    shared_buffers | 16384 | t
   (1 row)
   ```

In the preceding log, you can see that the `shared_buffers` parameter is pending a restart, which means that we have performed a change that has not got into effect yet. In this case, you can restart the PostgreSQL cluster so that the parameter change gets into effect using the following command:

```
$ pg_ctl -D $PGDATA restart -mf
```

There's more...

`postgresql.auto.conf` is the last file that is read when you start a PostgreSQL server. So, if a parameter has one value in the `postgresql.conf` file and another value in the `postgresql.auto.conf` file, the value specified in the `postgresql.auto.conf` file is considered by Postgres. Since the `ALTER SYSTEM` command writes the modified parameters to this file, the changes that are made using `ALTER SYSTEM` are considered to be persistent upon restart.

You need to be very careful while manually editing a parameter in the `postgresql.conf` file. This is because if the same parameter has a different value set in the `postgresql.auto.conf` file, the modifications that are made in the `postgresql.conf` file have no effect.

While automating the PostgreSQL installation and configuration using Ansible-like DevOps tools, you can add some environment-specific default parameters to the `postgresql.auto.conf` file. This way, you maintain all the modified parameters in one place, which will be helpful while you're troubleshooting.

Enable archiving in PostgreSQL

Archiving is the concept of storing history in a safe location for recovery. Similarly, in database technologies, we see transaction logs (WALs in PostgreSQL) being archived to a remote backup server or cloud to allow a database to be recovered during disasters. As WAL segments get recycled after a certain threshold, it is important to archive them to safe storage before they are gone from the server. This also helps with **Point In Time Recovery** (**PITR**) and also in situations where a standby is lagging behind the primary (or master) and requires the recently removed WAL segments to get back to sync. In this recipe, we shall see the steps involved in enabling archiving in PostgreSQL.

Getting ready

In PostgreSQL, archiving is not enabled by default. To enable archiving, the PostgreSQL instance needs to be restarted. So, we need to make sure to enable archiving before going live with a production PostgreSQL server. We must also ensure that we choose a piece of storage that is redundant and safe from disasters, for storing the archives.

How to do it...

Follow these steps to complete this recipe:

1. Verify `archive_mode` by running the following command:

```
$ psql -c "show archive_mode"
```

2. Set `archive_mode` to `ON` to enable archiving using `ALTER SYSTEM`:

```
$ psql -c "ALTER SYSTEM SET archive_mode TO 'ON'"
```

3. Restart PostgreSQL by running the following command:

```
$ pg_ctl -D $PGDATA restart -mf
```

4. Create the archive location and set the ownership to `postgres`:

```
$ mkdir -p /backups/archive
$ chown postgres:postgres /backups/archive
```

5. Set `archive_command` with the appropriate shell command or a script that copies archives to a safe location. Create the archive location and set the ownership to `postgres`:

```
$ mkdir -p /backups/archive
$ psql -c "ALTER SYSTEM SET archive_command TO 'cp %p
/backups/archive/%f'"
```

6. Run either `reload` or `SIGHUP` for the changes that were made to the `archive_command` parameter to take effect:

```
$ psql -c "select pg_reload_conf()"
```

How it works...

To enable WAL segments to be archived to permanent storage, follow these steps:

1. Set the `archive_mode` parameter to ON (requires restart).
2. Set the `archive_command` parameter to a shell command or a script that can send archives to an archive location.

Before setting the archiving to a location, we must validate whether `archive_mode` is set to ON, as shown in *Step 1*. If it is not set to ON, we can set it to ON using the command shown in *Step 2*. As a change to `archive_mode` requires a restart, we need to restart the PostgreSQL cluster using a command similar to what we saw in *Step 3*.

To copy WAL segments to a different location for archiving, we need to provide the appropriate shell command, which can be used to perform the copy. In my setup, I am trying to safely archive the WAL segment to a NAS mounted named `/backups`. So, I could just let the archiver process issue a simple copy command to copy the WAL segment to the NAS mount point, as shown in *Step 5*.

Here, %p => refers to the path of the WAL segment to be archived, while %f => refers to the WAL segment's name.

These two values are substituted by Postgres.

Now, to get the changes to `archive_command` into effect, we must perform either a `reload` or a `SIGHUP`, as seen in *Step 5*. Once done, archiving will be in effect.

There's more...

As an example, after setting `archive_command` with the previously mentioned shell command, the command that's executed by Postgres to archive one of the WAL segments may look as follows:

```
cp /var/lib/pgsql/12/data/pg_wal/00000001000000D2000000C9
/backups/archive/00000001000000D2000000C9
```

As you can see, it copies the WAL segment to the location specified in the shell command.

Cluster Management Techniques 2

This chapter consists of several recipes to c. We shall start this chapter with recipes that show some of the utilities available for creating and dropping databases. We will see how a database and a table can be located on a file system and then see how a schema can be created. We shall also understand the advantages of using schemas, along with the steps involved in assigning the ownership of a schema to a user. We'll then move on to discuss the methods involved in looking at the size of a table and an index in PostgreSQL.

Over a period of time, database activity may cause objects to grow huge in size. This is the time when we wish to move tables and indexes across different tablespaces to distribute the IOPS across multiple disks. Additionally, you may wish to create archive tables to store old data that is not heavily accessed but only kept for satisfying compliances. For this purpose, we shall discuss the steps involved in creating a tablespace and how to move a table to a tablespace.

We will then move on to user management in PostgreSQL, where we will see how to create and drop a user, how to assign and revoke a privilege from a user, and how to properly manage the segregation of privileges using roles.

Finally, we will end the chapter by discussing how the MVCC implementation is different in PostgreSQL, along with an introduction to VACUUM.

The following are the recipes that will be discussed in this chapter:

- Creating and dropping databases
- Locating a database and a table
- Creating a schema
- Checking table and index sizes
- Creating tablespaces
- Moving tables to a different tablespace

- Creating a user
- Dropping a user
- Assigning and revoking privileges
- Creating a group role for role-based segregation
- MVCC implementation and VACUUM

Technical requirements

In order to test the code you'll see in this chapter, you'll need the following:

- You must have a Linux server with PostgreSQL installed and running.
- You must be able to connect as root or have `sudo` access to perform some commands as root.
- You must be able to connect to the server as the OS user (`postgres`) who owns the data directory.

Creating and dropping databases

So far, we have seen how to install PostgreSQL, initialize a PostgreSQL cluster, and start and stop a cluster. In this recipe, we shall discuss how to create or drop a database using the `createdb` and `dropdb` utilities.

There are multiple ways to create and drop a database in PostgreSQL. Upon successful installation of PostgreSQL, you have two utilities, called `createdb` and `dropdb`, that can be used to create and drop databases in PostgreSQL. The same can also be done using the `psql` utility.

Let's look at this in detail in these recipes.

Getting ready

In order to create or drop databases, we must either be a superuser or have the role `CREATEDB`. Also, the user who is dropping the database should either be a superuser or the `OWNER` of the database.

How to do it...

The following are the steps involved in creating and dropping a database using the createdb and dropdb utilities:

1. We will use help to list all the arguments for the createdb utility:

```
$ createdb --help
createdb creates a PostgreSQL database.

Usage:
  createdb [OPTION]... [DBNAME] [DESCRIPTION]

Options:
  -D, --tablespace=TABLESPACE   default tablespace for the database
  -e, --echo                    show the commands being sent to the
server
  -E, --encoding=ENCODING       encoding for the database
  -l, --locale=LOCALE           locale settings for the database
      --lc-collate=LOCALE       LC_COLLATE setting for the database
      --lc-ctype=LOCALE         LC_CTYPE setting for the database
  -O, --owner=OWNER             database user to own the new
database
  -T, --template=TEMPLATE       template database to copy
  -V, --version                 output version information, then
exit
  -?, --help                    show this help, then exit

Connection options:
  -h, --host=HOSTNAME           database server host or socket
directory
  -p, --port=PORT               database server port
  -U, --username=USERNAME       user name to connect as
  -w, --no-password             never prompt for password
  -W, --password                force password prompt
      --maintenance-db=DBNAME   alternate maintenance database
By default, a database with the same name as the current user is
created.Report bugs to <pgsql-bugs@postgresql.org>.
```

2. We will run the following command to create a database using createdb:

```
$ createdb -e pgtest -O user1
SELECT pg_catalog.set_config('search_path', '', false)
CREATE DATABASE pgtest OWNER user1;
```

3. We will then create a database using a template as follows:

```
$ createdb -e pgtest -O user1 -T percona
SELECT pg_catalog.set_config('search_path', '', false)
CREATE DATABASE pgtest OWNER user1 TEMPLATE pg11;
```

4. We will use `help` to list all the arguments for the `dropdb` utility:

```
$ dropdb --help
dropdb removes a PostgreSQL database.

Usage:
  dropdb [OPTION]... DBNAME

Options:
  -e, --echo                   show the commands being sent to the
server
  -i, --interactive            prompt before deleting anything
  -V, --version                output version information, then exit
  --if-exists                  don't report error if database doesn't
exist
  -?, --help                   show this help, then exit

Connection options:
  -h, --host=HOSTNAME          database server host or socket
directory
  -p, --port=PORT              database server port
  -U, --username=USERNAME      user name to connect as
  -w, --no-password            never prompt for password
  -W, --password               force password prompt
  --maintenance-db=DBNAME      alternate maintenance database
Report bugs to <pgsql-bugs@postgresql.org>.
```

5. We will now drop a database using `dropdb`:

```
$ dropdb -i pgtest
Database "pgtest" will be permanently removed.
Are you sure? (y/n) y
```

How it works

The best way to understand the options that can be passed to any utility is through `--help`. As seen in Step 1 and Step 4, we could list all the possible arguments we could pass to the `createdb` and `dropdb` utilities.

As seen in the options available with `createdb` in Step 1, we can use `-e` to print the commands sent to the server and `-O` to assign the ownership of the database to a user. Using `-e` does not stop it from running `createdb` but just prints the commands executed through `createdb`. As seen in Step 2, using `-e` and `-O` has created the database.

Another option available in PostgreSQL is creating a database using a template. Sometimes, we may create a template and wish to apply the same template to future databases. So, everything maintained inside the template database specified is copied to the database being created. As seen in step 3, we are creating a database named `pgtest` using a template database: `percona`.

When you wish to drop a database you have created, you could use the command seen in Step 5. It uses the `dropdb` utility to drop the database.

When you create a database or drop a database using any of the aforementioned utilities, you could simply use `psql` to list the databases you have created. We could either use the `psql` shortcut discussed in the previous recipe or query the catalog table: `pg_database`.

```
$ psql -c "\l"
 List of databases
 Name | Owner | Encoding | Collate | Ctype | Access privileges
-----------+-----------+-----------+-------------+-------------+-------------
-----------
 pgtest | user1 | UTF8 | en_US.UTF-8 | en_US.UTF-8 |
 postgres | postgres | UTF8 | en_US.UTF-8 | en_US.UTF-8 |
 template0 | postgres | UTF8 | en_US.UTF-8 | en_US.UTF-8 | =c/postgres +
 | | | | | postgres=CTc/postgres
 template1 | postgres | UTF8 | en_US.UTF-8 | en_US.UTF-8 | =c/postgres +
 | | | | | postgres=CTc/postgres
(4 rows)

$ psql -c "select oid, datname from pg_database"
 oid | datname
-------+-----------
 13881 | postgres
 16385 | pgtest
 1 | template1
 13880 | template0
(4 rows)
```

There's more

We have seen how to create and drop a database using the `createdb` and `dropdb` utilities.
The same can also be achieved using `psql` through CREATE and DROP commands. It is of
course very simple to run a simple CREATE DATABASE or DROP DATABASE command. But,
when you need to combine that with several parameters such as owner, encoding,
tablespace, and connection limit, you may need to find the correct syntax. In order to do
that, you could use `\help` as seen in the following example:

```
$ psql
psql (13.1)
Type "help" for help.

postgres=# \help CREATE DATABASE
Command: CREATE DATABASE
Description: create a new database
Syntax:
CREATE DATABASE name
    [ [ WITH ] [ OWNER [=] user_name ]
           [ TEMPLATE [=] template ]
           [ ENCODING [=] encoding ]
           [ LC_COLLATE [=] lc_collate ]
           [ LC_CTYPE [=] lc_ctype ]
           [ TABLESPACE [=] tablespace_name ]
           [ ALLOW_CONNECTIONS [=] allowconn ]
           [ CONNECTION LIMIT [=] connlimit ]
           [ IS_TEMPLATE [=] istemplate ] ]

postgres=# \help DROP DATABASE
Command: DROP DATABASE
Description: remove a database
Syntax:
DROP DATABASE [ IF EXISTS ] name
```

So, the command to create a database that is owned by `user2` with a connection limit of 200
should be as follows:

```
postgres=# CREATE DATABASE mydb WITH OWNER user2 CONNECTION LIMIT 200;
CREATE DATABASE


postgres=# \l+ mydb
                                    List of databases
 Name | Owner | Encoding | Collate | Ctype | Access privileges | Size |
Tablespace | Description
------+-------+----------+---------+-------+-------------------+-
--------+-----------+-------------
```

```
  mydb | user2 | UTF8 | en_US.UTF-8 | en_US.UTF-8 | | 7809 kB | pg_default |
(1 row)
```

Similarly, the command to drop a database, `mydb`, is as follows:

```
postgres=# DROP DATABASE mydb ;
DROP DATABASE


postgres=# \l+ mydb
                                     List of databases
 Name | Owner | Encoding | Collate | Ctype | Access privileges | Size |
Tablespace | Description
------+-------+----------+---------+-------+-------------------+------+----
--------+-------------
(0 rows)
```

Locating a database and a table on the file system

So far, we have seen how to create or drop a database and how to list all the databases or schemas or tables. We discussed earlier that there is a base subdirectory inside the data directory of a PostgreSQL cluster that contains the databases and their objects. In this recipe, we are going to discuss some of the interesting details, such as the file system layout of a database and a table in PostgreSQL.

Getting ready

To identify a table or a database, we should have a running PostgreSQL cluster that we could connect using `psql`. Additionally, it requires access to the data directory on the database server (through the Postgres OS user) to walk through the locations and see the files in reality.

How to do it...

In the following steps, we will see how we could identify the directory specific to the database and how the table appears on the filesystem by locating it:

1. We will create a database for test purposes:

```
$ psql -c "CREATE DATABASE testing"
CREATE DATABASE
```

2. Get the oid value of the database from pg_database as seen in the following command:

```
$ psql -c "select oid, datname from pg_database"
  oid  | datname
-------+-----------
 13878 | postgres
 16384 | testing
     1 | template1
 13877 | template0
(4 rows)
```

3. Locate the database directory using the oid value from the previous step:

```
$ ls -ld $PGDATA/base/16384
drwx------. 2 postgres postgres 8192 Sep 1 07:14
/var/lib/pgsql/13/data/base/16384
```

4. Create a table in the newly created database:

```
$ psql -d testing -c "CREATE TABLE employee (id int)"
CREATE TABLE
```

5. Get the oid value of the table created in the previous step from pg_class as seen in the following command:

```
$ psql -d testing -c "select oid, relname from pg_class where
relname = 'employee'"
  oid  | relname
-------+----------
 16385 | employee
(1 row)
```

6. Get the location of the table on the file system using the `pg_relation_filepath` function:

```
$ psql -d testing -c "select pg_relation_filepath('employee')"
 pg_relation_filepath
----------------------
 base/16384/16385
(1 row)
```

How it works...

In order to understand the location of a database in the file system, we shall create a database as seen in Step 1. Now, we could use the catalog `pg_database` to get the oid of the database we created, as seen in Step 2.

As you can see in the log of Step 2, there is a unique identifier for each database. While there are three default databases that are automatically created, the fourth database we have created (testing) has got a unique oid (object identifier) as well. In the previous recipes, we discussed that the base directory contains all the databases of the cluster. So, a subdirectory with the same name as the oid of the database is created inside this base directory. This directory contains all the objects created inside the database.

What this means is that when you create a database in PostgreSQL, a subdirectory with the same name as the oid of the newly created database is created inside the base directory, as seen in Step 3.

Now, let's understand the file system layout of a table. We can see that in action by creating an example table in the testing database as seen in Step 4.

In order to identify the file system layout of the table, there is a function called `pg_relation_filepath()`. This function can be used to know the location of the table and the file that corresponds to this table. But before using this function, let's see if there is a unique identifier for this table using `pg_class` as seen in Step 5.

So, from the log, we can see that 16385 is the oid of the `employee` table we have just created. Now, let's run the function to know where this was table created, as seen in Step 6.

As we can see in the log of Step 6, a file with the name 16385 (the same as the oid of the employee table) is created inside the 16384 directory. The directory 16384 corresponds to the oid of the database we created. So, this indicates that a table in PostgreSQL is created as a file inside the database directory inside the base directory. This base directory is, of course, one of the subdirectories of the data directory.

Creating a schema in PostgreSQL

A schema in PostgreSQL is a logical entity used to group together a list of tables, serving a specific purpose. It is not mandatory to create schemas in PostgreSQL. There exists a default **public** schema that can be used to create all tables. However, creating schemas has several advantages. Let's look at a few:

1. Let's say there are multiple applications writing to the same database. Each application's logic may serve a specific purpose. If we have a separate schema for each application's logic, it makes the lives of administrators and developers easier. This is because, if there is a need to perform maintenance on the tables related to a specific application, an admin can distinguish it using the schema.

2. In some applications, when a new user is created, the user is allocated a new set of objects that share the same name as the objects of another user in the same database. It is not possible to have two objects with the same name in a single schema. But, when we have two schemas, an object with the same name can exist in different schemas, for example:

   Table `employee` in `user1` schema ⇒ `user1.employee`
   Table `employee` in `user2` schema ⇒ `user2.employee`

3. User management can be simplified when we use schemas in PostgreSQL. If there are multiple application modules connecting to the same database, each module may need to access a certain set of tables. And each developer may need access to a specific set of objects related to that application module but not all. If schemas are used, users and applications can be granted read or read-write access to specific schemas through roles in a more simplified way.

In this recipe, we shall discuss the purpose of a schema and how it can be created.

Getting ready

To create a schema, we must have a PostgreSQL cluster that is running and can be connected using `psql`. Additionally, it requires either a user with the superuser role or ownership of the database to create a schema in the database.

 When you create a schema in PostgreSQL, it does not create a user with the same name as the schema name as it does in Oracle. Users need to be explicitly created.

How to do it...

The following are the steps involved in creating a schema in a PostgreSQL database:

1. Connect to the database:

```
$ psql -d percona
psql (13.1)
Type "help" for help.

percona=#
```

2. Create the schema using the CREATE SCHEMA command:

```
percona=# CREATE SCHEMA foo;
CREATE SCHEMA
```

3. Use IF NOT EXISTS for scripting purposes:

```
percona=# CREATE SCHEMA foo;
ERROR:  schema "foo" already exists
percona=# CREATE SCHEMA IF NOT EXISTS foo;
NOTICE:  schema "foo" already exists, skipping
CREATE SCHEMA
```

How it works...

In order to create a schema, you should first choose the database where you need to create the schema and connect to the database using psql, as seen in Step 1. Once you have connected to the database, you could simply use the command seen in Step 2 to create the schema.

Sometimes, you may wish to automate schema creation through scripting and avoid errors if the schema already exists. For that purpose, we could use the option seen in Step 3, to avoid printing an error when the schema already exists and create it only if it does not exist.

When you create a schema in PostgreSQL, the user who issued the CREATE SCHEMA command gets the ownership by default. This can be modified by using AUTHORIZATION. The following is the log that shows that the ownership is automatically assigned to current_user:

```
percona=# select current_user;
 current_user
```

```
--------------
 postgres
(1 row)

percona=# CREATE SCHEMA foo;
CREATE SCHEMA
percona=#
percona=# SELECT n.nspname AS "Name",
  pg_catalog.pg_get_userbyid(n.nspowner) AS "Owner"
FROM pg_catalog.pg_namespace n
WHERE n.nspname = 'foo';
 Name | Owner
------+----------
 foo  | postgres
(1 row)
```

In order to assign ownership of a schema to another user, either execute CREATE SCHEMA as that user or use AUTHORIZATION. You would need to grant the CREATE privilege to a user to execute CREATE SCHEMA. In the following log, user1 was already granted the CREATE privilege so CREATE SCHEMA succeeded with no errors:

```
$ psql -d percona -U user1
psql (13.1)
Type "help" for help.

percona=> select current_user;
 current_user
--------------
 user1
(1 row)

percona=> CREATE SCHEMA foo;
CREATE SCHEMA

percona=> SELECT n.nspname AS "Name",
  pg_catalog.pg_get_userbyid(n.nspowner) AS "Owner"
FROM pg_catalog.pg_namespace n
WHERE n.nspname = 'foo';
 Name | Owner
------+--------
 foo  | user1
(1 row)
percona=>
```

There's more...

When you are connecting as a superuser (`postgres`), you could grant the ownership to any user as you can see in the following log:

```
percona=# select current_user;
 current_user
--------------
 postgres
(1 row)
percona=# CREATE SCHEMA foo AUTHORIZATION user1;
CREATE SCHEMA
percona=#
percona=# SELECT n.nspname AS "Name",
  pg_catalog.pg_get_userbyid(n.nspowner) AS "Owner"
FROM pg_catalog.pg_namespace n
WHERE n.nspname = 'foo';
 Name | Owner
------+-------
 foo  | user1
(1 row)
```

When you use AUTHORIZATION to give ownership of a schema to a non-superuser (`user2`) as a non-superuser (`user1`), the user executing CREATE SCHEMA (`user1` here) should be a member of the role (`user2`) who should own the schema. In the following log, you can see an error when `user1` is giving authorization to `user2` without being a member of `user2`:

```
percona=> CREATE SCHEMA foo AUTHORIZATION user2;
ERROR:  must be member of role "user2"
postgres=# GRANT user2 to user1;
GRANT ROLE

percona=> CREATE SCHEMA foo AUTHORIZATION user2;
CREATE SCHEMA
```

Checking table and index sizes in PostgreSQL

In this recipe, we shall see some of the best ways to check the size of a table and index in PostgreSQL.

Getting ready

Creating a table in PostgreSQL requires you to have appropriate privileges. A newly created user can create a table in the public schema of any database. But, when you need to create a table inside another schema, it requires you to have sufficient privileges to do so. Similarly, it requires you to have sufficient privileges to read data from a table or perform writes to that table. However, it does not require you to have any privileges to see the size of a table in any schema.

How to do it...

The following are the steps involved in finding the size of a table and an index:

1. We will use \dt+ to get the table size:

```
percona=# \dt+ foo.dept
                    List of relations
 Schema | Name  | Type  |  Owner   |  Size   | Description
--------+-------+-------+----------+---------+-------------
 foo    | dept  | table | postgres | 3568 kB |
(1 row)

--- To get size of a table or a set of tables matching a pattern,
the following can be used.

percona=# \dt+ public.*bench*
                       List of relations
 Schema |       Name       | Type  |  Owner   |  Size   | Description
--------+------------------+-------+----------+---------+----------
---
 public | pgbench_accounts | table | postgres | 1281 MB |
 public | pgbench_branches | table | postgres | 40 kB   |
 public | pgbench_history  | table | postgres | 0 bytes |
 public | pgbench_tellers  | table | postgres | 80 kB   |
(4 rows)
```

2. We will use `\di+` to get the index size:

```
percona=# \di+ foo.dept_pkey
                       List of relations
  Schema |    Name    | Type  |  Owner   | Table |  Size  | Description
--------+-----------+-------+----------+------ |--------+---------
----
  foo     | dept_pkey | index | postgres | dept  | 2208 kB |
(1 row)
```

3. We will use `pg_relation_size` to get the table and index size:

```
percona=# select pg_relation_size('foo.dept');
 pg_relation_size
------------------
 3629056
(1 row)
```

How it works...

Database objects such as tables, indexes, views, materialized views, and so on may also be called relations in PostgreSQL. The three relations that can grow in size are tables, indexes, and materialized views. There are multiple ways to find the size of a table or an index in PostgreSQL. While one of them is using `psql` shortcuts, the other method is through a function called `pg_relation_size()`.

As seen in Step 1, we can pass the fully qualified table name `(schemaname.tablename)` to `\dt+` after connecting to the appropriate database using `psql`. And in order to find the size of an index, we can pass the fully qualified index name (that is, `chemaname.indexname`) to `\di+` after connecting to the appropriate database using `psql`, as seen in Step 2.

We can also find the size of these relations using `pg_relation_size()` easily, as seen in Step 3. We need to make sure that we pass a fully qualified relation name with the schema prefix to the `pg_relation_size()` function.

There's more...

When we used the function: `pg_relation_size()` earlier, we noticed that the size of a relation is displayed in bytes. This is not easily readable. For that purpose, we have the function `pg_size_pretty()`. This function converts the bytes into the nearest MB or GB or KB but not bytes, always. The following example should be helpful to understand this in reality:

```
postgres=# SELECT schemaname, relname,
pg_size_pretty(pg_relation_size(schemaname||'.'||relname)) as pretty_size
FROM pg_stat_user_tables where schemaname = 'foo' and relname IN
('employee','sales','bar');
 schemaname | relname | pretty_size
------------+----------+-------------
 foo | employee | 360 kB
 foo | bar | 640 MB
 foo | sales | 13 GB
(3 rows)
```

Creating tablespaces

A tablespace in PostgreSQL can be used to distribute database objects such as tables and indexes to different disks/locations. This is especially helpful in distributing the IO across multiple disks and avoiding IO saturation on a single disk. In this recipe, we shall see the steps involved in creating tablespaces in PostgreSQL.

Getting ready

A tablespace directory needs to be created on the file system before creating them in the database. We should have access to the operating system as a root user or a user with `sudo` access to create directories on the mount points that are owned by the root user.

When you create a tablespace in the master-slave replication cluster, which is using streaming replication, you must make sure that the tablespaces also exist on the standby server. Similarly, when you restore a backup from a PostgreSQL cluster that has got one or more tablespaces, you must make sure to consider creating the respective tablespace directories before performing the restore of the backup.

How to do it...

The following steps can be used to create a tablespace in PostgreSQL:

1. Create a directory as shown:

```
$ sudo mkdir -p /newtablespace
$ sudo chown postgres:postgres /newtablespace
```

2. Now create a tablespace using the newly created directory by running the following command:

```
$ psql -c "CREATE TABLESPACE newtblspc LOCATION '/newtablespace'"
```

3. Check the `pg_tblspc` directory to see a symlink to the new tablespace:

```
$ ls -l $PGDATA/pg_tblspc
 total 0
 lrwxrwxrwx. 1 postgres postgres 14 Nov 3 00:24 24611 ->
/newtablespace
```

How it works

To create a tablespace, we must specify a location in which the tablespace must be created, as seen in step 1. We will see the benefits of having a separate tablespace when it is created on a different disk other than the disk being used by the data directory. Now, to create a tablespace using the newly created directory, we could simply use the command as seen in step 2.

When we create a tablespace, we see a new entry in the `pg_tblspc` directory that has a symlink to the new tablespace location as seen in the output of step 3. There will be many such entries when we create more tablespaces.

Once you have created tablespaces, you could simply validate all the tablespaces and their location using the shortcut `\db` as seen in the following log:

```
$ psql
 psql (13.1)
 Type "help" for help.

postgres=# \db
 List of tablespaces
 Name | Owner | Location
 ------------+----------+----------------
 newtblspc | postgres | /newtablespace
```

```
pg_default | postgres |
pg_global | postgres |
(3 rows)
```

There's more...

In order to create a table in the new tablespace, we may just append the appropriate tablespace name to the CREATE TABLE command:

```
postgres=# create table employee (id int) TABLESPACE newtblspc;
CREATE TABLE
```

If you create a table inside the new tablespace, here is how the relation path appears. In the following log, it shows how the table is pointing to the appropriate tablespace:

```
postgres=# select pg_relation_filepath('employee');
pg_relation_filepath
-----------------------------------------------
pg_tblspc/24611/PG_13_201909212/14187/24612
(1 row)
```

And now, if you describe the table, you should be able to see the tablespace in which the table got created:

```
postgres=# \d employee
 Table "public.employee"
 Column | Type | Collation | Nullable | Default
--------+---------+-----------+----------+---------
 id | integer | | |
 Tablespace: "newtblspc"
```

With the preceding output, it is clear that the table is created inside the new tablespace.

Moving tables to a different tablespace

After a few months or years, you see the data in your database growing. And when the number of transactions increases along with the volume of data, you will wish to distribute objects, especially tables and indexes, across multiple tablespaces to scatter the IOPS. In this recipe, we shall see the steps involved in moving existing tables and indexes to different tablespaces.

Getting ready

To move tables and indexes to a different tablespace, we could use the `ALTER TABLE` syntax. We should be a superuser or an owner of the schema to run `ALTER TABLE`.

Running the `ALTER TABLE` command could cause downtime for the application as it acquires an exclusive lock on the table while moving it to a different tablespace. So the downtime needs to be planned appropriately before proceeding further. Additionally, we could use extensions such as `pg_repack`, which could be used to move tables and indexes to different tablespaces online. `pg_repack` will be discussed in future chapters.

How to do it...

The following steps can be performed to move a table to a different tablespace:

1. To move a table to another tablespace, the syntax looks like the following:

```
ALTER TABLE percona.foo SET TABLESPACE newtblspc;
```

2. To move an index to a new tablespace, the syntax looks like the following:

```
ALTER INDEX percona.foo_id_idx SET TABLESPACE newtblspc;
```

How it works

In order to move a table from one tablespace to another, we could simply use the `ALTER TABLE` command as seen in the following syntax:

```
ALTER TABLE <schemaname.tablename> SET TABLESPACE <tablespace_name>;
```

As an example, we could see the command that can be used to move a table, `percona.foo`, to a tablespace named `newtblspc` in step 1.

Similarly, in order to move an index to a tablespace, the syntax appears like the following:

```
ALTER INDEX <schemaname.indexname> SET TABLESPACE <tablespace_name>;
```

An example command to move the index `percona.foo_id_idx` to tablespace `newtblspc` can be seen in step 2.

Creating a user in PostgreSQL

In order to connect to a PostgreSQL database, we need to have a username. A PostgreSQL user is a role that has the CONNECT privilege. Both CREATE USER and CREATE ROLE work well to create a PostgreSQL user. The only difference between the two is that the LOGIN role is not assigned when we use CREATE ROLE to create a user. In this recipe, we shall see how a user can be created in PostgreSQL.

Getting ready

It requires a superuser or a CREATEROLE privilege for the database user to create a user or a role. So, we must use a user who has either of these privileges to create a user.

How to do it...

A user with a LOGIN role can be created using any of the following three methods:

1. **Method 1:** We can create a user using the CREATE USER command:

   ```
   CREATE USER percuser WITH ENCRYPTED PASSWORD 'secret';
   ```

2. **Method 2:** We can create a user using the CREATE ROLE .. WITH LOGIN command:

   ```
   CREATE ROLE percuser WITH LOGIN ENCRYPTED PASSWORD 'secret';
   ```

3. **Method 3:** We can create a user using the CREATE ROLE command and then assign the LOGIN privilege to that user:

   ```
   CREATE ROLE percuser;
   ALTER ROLE percuser WITH LOGIN ENCRYPTED PASSWORD 'secret';
   ```

The three aforementioned methods demonstrate the three different ways in which a user, percuser, can be created.

How it works

When you use CREATE USER with any of these commands, PostgreSQL automatically translates them internally with the following:

```
CREATE ROLE percuser
 WITH NOSUPERUSER INHERIT NOCREATEROLE NOCREATEDB LOGIN NOREPLICATION
NOBYPASSRLS
 ENCRYPTED PASSWORD 'secret';
```

In order to validate whether the user can log in (has the CONNECT privilege) or not, we may use the following query and substitute the username appropriately:

```
postgres=# select rolcanlogin from pg_roles where rolname = 'percuser';
 rolcanlogin
 -------------
 t
 (1 row)
```

There's more...

In order to list the users and roles created in a PostgreSQL server, we could either query the view (pg_roles) or use the shortcut "\du":

We can use the shortcut "\du" to get the list of users:

```
$ psql -c "\du"
 List of roles
 Role name | Attributes | Member of
 -----------------+-------------------------------------------------------
 -----+-----------
 app_user | | {}
 dev_user | | {}
 percuser | | {}
 postgres | Superuser, Create role, Create DB, Replication, Bypass RLS | {}
 read_only_scott | Cannot login | {}
 read_write_scott | Cannot login | {}
```

We can also use the pg_roles query to get the list of users:

```
$ psql -c "SELECT rolname, rolcanlogin FROM pg_roles where rolname NOT
LIKE 'pg_%'"
 rolname | rolcanlogin
 ------------------+-------------
 postgres | t
 percuser | t
```

```
read_write_scott | f
read_only_scott | f
app_user | t
dev_user | t
(6 rows)
```

Thus, we have learned how to create users with various privileges in PostgreSQL.

Dropping a user in PostgreSQL

We may need to drop the users who no longer need access to PostgreSQL. There will also be a great challenge when a user who is being dropped owns one or more objects. In this case, we may have to re-assign the ownership to another user before dropping the user without dropping the objects it owns. In this recipe, we shall see how a user can be dropped safely and the best practices you can follow to avoid dropping the objects a user owns.

Getting ready

To drop a user, a simple DROP USER or DROP ROLE command is sufficient. However, this only works without errors when there are no objects owned by the user that is being dropped. Otherwise, an error like the following appears in such cases:

```
postgres=# DROP USER percuser;
 ERROR: role "percuser" cannot be dropped because some objects depend on it
 DETAIL: privileges for database percona
 2 objects in database pmm
 2 objects in database percona
```

How to do it ...

The following steps need to be followed to complete the recipe:

1. When a user that does not own any objects has to be dropped, it could be done using a simple command, as follows:

    ```
    $ psql -c "DROP USER percuser"
    ```

2. Re-assign the ownership of objects that are owned by the user that needs to be dropped:

```
$ psql -U postgres -d percona -c "REASSIGN OWNED by percuser TO
pmmuser"
```

3. Revoke the privileges from the user that is being dropped:

```
$ psql
 psql (13.1)
 Type "help" for help.
 postgres=# REVOKE ALL PRIVILEGES ON DATABASE percona FROM
percuser;
 REVOKE
 postgres=# REVOKE ALL PRIVILEGES ON DATABASE pmm FROM percuser;
 REVOKE
```

4. Drop the user after the revocation is successful:

```
postgres=# DROP USER percuser ;
DROP ROLE
```

How it works ...

When the user who needs to be dropped does not own any objects, the command to drop a user as seen in step 1 would succeed without any errors. However, if the user is an OWNER of one or more objects of one or more databases, then the ownership of the objects owned by the user being dropped must be reassigned to another user. This can be done using REASSIGN OWNED as a superuser.

Dropping a user that owns one or more objects of one or more databases can be done using three simple steps. The first step is to reassign the ownership of the objects owned by the user to another user. This can be done using a simple command as seen in step 2.

If there exists another database that has some objects owned by the user being dropped, the ownership of the objects must be reassigned separately for the objects in that database as well:

```
$ psql -U postgres -d pmm -c "REASSIGN OWNED by percuser TO pmmuser"
```

Notice the difference in the two commands – the one we saw in step 2 and the preceding command. The first one connects to the percona database and the second command connects to the pmm database and reassigns ownership to pmmuser.

Once the ownership of the objects has been reassigned using the command mentioned in step 2, all the privileges owned by that user must be revoked using the command seen in step 3.

After revoking the privileges from the user being dropped, we can safely use the DROP USER command to drop the user as seen in step 4.

Assigning and revoking a privilege to/from a user or a role

Once a user is created, the next task is to grant privileges or sometimes to revoke granted privileges from the user. PostgreSQL supports several privileges that are similar to other relational databases. The following is a list of available privileges that can be granted to a user or revoked from a user/role:

```
SELECT
INSERT
UPDATE
DELETE
TRUNCATE
REFERENCES
TRIGGER
CREATE
CONNECT
TEMPORARY
EXECUTE
USAGE
```

In this recipe, we shall see how we can assign and revoke a privilege to/from a user.

Getting ready

To grant or revoke privileges from a user, GRANT and REVOKE commands are used. It will be wise to use a database user that has a superuser role or sometimes the owner of the schema and objects to perform GRANT or REVOKE.

How to do it

The following steps need to be followed to understand the recipe:

1. To grant a select privilege on a table, `employee`, to a user, `percuser`, the following `GRANT` command could be used:

   ```
   GRANT SELECT ON employee TO percuser;
   ```

2. Now we revoke `SELECT` from the user:

   ```
   REVOKE SELECT ON employee FROM percuser;
   ```

3. `GRANT` all the privileges possible on the employee table to `percuser`:

   ```
   GRANT ALL ON employee TO percuser;
   ```

4. `REVOKE` all the privileges on `employee` from `percuser`:

   ```
   REVOKE ALL ON employee FROM percuser;
   ```

5. `GRANT` all privileges on a database to a user:

   ```
   GRANT ALL ON DATABASE percona TO percuser ;
   ```

6. `REVOKE` all privileges from a user:

   ```
   REVOKE ALL ON DATABASE percona FROM percuser ;
   ```

How it works

In order to assign privileges, a `GRANT` command must be used. And to revoke the assigned privilege, a `REVOKE` command must be used. For example, to assign a `SELECT` privilege on the `employee` table to a user, `percuser`, the command seen in step 1 can be used. And to revoke the `SELECT` privilege on the `employee` table from `percuser`, the command seen in step 2 can be used.

When a privilege is granted to a user or a role, it takes effect immediately without the need for `SIGHUP` or a reload. At the same time, a user can also be granted all the privileges that can be assigned to an object depending on the object type.

The command seen in step 3 can be used to grant all the privileges possible on the `employee` table to `percuser`. And to revoke all the privileges, the command seen in step 4 can be used. We could similarly allocate all privileges on a database to a user as seen in step 5. And to revoke the privileges, the command seen in step 6 can be used.

Creating a group role for role-based segregation

It is a very challenging task for admins when there are several tens or hundreds of users in a database that need to be assigned privileges to access or modify database objects. It becomes a time-consuming task to individually manage each user and assign `SELECT` or `INSERT` privileges to hundreds of objects. For this reason, it is always recommended to provide access privileges to database users using `GROUP ROLES`. In this recipe, we shall see how `GROUP ROLES` can be used for role-based segregation.

Getting ready

A role in Postgres can **INHERIT** another role. This means one role can be granted the privileges of another role. This can be achieved using the **GRANT** or **INHERIT** keyword. So, there can be a read-only role and a read-write for each schema or for a set of objects belonging to a specific schema or an application's logic/module. So, if a user needs to access the objects of a specific application module, just the role belonging to that application module can be granted to the user. This helps in achieving better user management.

How to do it

The following steps need to be followed to complete the recipe:

1. Create the read-only and read-write roles for each schema respectively:

   ```
   CREATE ROLE scott_readonly;
   CREATE ROLE scott_readwrite;
   CREATE ROLE tiger_readonly;
   CREATE ROLE tiger_readwrite;
   ```

2. Grant the `SELECT` access in the schemas to their associated roles:

   ```
   GRANT USAGE, SELECT ON ALL TABLES IN SCHEMA scott TO
   scott_readonly;
   ```

```
GRANT USAGE, SELECT ON ALL TABLES IN SCHEMA tiger TO
tiger_readonly;
```

3. Grant usage and write access in the schemas to their appropriate read-write
   roles:

```
GRANT USAGE, SELECT, INSERT, UPDATE, DELETE ON ALL TABLES IN SCHEMA
tiger TO tiger_readwrite;
GRANT USAGE, SELECT, INSERT, UPDATE, DELETE ON ALL TABLES IN SCHEMA
scott TO scott_readwrite;
```

4. Assign read-write roles to application users and read-only roles to individual
   users:

```
GRANT scott_readwrite to appuser1;
GRANT tiger_readwrite to appuser2;

GRANT scott_readonly to devuser1;
GRANT tiger_readonly to devuser2;
```

How it works

In order to understand how to implement the group roles in a better way, consider an
example where there is a company that has one PostgreSQL database (salesdb) with two
schemas – scott and tiger.

Now, the following are the requirements:

- Create 100 individual user accounts and 5 application users.
- Grant read access on the 2 schemas to 100 individual user accounts.
- Grant read and write access on 2 schemas to 5 application users.

There are multiple ways to achieve this. One way is to grant access to each of these objects
to all the user accounts individually. But isn't that very time-consuming? The other way is
to use group roles.

In order to use group roles, we need to create two roles for each schema, as seen in step 1 –
one for read-only and the other for read-write for both scott and tiger schemas:

- scott_read_only: The READ-ONLY role to perform READS on the
  schema scott.
- scott_read_write: The READ-WRITE role to perform WRITES on the
  schema scott.

- `tiger_read_only`: The READ-ONLY role to perform READS on the schema `tiger`.
- `tiger_read_write`: The READ-WRITE role to perform WRITES on the schema `tiger`.

And then the reads and writes on the two schemas can be granted to their associated roles as seen in step 2 and step 3. And those roles can be granted to the individual users and the application users as seen in step 4.

By using the preceding approach, a role can be directly assigned to a new user instead of granting appropriate privileges on each object explicitly. This helps in achieving proper user management through role-based segregation.

MVCC implementation and VACUUM in PostgreSQL

MVCC implementation in PostgreSQL is unique when compared to Oracle and MySQL-like relational databases. MVCC stands for **Multi-Version Concurrency Control**. As the full form speaks for itself, MVCC is needed to support consistency while running transactions so that readers and writers do not block each other.

To understand it better, consider a hypothetical situation where transaction **A** started at 9:00 a.m. to get a count of all the records in a table: `foo.bar` (with 10,000,020 records). As it is a very huge table, let's say it is said to be completed in 20 minutes. Another transaction, **B**, started at 9:10 a.m. to delete 20 records from the same table. When transaction A, which started at 9:00 a.m., is completed at 9:20 a.m., it still should be able to see the same records as it did at 9:00 a.m., that is 10,000,020 records, without considering transaction B, which deleted some records at 9:10 a.m. Though the behavior always depends on the isolation levels, it is still able to provide a consistent view of the data as to how it was when the query actually ran. How does it work? What is happening internally? We will discuss these things in this recipe.

 Throughout this book, you shall see the words records or tuples (of a table). A record in PostgreSQL is mostly referred to as a tuple. Also, PostgreSQL may be referred to as Postgres or PG in many places. They are one and the same.

Getting ready

Oracle and MySQL-like databases have separate UNDO storage that stores the past images required for consistency. If an existing record of a table is modified (updated or deleted), the past image is copied to a separate location. This way, if there is an existing transaction that started before the record got modified, it can still access the record as it was before it got modified. However, this UNDO is maintained in a separate location, not within the same table.

In PostgreSQL, UNDO is maintained in its own table. What this means is that the tuple before modification and the modified tuple are both stored in the same table.

How to do it...

In the following steps, we shall understand how PostgreSQL implements MVCC by explaining some of the system columns in detail. We shall also consider a simple example where we create a table with two columns, insert some records, and see the transaction IDs assigned to these records. We shall then query system columns such as xmin and xmax and understand how multiple versions of rows are maintained within the same table. This exercise will not only help you understand MVCC but will also show you some of the common queries that are useful in your daily admin life:

1. Create a schema and a table with two columns and insert some records into it:

```
postgres=# CREATE SCHEMA foo;
CREATE SCHEMA
postgres=# CREATE TABLE foo.bar (id int, name varchar(5));
CREATE TABLE
postgres=# INSERT INTO foo.bar VALUES (generate_series(1,5),'avi');
INSERT 0 5
```

2. Query the pg_attribute table to see the system columns that got added to the table along with the two columns id and name:

```
postgres=# SELECT attname, format_type (atttypid,atttypmod)
FROM pg_attribute
WHERE attrelid = 'foo.bar'::regclass::oid
ORDER BY attnum;

 attname  | format_type
----------+---------------------
 tableoid | oid
 cmax     | cid
 xmax     | xid
```

```
        cmin      | cid
        xmin      | xid
        ctid      | tid
        id        | integer
        name      | character varying(5)
        (8 rows)
```

3. We shall then select all the columns from the table using the `select * from table` command and understand that we don't see any data related to the system column:

```
postgres=# SELECT * FROM foo.bar LIMIT 1;
 id | name
----+------
  1 | avi
(1 row)
```

4. Now, to select the values of a system column exclusively, we shall include the system column name in the `select` command and see what it stores:

```
postgres=# select xmin,* from foo.bar limit 1;
 xmin  | id | name
-------+----+------
 11705 | 1  | avi
(1 row)
```

5. Let's query the `pg_class` table to see the `oid` of the table created in step 1:

```
postgres=# SELECT oid, relname FROM pg_class WHERE relname = 'bar';
  oid  | relname
-------+---------
 31239 | bar
(1 row)
```

6. If we have two tables with the same name, `bar`, but in different schemas, they do not share the same oid, as seen in the following example. In this example, we shall create another table in a different schema than the one created in step 1 and see that the oid is different for both:

```
postgres=# CREATE TABLE public.bar (id int, name varchar(5));
CREATE TABLE

postgres=# SELECT oid, relname FROM pg_class WHERE relname = 'bar'
and relkind = 't';
  oid  | relname
-------+---------
 31242 | bar
```

```
31239 | bar
(2 rows)
```

7. To properly identify the table that belongs to a specific schema, we could join `pg_namespace` with `pg_class` as seen in the following log:

```
postgres=# SELECT pc.oid, pn.nspname, pc.relname
           FROM pg_class pc
           JOIN pg_namespace pn ON pc.relnamespace = pn.oid
               WHERE pn.nspname = 'foo'
               AND pc.relname = 'bar';
  oid   | nspname | relname
--------+---------+---------
 31239  | foo     | bar
(1 row)
```

8. We could also use `regclass` to identify the oid of a fully qualified table. A fully qualified table is a table specified along with its `schemaname` (`schemaname.tablename`):

```
postgres=# select 'foo.bar'::regclass::oid;
  oid
-------
 31239
(1 row)
```

9. In this step, we will see how the system column `tableoid` can be seen from the table for each record and understand that it is the same as the oid of the table:

```
postgres=# select tableoid, id, name from foo.bar limit 1;
 tableoid | id | name
----------+----+------
    31239 |  1 | avi
(1 row)
```

10. Every transaction in PostgreSQL has a unique transaction ID. In this step, we shall see how a transaction ID remains the same within a transaction block and changes for a new transaction:

```
postgres=# BEGIN;
BEGIN
postgres=# select txid_current();
 txid_current
--------------
        11902
(1 row)
```

```
postgres=# select txid_current();
 txid_current
--------------
        11902
(1 row)
postgres=# END;
COMMIT

postgres=# select txid_current();
 txid_current
--------------
        11903
(1 row)
```

11. By querying `xmin` explicitly, we can see the transaction ID that inserted the records by finding the `xmin` value of each record. Notice the `xmin` values of all the records in the following log:

```
postgres=# select xmin,* from foo.bar;
 xmin  | id | name
-------+----+------
 11705 |  1 | avi
 11705 |  2 | avi
 11705 |  3 | avi
 11705 |  4 | avi
 11705 |  5 | avi
 11905 |  6 | avi
(6 rows)
```

12. We could also find the `xmax` of each record by explicitly selecting it. If `xmax` is set to `0`, it was never deleted and is visible:

```
postgres=# select xmin, xmax, * from foo.bar ;
 xmin  | xmax | id | name
-------+------+----+------
 11705 |    0 |  1 | avi
 11705 |    0 |  2 | avi
 11705 |    0 |  3 | avi
 11705 |    0 |  4 | avi
 11705 |    0 |  5 | avi
 11905 |    0 |  6 | avi
 11907 |    0 |  7 | avi
(7 rows)
```

13. If we perform a `delete` operation to delete a record, subsequent select queries cannot see the deleted record anymore:

```
postgres=# BEGIN;
BEGIN
postgres=# DELETE FROM foo.bar WHERE id = 7;
DELETE 1
postgres=# COMMIT;
COMMIT
postgres=# select xmin, xmax, * from foo.bar ;
 xmin  | xmax | id | name
-------+------+----+------
 11705 |    0 |  1 | avi
 11705 |    0 |  2 | avi
 11705 |    0 |  3 | avi
 11705 |    0 |  4 | avi
 11705 |    0 |  5 | avi
 11905 |    0 |  6 | avi
(6 rows)
```

14. Now, let's use two terminals in parallel. In one terminal, we shall delete a record and then observe the `xmin` and `xmax` values of the record being deleted from another terminal, before committing `delete`:

- **Terminal 1**: Running `delete` but not committing it. Note the transaction ID that performed `delete`:

```
postgres=# BEGIN;
BEGIN
postgres=# select txid_current();
 txid_current
--------------
        11911
(1 row)

postgres=# DELETE FROM foo.bar WHERE id = 6;
DELETE 1
```

- **Terminal 2:** We can see the `xmax` value changed to the transaction ID that executed `delete` in terminal 1:

```
postgres=# select xmin, xmax, * from foo.bar ;
 xmin  | xmax  | id | name
-------+-------+----+------
 11705 |     0 |  1 | avi
 11705 |     0 |  2 | avi
 11705 |     0 |  3 | avi
```

```
11705 |      0 | 4 | avi
11705 |      0 | 5 | avi
11905 | 11911 | 6 | avi
(6 rows)
```

15. Roll back the delete and now see the xmax value:

- **Terminal 1**: Let's issue rollback instead of commit so that the record is not deleted:

```
postgres=# BEGIN;
BEGIN
postgres=# select txid_current();
 txid_current
--------------
        11911
(1 row)

postgres=# DELETE FROM foo.bar WHERE id = 6;
DELETE 1
postgres=# ROLLBACK;
ROLLBACK
```

- **Terminal 2:** We can see that the xmax still remains the same but internally the hint bits xact_rolled_backed will be set to true:

```
$ psql -d postgres -c "select xmin, xmax, id, name from
foo.bar"
 xmin  | xmax  | id | name
-------+-------+----+------
 11705 |     0 | 1  | avi
 11705 |     0 | 2  | avi
 11705 |     0 | 3  | avi
 11705 |     0 | 4  | avi
 11705 |     0 | 5  | avi
 11905 | 11911 | 6  | avi
(6 rows)
```

16. We could query the location of each tuple by querying the system column, `ctid`:

```
postgres=# select xmin, xmax, ctid, * from foo.bar ;
 xmin  | xmax  | ctid  | id | name
-------+-------+-------+----+------
 11705 |     0 | (0,1) |  1 | avi
 11705 |     0 | (0,2) |  2 | avi
 11705 |     0 | (0,3) |  3 | avi
 11705 |     0 | (0,4) |  4 | avi
 11705 |     0 | (0,5) |  5 | avi
 11905 | 11911 | (0,6) |  6 | avi
(6 rows)
```

How it works...

In order to understand how MVCC works in PostgreSQL, it is important to understand some of the system columns of a table in PostgreSQL. The preceding example contains a demonstration of the hidden columns of a table in PostgreSQL along with the changes to their values when their corresponding records are modified.

If you observe Step 1, it is visible that a table with the name `foo.bar` has been created with just two columns. However, when you see the output in Step 2, it is interesting to see that it is not just two columns but there are some additional columns that are automatically created by PostgreSQL.

Well, through the output, it is clear that there are six additional columns to what is assumed to be created when we create a table using the CREATE TABLE syntax. To understand how these columns make a significant difference to the way *MVCC* is implemented in PostgreSQL, let's learn about these system columns in detail.

Though these columns are considered to be hidden, it doesn't mean that the values in the columns are a mystery to an admin. The reason why these columns are considered hidden columns is they are excluded from the output of `select * from table`, as seen in the output of Step 3.

In order to see what values are stored in these hidden columns, these columns need to be exclusively used in the SELECT statement as seen in Step 4. In this example, we see the difference between selecting all the columns of a table versus selecting a system column exclusively along with the actual columns.

tableoid

Now, before learning about `tableoid`, it is important to understand what an OID is. An OID in PostgreSQL stands for an Object Identifier. When a table is created in PostgreSQL, a new record with the table name and the schema name is inserted into the system tables – `pg_class` and `pg_namespace`. OIDs are used by PostgreSQL internally as a primary key for such system tables. In order to find the oid of the table `foo.bar` that was created earlier, the easiest way is to query the `pg_class` system table as seen in Step 5.

But, what if there is more than one table with the same name but in two different schemas? In PostgreSQL, it is possible to have more than one schema in a single database. For example, if we observe the output in Step 6, it is visible that a table with the same name as the table created in Step 1 was created in a different schema as well.

Thus, in order to find the oid of the table that corresponds to the appropriate schema, `pg_class` can be joined with the system table `pg_namespace` (which contains the schema name and the oid of the schema). For every relation in `pg_class`, the oid of its schema is also inserted. To see that in action, the log in Step 7 contains simple SQL to identify the oid of a specific table that belongs to a specific schema.

There is another easy way to find the OID of a table, using `regclass`. Substitute `foo.bar` with the schema name and table name as seen in Step 8.

Now to understand tableoid in a simple way, it is nothing but a column that contains the oid of the table, which is the same as the oid visible in the `pg_class` table. See Step 9, which illustrates how we can select the tableoid along with the other columns of a table.

xmin

`xmin` is one of the important columns that a PostgreSQL admin should be fully aware of. An admin's day-to-day activity totally depends on understanding xmin very well. To understand xmin better, let's learn about transaction IDs in PostgreSQL. We are not going to discuss problems with transaction IDs in this chapter; this is just an introduction. For now, let's remember that a transaction ID is a unique identifier assigned to a transaction.

A transaction ID in PostgreSQL is a 32-bit unsigned integer. It is cyclic, which means that it starts from 0 and goes up to 4.2 billion (4,294,967,295) and then starts from 0 again. The function `txid_current()` shows the ID of the current transaction. If we observe the output in Step 10 carefully, we see that the transaction ID stayed the same within the entire transaction (between `BEGIN` and `END`) but it changed incrementally for another new transaction.

As we've understood the transaction ID now, *xmin* is nothing but the transaction ID that inserted that tuple. For example, in the output of Step 11, we can see that the first five records were inserted by a transaction with the ID 11705 and the last record was inserted by a transaction with the ID 11905.

This difference in *xmin* is essential in determining what tuples are visible to a transaction. For example, an SQL statement in a transaction that started before 11905 may not be able to see the records inserted by its future transactions.

xmax

The xmax value makes a significant difference when there are tuples that are being deleted or updated. Before we start to learn about xmax, see the log in Step 12, which shows the xmax value of the records in the foo.bar table.

In the log, we see that the value of xmax is 0. The value of xmax is 0 when it is a row that was never deleted or attempted for delete. There are two scenarios that could happen when you consider deleting a record:

1. A delete command was issued by a transaction and it was committed.
2. A delete command was issued by a transaction but it hasn't been committed yet, after it.

In the first scenario, it is quite understandable that when a delete was issued and committed, the record was no more visible, as seen in Step 13. So, there is no point in discussing the xmax value for that record.

But, what about the second scenario, where the delete has not been committed yet? To demonstrate that, I have issued a delete in one terminal and looked at the xmax value in another terminal, as seen in Step 14. If you look at the terminal 2 log carefully, the xmax value has been updated with the transaction ID that issued the delete. Please note that the xmax value remains the same as the transaction ID that issued the delete when a ROLLBACK is issued. And when the delete is committed, as discussed earlier, the record is no longer visible to the future selects.

As seen in Step 15, if I issue a ROLLBACK instead of COMMIT, the xmax value remains the same as the transaction ID that issued a delete before the rollback.

As we understood xmin and xmax now, when a transaction runs SELECT on a table, the records that are visible to the transaction are the tuples with (xmin <= txid_current()) and (xmax = 0 OR txid_current() < xmax):

```
select * from foo.bar where id = 2 ;
```

The preceding SQL issued by a transaction internally uses the following logic:

```
select * from foo.bar where id = 2 (and xmin <= txid_current() AND (xmax =
0 OR txid_current() < xmax));
```

ctid

ctid is the field that denotes the location of a tuple in a Postgres table. It is unique for each tuple. It contains the page/block number along with the tuple index within that page for the tuple. For example, the log in Step 16 shows that all the tuples are stored in page 0 and it also shows their locations within the page.

pageinspect

We are going to discuss extensions in PostgreSQL in future chapters. For now, consider them as a piece of external code that can be attached to existing Postgres code to achieve a specific functionality. pageinspect is an extension that is included with the *contrib* module, which is useful in showing the contents of a page. All the tuples of a table are stored in one or more pages. This extension gives granular visibility to the contents stored inside each page.

To create this extension, we shall just issue the command seen in Step 17:

```
postgres=# CREATE EXTENSION pageinspect ;
CREATE EXTENSION

-- Verify
postgres=# \dx
                          List of installed extensions
    Name      | Version |  Schema  |                Description
--------------+---------+----------+-------------------------------------
------------------
 pageinspect  | 1.6     | public   | inspect the contents of database pages at
a low level
 plpgsql      | 1.0     | pg_catalog | PL/pgSQL procedural language
(2 rows)
```

This extension provides two functions:

```
get_raw_page          : reads the specified 8KB page
heap_page_item_attrs : shows metadata and data of each tuple
```

From the previous log, we saw that there are six records after deleting one record from the table. But, has the record really been deleted from the table? Let's look at what is stored inside the page.

As there are very few tuples inside the table, we can see from the following output that there is only 1 page of size 8 KB for this table:

```
$ psql -d postgres -c "select relname, relpages from pg_class where oid =
'foo.bar'::regclass::oid"
 relname | relpages
---------+----------
 bar     | 1
(1 row)

$ psql -c "show block_size"
 block_size
------------
 8192
(1 row)
```

The page sequence starts from 0. So, we shall use *pageinspect* to see what is inside page 0:

```
$ psql -d postgres -c "SELECT t_xmin, t_xmax, t_field3 as t_cid, t_ctid
FROM
heap_page_items(get_raw_page('foo.bar',0))"
 t_xmin | t_xmax | t_cid | t_ctid
--------+--------+-------+--------
  11705 |      0 | 0 | (0,1)
  11705 |      0 | 0 | (0,2)
  11705 |      0 | 0 | (0,3)
  11705 |      0 | 0 | (0,4)
  11705 |      0 | 0 | (0,5)
  11905 |  11911 | 0 | (0,6)
  11907 |  11910 | 0 | (0,7)
(7 rows)
```

In the previous log, we saw that there is no such tuple with *ctid = (0,7)*. But we have deleted the record (committed) with id = 7. Is it still quite surprising that is not gone from the page? I don't think it is anymore, because we discussed earlier that UNDO is stored in its own table. So, a tuple that was deleted earlier is still stored in the table until a cleanup process removes it. The cleanup process (*VACUUM*) removes it only when there are no transactions dependent on the deleted record. In the following log, we saw that the record with this *ctid* has its *xmax_committed* set to t (true). What this means is that a delete was issued by transaction ID *11910* and it got committed:

```
postgres=# \x
Expanded display is on.

postgres=# SELECT lp,
        t_ctid AS ctid,
        t_xmin AS xmin,
        t_xmax AS xmax,
        (t_infomask & 128)::boolean AS xmax_is_lock,
        (t_infomask & 1024)::boolean AS xmax_committed,
        (t_infomask & 2048)::boolean AS xmax_rolled_back,
        (t_infomask & 4096)::boolean AS xmax_multixact,
        t_attrs[1] AS p_id,
        t_attrs[2] AS p_val
FROM heap_page_item_attrs(
        get_raw_page('foo.bar', 0),
        'foo.bar'
    ) WHERE lp = 7;
-[ RECORD 1 ]----+------------
lp               | 7
ctid             | (0,7)
xmin             | 11907
xmax             | 11910
xmax_is_lock     | f
xmax_committed   | t
xmax_rolled_back | f
xmax_multixact   | f
p_id             | \x07000000
p_val            | \x09617669
```

There's more...

So far, in the previous sections, we have understood how MVCC works in PostgreSQL. The final conclusion is that there may be several row versions maintained within each table due to deletions or updates. Over a period of time, there may be many such deleted records still stored in each page. Such records/tuples are called dead tuples. And the tuples that are inserted and remain unmodified are called live tuples. Dead tuples occupy more space and may decrease the performance of queries in the database. How should we manage these dead tuples? Should we perform any periodic manual maintenance or is it taken care of automatically? If it's automatic, what does that job? The answer to all of these questions is VACUUM. Let's learn about it in detail now.

When you start Postgres, you should see that there is a list of background processes running, as seen in the following screenshot. These processes (aka u*tility processes*) take some responsibility each to help users in the best possible way. One of these processes is the *autovacuum launcher* process. This process takes the responsibility of starting *VACUUM* and *ANALYZE* tasks on tables:

```
[avi@percona] $ps -eaf | grep postgres
postgres  2962     1  0 21:30 ?        00:00:00 /usr/pgsql-10/bin/postgres -D /var/lib/pgsql/10/data
postgres  2963  2962  0 21:30 ?        00:00:00 postgres: logger process
postgres  2965  2962  0 21:30 ?        00:00:00 postgres: checkpointer process
postgres  2966  2962  0 21:30 ?        00:00:00 postgres: writer process
postgres  2967  2962  0 21:30 ?        00:00:00 postgres: wal writer process
postgres  2968  2962  0 21:30 ?        00:00:00 postgres: autovacuum launcher process
postgres  2969  2962  0 21:30 ?        00:00:00 postgres: archiver process
postgres  2970  2962  0 21:30 ?        00:00:00 postgres: stats collector process
postgres  2971  2962  0 21:30 ?        00:00:00 postgres: bgworker: logical replication launcher
```

VACUUM cleans up dead tuples so that the space occupied by them can be reused by future inserts (an update does a deletion and an insertion). Whereas an *ANALYZE* collects the statistics of a table so that the execution plan prepared by the parser for a query using this table is optimal. There are certain parameters in PostgreSQL (*postgresql.conf*) that are used by this process to determine when to run an *autovacuum vacuum* or an *autovacuum analyze* on a table. We shall learn about tuning autovacuum and the internals of autovacuum in future chapters.

Backup and Recovery 3

One of the most important requirements in any database technology is the ability to perform backup and recovery. Some of the commercial databases require you to pay a huge license fee to use backups. But, PostgreSQL includes robust backup methods built into the source at no cost. These built-in tools are well-known tools that serve different use cases.

Backup and recovery is important to achieve a number of requirements that are not limited to the following:

- Performing a schema refresh or a data refresh from one database to another
- Copying or moving a database from one server to another server
- Recovering a table or a database from a backup upon corruption
- Performing point-in-time recovery when the database has to be restarted from a certain point in time due to an accidental change or human error

Similar to many other databases, PostgreSQL supports both logical and physical backups. We have `pg_dump`/`pg_restore` for logical backup/restore and `pg_basebackup` for physical backups.

Depending on the size of your database, you may consider using the most popular open-source backup tools, such as pgBackRest, Barman, or WAL-g as alternatives. These are stable, open-source backup solutions that have been contributed and are continuously being maintained by a wider community. These external backup tools help us to achieve one or more of the following features:

- Parallel backup and restore
- Incremental backups
- Differential backups
- Features for building standby replicas
- The ability to stream backups to another server

- Streaming backups to AWS S3 or object store, removing the need to store backups locally or on locally mounted network shares before uploading to the cloud

In this chapter, we will learn about several methods available to back up and restore a PostgreSQL database. We will cover the following recipes in this chapter:

- Backing up and restoring a database using pg_dump and pg_restore
- Backing up and restoring one or more tables using pg_dump and pg_restore
- Backing up and restoring globals or an entire cluster using pg_dumpall and psql
- Parallel backup and restore using pg_dump and pg_restore
- Backing up a database cluster using pg_basebackup
- Restoring a backup taken using pg basebackup
- Installing pgBackRest on CentOS/Red Hat OS
- Installing pgBackRest on Ubuntu/Debian OS
- Backing up a database cluster using pgBackRest
- Restoring a backup taken using pgBackRest

Technical requirements

In order to follow along with the steps discussed in the following recipes, you will need the following:

- You must have a Linux server with PostgreSQL installed and running.
- You should be able to connect as root or should have sudo access to perform some commands as root.
- You should be able to connect to the server as the OS user (Postgres) who owns the data directory.

Backing up and restoring a database using pg_dump and pg_restore

Logical backups in PostgreSQL can be taken using pg_dump. These backups are portable across different operating systems and versions. Consider an example of moving a database from one server to another in order to upgrade it from PostgreSQL 9.6.x to PostgreSQL 13.x. In this case, we could use the binaries of PostgreSQL 13 to back up the database in version 9.6 and restore it using the version 13 binaries.

A backup taken using pg_dump can exist in both a text file (human-readable script file) format or a custom format (compressed). If a backup is taken in a plain text format, then we use psql to restore it. If a backup is taken in the custom format, then pg_restore must be used to restore that backup.

pg_dump helps in taking a consistent snapshot of the database without causing any waits to the usual database traffic. However, there are certain things to remember before considering a pg_dump for your backup strategy:

- pg_dump cannot be used to back up multiple databases at the same time. It can back up one database at a time.
- Backups taken using pg_dump are not useful for point-in-time recovery that needs some more WAL segments to be replayed. It is not possible to replay transaction logs (WALs) after restoring such backups.
- It is important to have periodic logical backup testing as it ensures that all the data from the disk is readable and thus proves there are no corrupted pages when the checksum is not enabled.
- Attempt to maintain a periodic schema dump of a database using pg_dump. It could be helpful in the case of catalog corruption, which may not allow you to perform a backup using pg_dump. If there is a catalog corruption, you could restore the schema to another cluster and then use the COPY command to copy the table to the filesystem to dump the corrupt data to a new cluster.

Getting ready

In order to use pg_dump, pg_restore, or psql, we need to have these binaries in place. If pg_dump needs to run locally on the database server, then nothing special needs to be done to use pg_dump as it is available in the bin directory. However, if the backup needs to be taken remotely, then the following rpm or deb will be needed.

The RPM package for CentOS/Red Hat distributions

To use `pg_dump` on Red Hat or the CentOS OS, the `postgresql13` package is required, which can be installed using the following command:

```
$ sudo yum install postgresql13
```

To make sure that the preceding command works, you could install the latest repository, `pgdg-redhat-repo-latest.noarch.rpm`, which is available at `https://www.postgresql.org/download/linux/redhat/` for Red Hat and CentOS.

Debian and Ubuntu

In order to use `pg_dump` and `pg_restore`, we require the `postgresql-client-13` package, which can be installed using the following command:

```
$ sudo apt-get install postgresql-client-13
```

In order to use the appropriate repository that suits your distribution, you could follow the instructions available at `https://www.postgresql.org/download/linux` or Ubuntu and Debian.

`pg_dump` can run on both the local database server and from a remote server.

How to do it

A backup can be taken using `pg_dump` in two formats, hence there are two sections in this recipe – Section A for a custom format and Section B for the plain format. If we observe the syntax for backup – 3a, the format of a backup can be specified using the command-line argument -F. Depending on the format specified, we could either use `pg_restore` or psql to restore the dump. If the backup needs to be performed remotely, the command should include the additional command-line arguments, such as -h for hostname, -p for port number, and -U for username.

1. The following is the syntax for taking a backup using `pg_dump` in the custom format:

    ```
    $ pg_dump -h <source_server> -p <source_port> -U <username>
    database_name -F<format> -f <backup_location>/<dumpfile_name>.dmp
    ```

2. The following is the syntax for performing a restore of a backup using `pg_restore` and `psql`. When a custom format is used while taking a backup using `pg_dump`, `pg_restore` should be used for restoring the dump. If the format used is plain text, then `psql` can be used for the restore but not `pg_restore`:

```
For restore of a custom format dump
$ pg_restore -h <target_server> -p <target_port> -U <username>
database_name <backup_location>/<dumpfile_name>.dmp
For restore of a plain format dump
$ psql -h <target_server> -p <target_port> -U <username>
database_name <backup_location>/<dumpfile_name>.dmp
```

Section A

This section will show the steps to back up the database `percdb` in a custom format from the source server and restore the dump to another database, `mypgdb`, on the target server:

1. Backing up of the `percdb` database is done in the custom format from the source:

```
$ pg_dump -h <source_server> -p <source_port> -U <username> percdb
-Fc -f /backup_dir/percdb.dmp
```

2. Create the database to which the dump needs to be restored on the target server. The database name need not be the same as the database that the backup belongs to:

```
$ psql -c "CREATE DATABASE mypgdb"
```

3. Now restore the dump of the `percd` database to the newly created database `mypgdb`. In this step, all the objects of the `percdb` database will be restored to the `mypgdb` database:

```
$ pg_restore -h <target_server> -p <target_port> -U <username>
mypgdb /backup_dir/percdb.dmp
```

Section B

This section will show the steps to back up the database `percdb` in plain format from the source server and restore the dump to another database, `mypgdb`, on the target server:

1. Backing up the `percdb` database is done in the plain format as follows:

   ```
   $ pg_dump -h <source_server> -p <source_port> -U <username> percdb
   -Fp -f /backup_dir/percdb.dmp
   ```

2. Create the database to which the dump needs to be restored. In this case, we are creating the database `mypgdb`:

   ```
   $ psql -c "CREATE DATABASE mypgdb"
   ```

3. Restore the dump that contains objects of the `percd` database to another database, `mypgdb`:

   ```
   $ psql -h <source_server> -p <source_port> -U <username> mypgdb -f
   /backup_dir/percdb.dmp
   ```

How it works

Under Section A, you might notice that the backup of database `percdb` was taken using the custom format (-Fc) in *Step 1*. As the backup was taken using the custom format, it can only be restored using `pg_restore`. If the backup was taken in the source server locally, the `dumpfile` must be copied using `scp` or `rsync` or other possible methods to the target server. We can then create the database before performing the restore as seen in step 2, because the restore fails if the target database does not exist. In step 3, `pg_restore` was used to restore the backup of the database `percdb` to the database `mypgdb`.

In Section B, we could see that `pg_dump` was used to take a backup in the plain format. When a plain-format backup is generated, psql can be used to restore the dump, as it is nothing but a script file.

Backing up and restoring one or more tables using pg_dump and pg_restore

In the previous recipe, we saw how `pg_dump` can be used to take a backup of an entire database. In this recipe, we will see how `pg_dump` can be used to take a backup of one or more tables from a database and restore those tables into another database.

Getting ready

`pg_dump` can be used to take a logical backup of single or multiple tables from a database. However, we cannot dump one table from one database and another table from a different database at once. `pg_dump` can only work on one database at a time. At the same time, it is also possible to take a dump of the entire database excluding one or more tables.

In order to perform the backup, the user should be able to connect to the database and access the tables being considered for backup. If the user is a superuser, then it does not need any additional privileges to perform the backup.

How to do it

In order to back up and restore a table, we use the flag `-t`. We could see an example syntax to back up a table using `pg_dump` and restore a table using `pg_restore` and `psql` here:

The following is the syntax for backing up the table:

```
$ pg_dump -h <source_server> -p <source_port> -U <username> database_name -F<format> -t tablename -f <location>/<dumpfile_name>.dmp
```

The following is the syntax to restore a custom format dump:

```
$ pg_restore -h <target_server> -p <target_port> -U <username> -d database_name -t tablename <backup_location>/<dumpfile_name>.dmp
```

The following is the syntax to restore a plain format dump:

```
$ psql -h <target_server> -p <target_port> -U <username> mypgdb -f <backup_location>/<dumpfile_name>.dmp
```

Let's see the steps involved in taking a backup of one or more tables:

1. In the following example, the tables being backed up are `accounts.infra` and `public.pgbench_history`:

   ```
   $ pg_dump percdb -t accounts.infra -t public.pgbench_history -Fc -f
   /backup_dir/tables.dmp
   ```

   The other alternative method is the following:

   ```
   $ pg_dump percdb -t accounts.infra -t public.pgbench_history -Fp -f
   /backup_dir/tables.dmp
   ```

2. Create the database to which the table dump needs to be restored on the target server. If the database already exists, you may ignore this step:

   ```
   $ psql -c "CREATE DATABASE mypgdb"
   ```

3. The next step is restoring two tables from backup to another database, `mypgdb`:

   The syntax to perform the restore using a custom format dump is as follows:

   ```
   $ pg_restore -h <target_server> -p <target_port> -U <username> -d
   mypgdb -t accounts.infra -t public.pgbench_history
   /backup_dir/tables.dmp
   ```

   The syntax to perform the restore using a plain format dump is as follows:

   ```
   $ psql -h <target_server> -p <target_port> -U <username> -d mypgdb
   -f /backup_dir/tables.dmp
   ```

How it works

As seen in syntax 3c, the command to back up a table looks the same as the command used to take a backup of a database, but with a minor difference: it includes another command-line argument, `-t`. Using `-t` or `--table`, we can specify one table or a pattern, using which multiple tables or a set of tables can be considered for backup.

For example, the following syntax can take a backup of all tables in the schema `accounts` from the database `percdb`. This syntax has `accounts.*` passed as a value to `-t`. It means all tables in the schema `accounts`:

```
$ pg_dump percdb -t accounts.* -Fp -f /backup_dir/accounts.dmp
```

In step 1, we see that there are two tables from two different schemas considered for backup. In such a case, drawing a pattern and simplifying the `pg_dump` command may be difficult. So, there is no other option than passing both the table names separately using `-t`.

While taking a backup, both custom and plain format can be chosen. But, a plain format dump is the same as a script file. So, all the tables backed up using `pg_dump` will be restored when we choose plain format. But, a custom format offers the comfort of choosing one table from an entire database dump.

In step 3, we see that `pg_restore` was specified when the backup format is custom format. If the backup format is plain, `psql` must be used to execute the script file. One more important point to consider is that `pg_restore` need not contain the `-t` command-line argument if the dump file just contains the tables that need to be restored. If it is a dump file that contains the entire database, then, `pg_restore` can use `-t` to selectively restore the required tables.

Backing up and restoring globals or an entire cluster using pg_dumpall and psql

In the previous recipes, we have seen how a logical backup of a database or tables can be taken using `pg_dump`.

`pg_dump` cannot serve the purpose of taking a logical backup of all the databases in the cluster in one go. For that reason, there is the `pg_dumpall` utility. This can be used to dump all the databases into a single dump file.

`pg_dumpall` can also be used to take a backup of only globals, excluding databases. Globals in PostgreSQL are the users/roles and tablespaces.

In this recipe, we shall see the steps involved in taking a cluster dump and globals dump and then proceed to the steps that show how the dumps can be restored.

Getting ready

In order to perform the globals or the entire cluster backup using `pg_dumpall`, it is recommended to use a database user who has superuser privilege.

How to do it

As `pg_dumpall` can be used to take a backup of the entire cluster or just the globals, we shall discuss these separately in Sections A and B.

In the following section, we shall see the steps involved in performing a backup and restore of a cluster using `pg_dumpall`:

1. The first step is to perform a full cluster using `pg_dumpall`. This can be seen in the following syntax:

   ```
   $ pg_dumpall -h <source_server> -p <source_port> -U <superuser> -f
   /backup_dir/dumpall.sql
   ```

   The example command to perform `pg_dumpall` on a server with IP 192.168.110.10 is as follows:

   ```
   $ pg_dumpall -h 192.168.110.10 -U postgres -p 5432 -f
   /backup_dir/dumpall.sql
   ```

2. The backup was taken using `pg_dumpall` needs to be restored using `psql` using the following syntax:

   ```
   $ psql -h <target_server> -p <target_port> -U <superuser> -f
   /backup_dir/dumpall.sql
   ```

   The example command to restore the dump file to a server with IP 192.168.110.10:

   ```
   $ psql -f /backup_dir/dumpall.sql
   ```

In this section, we shall see the steps involved in performing a backup and restore of globals but not the entire cluster using `pg_dumpall`:

1. The following command can be used to back up globals from a cluster using `pg_dumpall`:

   ```
   $ pg_dumpall -h <source_server> -p <source_port> -U <superuser> -g
   -f /backup_dir/dumpall.sql
   ```

   The following is an example command to take a globals dump from 192.168.110.10:

   ```
   $ pg_dumpall -h 192.168.110.10 -U postgres -p 5432 -f
   /backup_dir/dumpall.sql
   ```

2. The backup of globals taken using `pg_dumpall` can be restored using psql as seen in the following command:

   ```
   $ psql -h <target_server> -p <target_port> -U <superuser> -f
   /backup_dir/dumpall.sql
   ```

The following is an example command to restore the backup to a cluster using psql:

   ```
   $ psql -f /backup_dir/dumpall.sql
   ```

How it works...

`pg_dumpall` generates a human-readable plain text format dump file. As this is a script file, `psql` can be used to perform the restore. `pg_dumpall` can be executed remotely from a remote server or within the same server locally.

Section A includes the steps involved in performing a cluster dump and restore in two simple steps. The first step is to take the cluster backup using a simple `pg_dumpall` command and writing the output to a file. Once the file is generated, this file can be copied to the target server if required and restored simply using `psql`.

The only difference between Section A and Section B is that the second section contains the steps involved in taking a globals-only dump and how `psql` can be used to restore just the globals. The difference in the commands between a cluster and a global dump is that the global dump includes an additional flag, `-g`.

Parallel backup and restore using pg_dump and pg_restore

For a tiny database, `pg_dump` need not run in parallel using multiple connections. But, when there are databases of several GBs or TBs in size, you may wish to run `pg_dump` using more parallel jobs. If `pg_dump` can run in parallel using more CPUs without utilizing all the available server resources, it can complete faster.

Multiple processes are spawned when `pg_dump` is invoked in parallel mode. For that reason, it is not wise to allocate all the available CPUs on the database server to `pg_dump`, if the database server is serving any traffic.

In this recipe, we shall discuss how a large database's backup and restore can be performed faster using parallel features in `pg_dump`.

Getting ready

In order to use `pg_dump` either locally or remotely, the `postgresql-13` package must be installed on the server from the `pg_dump` being performed.

Additionally, it is better to observe the CPU load and allocate the safest number of parallel processes so that the load on the server doesn't become high.

How to do it

The following is the syntax that can be used as a reference to perform a parallel backup and restore:

The syntax for parallel backup is as follows:

```
$ pg_dump -Fd <database_name> -j <no_of_cores> -f
<location>/<parallel_dump_dir>
```

The syntax for parallel restore is as follows:

```
$ pg_restore -d <database_name> -j <no_of_cores>
<location>/<parallel_dump_dir>
```

The following are the steps involved in performing a parallel backup and restore using the directory format in `pg_dump`:

1. Create a directory for storing the backup. A parallel backup requires a unique directory unlike a custom or a plain format `pg_dump` backup:

    ```
    $ mkdir -p /backup_dir/percdb
    ```

2. We need to use the directory format to perform a parallel backup using `pg_dump`. The following command is an example of a parallel backup of a database, `percdb`, using the directory format. `-j` represents the number of parallel jobs:

    ```
    $ pg_dump -Fd percdb -j 8 -f /backup_dir/percdb
    ```

3. To perform a parallel restore of the database `percdb`, we could only use `pg_restore` but not `psql`. As seen in the following command, it requires the directory that was created to store the dumps generated out of the parallel backup. We could additionally use `-j` to mention the number of parallel connections to the database while performing the restore:

```
$ pg_restore -d percdb -j 4 /backup_dir/percdb
```

How it works

If we observe the syntax to take a parallel `pg_dump`, there is a command-line argument, `-Fd`. It means that it needs to be a directory format backup. In order to choose the number of parallel processes, we use `-j`.

Unlike the other backup formats, the directory format does not create a single dump file or a tar file. It creates one file for each table and blob being dumped. For this reason, the first step is to make sure that there is an exclusive empty directory for storing the parallel dump, as seen in step 1.

In Step 2, the database `percdb` was being backed up using 8 CPU cores to the location: `/backup_dir/percdb`. The dump generated for each table in the directory is in the custom format, which is compressed. So, the size of the custom format and the directory are comparatively similar.

In order to restore the backup to a parallel `pg_dump`, we must use `pg_restore` but not `psql`. A directory format backup creates a `toc.dat` file (table of contents datafile) that contains the details of the dumped objects, which can be read by `pg_restore`. As seen in step 3, `pg_restore` was used to restore the directory format backup from the location `/backup_dir/percdb` to the database `percdb` using four CPU cores. The number of cores used for backup and the number of cores used for restore need not be the same.

Backing up a database cluster using pg_basebackup

`pg_basebackup` is the built-in binary format backup tool available with PostgreSQL. Only the backups taken using `pg_basebackup` can be used for point-in-time recovery and not `pg_dump` or `pg_dumpall`.

This can also be performed from the standby and not just the master. So, we can offload the backups to a standby that is always in sync and on a faster network.

`pg_basebackup` cannot run in parallel mode and does not support incremental or differential backups. So, it may be a great tool when the backup is a few hundred gigabytes and stored in the same data center. If the backup is several terabytes in size and needs to be pushed over the network to the cloud or a remote backup server, then it is wise to try alternate open source backup tools upon testing `pg_basebackup`.

Getting ready

In order to run a backup using `pg_basebackup`, it requires an empty directory. If we have a requirement of running a daily or a weekly backup job, maybe scheduled using a cron job, it is wise to have a dated directory created to store the backup for each day.

The privileges required to run a backup using `pg_basebackup` are simple. It just needs the REPLICATION role to be assigned to the user. The backup user must be created on the database cluster that is being backed up. If the backup is running from a standby, the user must be created on the master.

As `pg_basebackup` runs using the replication protocol, the user must be allowed to connect from the server from where the backup is running, using the replication protocol. The following is an example entry that needs to exist in the `pg_hba.conf` of the database server that is being backed up.

How to do it

The following are the steps involved in performing a backup using `pg_basebackup`, from either the primary/master server or from a standby:

1. Create a directory to store the backup. It requires an empty target directory to perform the backup:

```
$ sudo mkdir -p /backup_dir/`date +"%Y%m%d"`
$ sudo chown -R postgres:postgres /backup_dir/`date +"%Y%m%d"`
```

2. Create the user using which the backup needs to be performed. This user requires a `REPLICATION` role to perform the backup:

```
$ psql -U postgres -c "CREATE USER backup_user WITH REPLICATION
PASSWORD 'secret'"
```

3. Add appropriate entries in the `pg_hba.conf` file to allow replication connections and perform a reload:

```
$ echo "host replication backup_user <backup_server_hostname>/32
md5" >> $PGDATA/pg_hba.conf
$ psql -c "select pg_reload_conf()"
```

4. Prepare a command using the following syntax to perform a backup using `pg_basebackup`:

```
$ pg_basebackup -h <hostname> -U <user> -p <port> -D
<target_directory> -c <checkpoint_mode> -F<format> -P -
X<wal_method> -l <backup_label>
```

The following is an example command to generate a backup of a PostgreSQL cluster running on `192.168.90.70` using `pg_basebackup`:

```
$ pg_basebackup -h 192.168.90.70 -U backup_user -p 5432 -D
/backup_dir/`date +"%Y%m%d"` -c fast -Ft -z -P -Xs -l backup_label
```

How it works...

In step 1, we are creating a new directory to store the backup. Though `pg_basebackup` automatically creates the target directory, it will fail when it lacks privileges.

The next step is to create the user using which `pg_basebackup` can be executed. Even the superuser Postgres can be used to take a backup. But, a superuser is always recommended to be limited to administrative operations only. For that reason, we are creating a `backup_user` in step 2, on the master database server.

As `pg_basebackup` uses a replication protocol, the user needs to be allowed to make replication connections from the backup server. In step 3, we are appending the entry to allow replication connections from `192.168.90.70` using `backup_user` to the `pg_hba.conf` of the database server. This entry must exist on the server to which `backup_user` is connecting to take a backup. And then, we need to perform a reload to get the changes to take effect.

And the final step is the backup. In step 4, we saw the syntax that can be used to perform a backup. It starts with the hostname, which can either be the IP or the hostname of the database server to which `backup_user` connects, and then the username followed by the port on which the database cluster is running. Using `-D`, we specify the directory in which the backup needs to be created.

As `pg_basebackup` waits for a checkpoint to complete, we can either issue a fastboot or a checkpoint that is spread within the command itself, instead of waiting. And then we go onto the format of the backup. It can be taken in tar or plain format. And we could also use `-z` to compress it to a tar format backup. `-Ft` stands for tar format and `-Fp` for plain. In order to display the progress, we can use `-P` so we know how long we need to wait for the backup to finish.

`pg_basebackup` may be used to set up replication as well. In that case, using `-R` makes our job very simple. It creates required entries for the parameters in `postgresql.auto.conf` to set up replication.

As the backup needs to be performed online, there may be the usual database transactions that are generating a lot of WAL segments. In order to make `pg_basebackup` consistent, it also needs the WALs that are generated during the backup. We can either stream the WALs using a parallel stream or fetch them all after the backup is finished. As the WAL segments are recycled after a certain threshold, it may sometimes be safe to stream them using `-Xs`. Otherwise, we could use `-Xf`, which fetches the WAL segments after the backup is completed. And finally, to give a label to the backup, we could use `-l`.

Restoring a backup taken using pg basebackup

In the previous recipe, we discussed how `pg_basebackup` can be used to take a physical backup of the PostgreSQL cluster. We may restore this backup in various situations, such as creating a standby server in replication or recovering a database to a point in time. In this recipe, we shall see the steps required to restore a backup taken using `pg_basebackup`.

Getting ready

In order to restore a backup taken using pg_basebackup, there should be a new directory that has available storage equivalent to the original data directory. Additionally, the backup should be copied over the network, if required, to the target server where it needs to be restored.

The backup needs to be extracted to the targeted data directory as a Postgres user. So, it is important to have access to the Postgres OS user to perform the restore of the database cluster.

How to do it

The following are the steps involved in restoring a backup to the /pgdata directory and starting PostgreSQL using the restored backup:

1. Create a directory to which the backup needs to be restored. This directory needs to be empty before we proceed to step 2:

   ```
   $ sudo mkdir -p /pgdata
   ```

2. Extract the base.tar.gz file to the target directory:

   ```
   $ tar xzf /backup_location/base.tar.gz -C /pgdata
   ```

3. If the database server contains one or more tablespaces, then the individual tablespaces should also be extracted to different directories. As is visible in the following log, we see a tar file (named with the oid of the tablespace) for each tablespace when a backup is completed:

   ```
   $ ls -l /backup_dir/20201027/
   total 16816
   -rw-------. 1 postgres postgres 1006685 Oct 27 11:48 16575.tar.gz
   -rw-------. 1 postgres postgres 1006657 Oct 27 11:48 16576.tar.gz
   -rw-------. 1 postgres postgres 15183012 Oct 27 11:48 base.tar.gz
   -rw-------. 1 postgres postgres 17094 Oct 27 11:48 pg_wal.tar.gz
   ```

A tablespace_map file exists in the data directory that is extracted using base.tar.gz after step 2:

   ```
   $ cat /pgdata/tablespace_map
   16575 /data_tblspc
   16576 /index_tblspc
   ```

So, each of these tablespaces must be extracted to the directories mentioned in the `tablespace_map` file:

```
$ tar xzf 16575.tar.gz -C /data_tblspc
$ tar xzf 16576.tar.gz -C /index_tblspc
```

4. Extract the WAL segments generated during the backup to the `pg_wal` directory:

```
$ tar xzf pg_wal.tar.gz -C /pgdata/pg_wal
```

5. Start PostgreSQL using the data directory restored using the backup:

```
$ pg_ctl -D /pgdata start
```

How it works

In Step 1, we are creating a directory that needs to be considered a data directory or a target directory for the restore task.

And then proceed to Step 2 by extracting the `base.tar.gz` file to the target directory.

As seen in step 3, we use the tablespace mapping to extract the tablespace contents to the same locations. If the locations need to be modified, it can be done by just modifying the `tablespace_map` file manually and adding the new locations for each tablespace.

And we then proceed to step 4 to extract the WAL segments to the `pg_wal` directory of the target directory. Once all four steps are successfully completed, we can proceed to start the database cluster using the backup as seen in step 5.

Installing pgBackRest on CentOS/RedHat OS

pgBackRest is a widely used open source backup tool that offers several capabilities, such as parallel backup, incremental and differential backup, and the ability to stream a backup to the cloud from both master and standby databases. This is very suitable for database environments that are several terabytes in size. In this recipe, we shall see the steps involved in installing pgBackRest on Red Hat or CentOS operating systems.

Getting ready

In order to install pgBackRest, the PGDG repository should be configured. Visit
www.postgresql.org/downloads to download the appropriate PGDG repo for the Linux
distribution. It requires internet connectivity to download the repository and the packages.
Otherwise, the pgbackrest packages need to be downloaded to any other server that has
internet connectivity and then copied to the database server.

How to do it

The following are the steps involved in installing pgBackRest on the CentOS/Red Hat
family of operating systems. In this recipe, we have included the steps for 7.x and 8.x
releases:

1. Create the PGDG repository using the generic rpm:

   For Red Hat or CentOS 7.x:

   ```
   # yum install
   https://download.postgresql.org/pub/repos/yum/reporpms/EL-7-x86_64/
   pgdg-redhat-repo-latest.noarch.rpm
   ```

   For Red Hat or CentOS 8:

   ```
   # dnf install
   https://download.postgresql.org/pub/repos/yum/reporpms/EL-8-x86_64/
   pgdg-redhat-repo-latest.noarch.rpm
   ```

2. Install pgBackRest using yum using the following command:

   ```
   $ sudo yum install pgbackrest

   # You may need epel-release if it fails with dependency issues for
   some packages.
   $ sudo yum install epel-release
   ```

How it works

The PGDG repository must be set up in the database server to download the pgBackRest
packages as seen in step 1. Depending on the version, we could choose either the repo for
version 7 or 8. Once that is completed, we could proceed to the next step to install
pgbackrest using yum or dnf as seen in step 2.

Installing pgBackRest on Ubuntu/Debian OS

In this recipe, we shall see the steps involved in installing `pgBackRest` on Ubuntu or Debian operating systems.

Getting ready

The PGDG repository for a specific Ubuntu or Debian release should be installed on the operating system. It requires internet connectivity to download the repository and the packages. Otherwise, the `pgbackrest` packages need to be downloaded to any other server that has internet connectivity and then copied to the database server.

How to do it

The following are the detailed steps involved in installing `pgbackrest` on Debian/Ubuntu operating systems:

1. Import the PGDG repository to your database server. The steps for different releases of Debian and Ubuntu are listed here:

   For Debian Buster (10.x):

   ```
   # echo "deb http://apt.postgresql.org/pub/repos/apt/ buster-pgdg
   main" >> /etc/apt/sources.list.d/pgdg.list
   ```

   For Debian Stretch (9.x):

   ```
   # echo "deb http://apt.postgresql.org/pub/repos/apt/ stretch-pgdg
   main" >> /etc/apt/sources.list.d/pgdg.list
   ```

   For Debian Jessie (8.x):

   ```
   # echo "deb http://apt.postgresql.org/pub/repos/apt/ jessie-pgdg
   main" >> /etc/apt/sources.list.d/pgdg.list
   ```

   For Ubuntu Bionic 18.04:

   ```
   # echo "deb http://apt.postgresql.org/pub/repos/apt/ bionic-pgdg
   main" >> /etc/apt/sources.list.d/pgdg.list
   ```

   For Ubuntu Xenial 16.04:

   ```
   # echo "deb http://apt.postgresql.org/pub/repos/apt/ xenial-pgdg
   main" >> /etc/apt/sources.list.d/pgdg.list
   ```

2. Import the signing key and update the list of packages using the latest keys:

```
$ wget --quiet -O -
https://www.postgresql.org/media/keys/ACCC4CF8.asc | sudo apt-key
add -
```

3. We could now use `apt` to install `pgbackrest` as seen in the following command:

```
$ apt-get install pgbackrest
```

How it works

In order to install `pgbackrest` on Ubuntu or Debian, the first step is to import the repository by adding a line to a file in `sources.list.d` as seen in step 1. However, it is important to append the line that suits the operating system version as seen in the `/etc/os-release` file.

The next step is to import the signing key as seen in step 2. This key may change, so it is important to validate it from the official PostgreSQL website: `https://www.postgresql.org/download/linux/`.

Once the key is imported, we can proceed to update the list of packages available for `apt` to install. After finishing the update in step 2, we can use step 3 to install `pgbackrest`.

Backing up a database cluster using pgBackRest

pgBackRest can be used to perform faster backups using its parallel backup feature along with the support to perform incremental and differential backups. As pgBackRest can be performed remotely, it can also be used to take a backup from a standby server. In this recipe, we shall see how pgBackRest can be used to perform a full backup from a primary/master or a standby server.

Getting ready

In order to perform a backup using pgBackRest, it needs to be installed both on the local and also the remote server from where the backup is being performed (if the backup is being performed from a remote server).

The backup user should have the REPLICATION role to perform the backup. Even a superuser could perform the backup but it is always recommended to limit SUPERUSER to administrative tasks. Additionally, enable trusted SSH authentication using public keys between the database server and the backup server.

How to do it

The following are the steps involved in performing a backup using pgBackRest:

1. Create the pgbackrest configuration file where the name and locations of the target server along with the retention are set. This file also includes the hostname of the database server and other variables required to connect and perform the backup:

```
$ sudo bash -c 'cat << EOF > /etc/pgbackrest.conf
[global]
repo1-host=backupserver.percona.com
repo1-path=/backup_directory
repo1-retention-full=2
log-level-stderr=error
log-path=/backup/db/log

[percdb]
pg1-host=192.168.70.10
# The above line must be removed when the backup is performed
locally.
pg1-path=/var/lib/pgsql/13/data
pg1-port=5432
EOF'
```

2. Ensure that the following parameters are set on the master followed by a restart. A reload instead of a restart is required to modify archive_command when archive_mode is already set to on:

```
$ psql -c "ALTER SYSTEM SET archive_mode = 'on'"
$ psql -c "ALTER SYSTEM SET archive_command = 'pgbackrest --
stanza=percdb archive-push %p'"
$ sudo systemctl restart postgresql-12
```

3. Once a stanza for the Postgres database cluster being backed up is configured in the file as seen in step 1, we could use the following `stanza-create` option to initialize a stanza and then validate to see any errors:

```
$ pgbackrest stanza-create --stanza=percdb --log-level-console=info
$ pgbackrest check --stanza=percdb --log-level-console=info
```

4. We could now run a full backup using a simple command as seen in the following:

```
$ pgbackrest backup --stanza=percdb --log-level-console=info
```

5. In order to list the backups, we could use the following command:

```
$ pgbackrest info
```

How it works

`pgBackRest` can be used to run a backup remotely and also from a local server. Upon installation of the pgBackRest tool, the first step is to create the configuration file that has the details of the backup directory and also the database cluster that needs to be considered for backup.

While creating the configuration file, it is important to know about stanzas. A stanza is used to define the backup configuration for a specific PostgreSQL database cluster. It can be named with any name to distinguish the database cluster. There also exists a global stanza that stores the repository information.

For example, `repo1-path` indicates the location where the backups and archives need to be stored.

`repo1-retention-full` indicates how many full backups should be retained. `pg1-host` indicates the remote PostgreSQL cluster that is being backed up, whereas `pg1-path` is to set the location of the data directory of the cluster.

Once the configuration file is created, step 2 is to enable archiving using pgBackRest. If `archive_mode` needs to be changed, a restart is required, else, just a reload should be sufficient.

After making the parameter changes, we need to create the stanza as defined in the configuration file of the backup server or the local database server if the backup is running locally.

After creating and validating the stanza, the command-line argument – `backup` can be used to perform the full database backup.

Restoring a backup taken using pgBackRest

In the previous recipe, we saw how `pgBackRest` can be used to perform a backup of a PostgreSQL cluster either locally or remotely. In this recipe, we shall see the steps involved in restoring a backup taken using `pgBackRest`.

Getting ready

In order to perform the restore of a backup taken using `pgBackRest`, we must have `pgBackRest` installed on the target server where the backup is being restored to. We should have a new or an empty directory available for the database backup to be restored. Additionally, we need to make sure to enable trusted SSH authentication using public keys between the target server and the backup server.

How to do it

The following are the steps involved in performing the restore of a backup taken using pgBackRest:

1. Create the new data directory on the target server where the backup is being restored:

   ```
   $ sudo mkdir /var/lib/pgsql/13/data/
   $ sudo chmod 0700 /var/lib/pgsql/13/data
   ```

2. Create the `pgBackRest` configuration file that is the same as the backup server. In this file, we see the `global` stanza and also a stanza for the target database server. If the target server (here, `[percdb]`) is not the same as the one specified in the backup server, you may need to modify it appropriately:

   ```
   $ sudo bash -c 'cat << EOF > /etc/pgbackrest.conf
   [global]
   repo1-host=backupserver.percona.com
   ```

```
repo1-path=/backup_directory
repo1-retention-full=2
log-level-stderr=error
log-path=/backup/db/log

[percdb]
pg1-host=192.168.70.10
pg1-path=/var/lib/pgsql/13/data
pg1-port=5432
EOF'
```

3. Restore the backup of the respective stanza to the target database server:

```
$ pgbackrest restore --stanza=percdb --log-level-console=info
```

4. Start PostgreSQL using the following service upon restoring the backup:

```
$ sudo systemctl start postgresql-13
```

How it works

When we need to restore the backup on a database server, we need to install pgBackRest on that server and create the data directory to store the backup, as seen in step 1. Once the permissions of the directory have been appropriately set in step 1, we can proceed to create the configuration file that contains the information on the backup server and the database server to which the backup belongs.

If the database server to which the backup is different from the server from where the backup was taken, it is important to add another stanza for the new database server. Once that is completed in step 2, we can proceed to perform the restore using the stanza name as seen in step 3. It will perform the restore to the data directory from the backup server specified under the globals stanza. After the restore is completed, we can proceed to start the PostgreSQL service.

4
Advanced Replication Techniques

Replication is one of the most important aspects of achieving high availability. Any unexpected failures on a database server could cause downtime for an application or a business. Configuring replication is thus the right practice to ensure that there is an option to perform failover in the event of disasters.

PostgreSQL is known for providing robust replication features for high availability without the need for an enterprise license or additional fees. There are two types of replication methods that are built into the community PostgreSQL source, namely streaming replication and logical replication.

Here are some of the differences between the two replication types:

- A standby in streaming replication does not allow writes whereas a standby (subscriber) in logical replication allows writes unless explicitly disabled.
- You cannot have selective replication of tables while using streaming. The only way that a table does not get replicated to a standby is when the table is set as UNLOGGED. Thus, a standby is a blind copy of a master in streaming replication.
- Logical replication offers selective replication of tables when they satisfy certain conditions.
- DDLs do not get replicated in logical replication, but streaming replication replicates every DDL and DML done on the master.
- Users created on the master also exist on a standby in streaming replication. This is not the case with logical replication; it must be explicitly created on the standby.
- It is streaming replication that satisfies the true purpose of high availability in the event of a disaster.

In this chapter, we will learn how to configure both streaming and logical replication and about some more crucial tasks in a production database environment.

We will cover the following recipes in this chapter:

- Setting up streaming replication in PostgreSQL 13
- Adding a delayed standby for faster point-in-time recovery
- Promoting a standby to a master
- Adding a cascaded streaming replica
- Promoting a standby in cascaded replication
- Using pg_rewind to re-synchronize a demoted master
- Enabling synchronous streaming replication
- Setting up logical replication in PostgreSQL 13

Setting up streaming replication in PostgreSQL 13

Streaming replication (physical replication), which is byte-by-byte replication, involves a continuous application of WAL records from Primary to Standby. As it uses a file-based log shipping method, it is one of the fastest replication methods when compared with logical replication or other trigger-based methods. It is asynchronous by default. For every replica/standby, there exists a WAL sender process on the primary server and a WAL receiver process on the standby server in streaming replication. These processes are responsible for streaming and applying the WAL records from the WAL segments, including the segments that are not full.

Starting from PostgreSQL 13, there have been some changes in how we perform streaming replication. For example, we don't see a `recovery.conf` file with PostgreSQL 13, unlike version 11 and earlier. Instead, the parameters that were initially added to `recovery.conf` can now be set in `postgresql.conf` or `postgresql.auto.conf` directly.

In this recipe, we shall see the steps involved in setting up streaming replication with PostgreSQL 13.

Getting ready...

We can set up streaming replication within two instances running on different ports on the same server. But that doesn't solve the purpose of high availability. So, it is recommended to build replication between servers that are geographically distributed. In order to get started with the steps being discussed, we need two servers (a master and a standby) with PostgreSQL 13 installed and with PostgreSQL running on the master.

How to do it ...

We will set up the replication using the following steps:

1. Create a replication user on the master:

   ```
   $ psql -c "CREATE USER replicator WITH REPLICATION ENCRYPTED
   PASSWORD 'secret'"
   ```

2. Add necessary entries to the pg_hba.conf file of the master:

   ```
   $ echo "host replication replicator <slave_ip_address>/32 md5" >>
   $PGDATA/pg_hba.conf
   $ psql -c "select pg_reload_conf()"
   ```

3. On the master, validate the parameters required to set up replication. The best way is as follows:

   ```
   $ psql -c "select name, setting from pg_settings where name IN
   ('listen_addresses','archive_mode','archive_command','wal_keep_segm
   ents','restore_command')"
   ```

4. Modify parameters that require modification on the master:

   ```
   $ psql -c "ALTER SYSTEM SET listen_addresses TO '*'";
   $ psql -c "ALTER SYSTEM SET archive_mode TO 'ON'";
   $ psql -c "ALTER SYSTEM SET archive_command TO 'cp %p
   /archives/%f'";
   $ psql -c "ALTER SYSTEM SET restore_command TO 'cp /archives/%f
   %p'";
   $ psql -c "ALTER SYSTEM SET wal_keep_segments TO '100'";
   ```

5. Restart the master if required or reload it, depending on the parameters modified:

   ```
   $ pg_ctl -D $PGDATA restart -mf
   ```

- Reload the master using the following command:

```
$ pg_ctl -d $PGDATA reload
```

6. Run `pg_basebackup` from the standby to take a backup of the master:

```
$ pg_basebackup -h <master_ip> -U replicator -p 5432 -D $PGDATA -Fp
-Xs -P -R
```

7. Validate the mandatory parameters needed for replication on the standby:

```
$ cat $PGDATA/postgresql.auto.conf
```

8. Add the `primary_conninfo` setting and `standby.signal` if they do not exist:

```
$ echo "primary_conninfo = 'user=replicator password=secret
host=<master_IP> port=5432 sslmode=prefer sslcompression=0
gssencmode=prefer krbsrvname=postgres target_session_attrs=any'" >>
$PGDATA/postgresql.auto.conf
```

```
$ echo "standby_mode = 'ON'" >> $PGDATA/postgresql.auto.conf
```

```
$ touch $PGDATA/standby.signal
```

9. Start the standby server or reload the configuration, depending on the parameter changes made:

```
$ pg_ctl -D $PGDATA start
```

Or, using the following command:

```
$ sudo systemctl start postgresql-13
```

How it works ...

The first step to setting up streaming replication is creating a replication user that has a REPLICATION role. We may use the superuser `postgres` for this purpose but it is not recommended. Once the user is created, we need to add an entry in the `pg_hba.conf` file of the master to allow replication connections from the standby, as seen in Step 2. It is important to replace `<slave_ip_address>/32` with the standby server IP or hostname/subnet so that the replication connections are allowed by the master.

As seen in Step 3, there are some parameters that play a vital role when we set up streaming replication. Except for `listen_addresses`, most of the default parameters hold good for replication. But, if all these parameters are set appropriately, then we shall have a perfect replication setup.

As an example, in Step 4, we see that `listen_addresses` is set to '*' to allow a specific IP interface or all (using *) to connect to the master. To enable archiving, as discussed in the previous chapters, we can set `archive_mode` to 'ON' and `archive_command` can be set to the shell command that can be used by the archiver process to copy the completed WAL segment to a safe location for recovery purposes.

Additionally, we can set `restore_command`, which will help when the master becomes a standby in the future. This parameter must set with the shell command that is used to fetch an archived WAL segment from the archive location. If this parameter is set on the master, it also gets replicated to the standby upon backup, so it need not be set twice. And finally, `wal_keep_segments` can be set with the number of WAL segments that are to be retained by the master server at any given time. This will help when the standby need not fetch WALs from the archive location if it gets lagged in replication by a few WALs.

Once all the parameters have been properly set, we can move on to Step 5 to restart the master server if the `listen_addresses` or `archive_mode` parameters have been modified, otherwise, this step can be skipped with just a reload of the configuration.

We can now proceed to Step 6, to back up the master's data directory from the standby. In Step 6, we used `pg_basebackup` with plain format (-Fp). If the master server is huge in size, we may use `pg_basebackup` with compressed tar format (-Ft -z) on the master and copy the backup to the standby to restore it. This was discussed in the *Restore of a backup taken using pg_basebackup* recipe of Chapter 3, *Backup and Recovery*.

If you noticed the command used in Step 6 carefully, it contains the command-line argument `-R`. This creates the replication of specific files and entries in the data directory of the standby. You may use multiple approaches such as rsync or any other disk backup methods to copy the master's data directory to the standby. Depending on the backup method we choose, we need to set a few parameters that are not automatically taken care of, as seen in the case of `pg_basebackup` with `-R`.

We then proceed to validate the mandatory parameters needed to set up streaming replication on the standby in Step 7. The parameter `primary_conninfo` is automatically added when we use `-R` with `pg_basebackup`. Otherwise, we need to add a similar entry as seen in Step 8, to tell the standby how to connect to the master. We must replace `<master_IP>` with the master server's IP address or hostname. There is an important file (`standby.signal`) that must exist in a standby data directory to help Postgres determine its state as a standby. It is automatically created when we use the `-R` option while performing `pg_basebackup`. If not, we may simply use `touch` to create this empty file as seen in Step 8. And then, to tell that the database is in standby mode, we need to set `standby_mode` to ON.

And the last step, Step 9, is to start the standby server using `pg_ctl`.

Adding a delayed standby for faster point-in-time recovery

PostgreSQL does not have a feature like FLASHBACK, as seen in Oracle. Flashback in Oracle is used to take the database back to a certain point in time when some accidental changes were performed. It relies on redo logs, undo, and the flash recovery area. However, for faster point-in-time recovery in PostgreSQL, we can always set up a delayed replica/standby so that the standby is always lagging by a certain amount of time. We can always delay the replica by a certain amount of time – let's say, hours, minutes, days, or even seconds. This way, if someone dropped a table accidentally, we could perform a switchover to the standby that is lagging by a certain amount of time.

In this recipe, we shall discuss how a delayed standby can be set up. In order to avoid duplication, I am going to skip the steps involved in setting up streaming replication, which was discussed in the previous recipe, *Setting up streaming replication in PostgreSQL 13*.

Getting ready...

In order to set up a delayed standby, we need a master Postgres server that is configured with all the appropriate parameters, as discussed in the previous recipe, *Setting up streaming replication in PostgreSQL 13*. The WAL sender process sends all the WAL segments from the master to the delayed replica. So, it is important to have sufficient storage on the standby that can accommodate the WAL segments generated during that period. As the replication relies on WALs, all the WAL segments during the delay period must be safely archived, to be safe.

How to do it...

Let's get started, using the following steps:

1. On the standby, add the following parameter:

```
$ echo "recovery_min_apply_delay = '12h' # or '1min' or 1d'" >>
$PGDATA/postgresql.auto.conf
```

2. Restart PostgreSQL:

```
$ pg_ctl -D $PGDATA restart -mf
```

How it works...

Upon setting up the streaming replication successfully, the
parameter `recovery_min_apply_delay` can be used to tell the standby to delay
replication. In Step 1, we set `recovery_min_apply_delay` to 12 hours. This means that
the replication is being by 12 hours. For PostgreSQL 11 or older releases, this parameter
should be added to the `recovery.conf` file. Since PostgreSQL 13, `recovery.conf` does
not exist, so it can be added to the `postgresql.auto.conf` file.

Any changes to recovery settings require a restart. So, the delay will be, in effect, upon the
restart of the PostgreSQL server using `pg_ctl`, as seen in Step 2.

Once these two steps are performed, we have successfully configured a delayed standby.

Promoting a standby to a master

In the event of a disaster, a standby should be promoted to a master. This is to limit the
amount of downtime involved when the master cannot be brought up for a longer period.
While it is tricky to perform failover in some relational databases, it is very easy with
PostgreSQL. We shall discuss how a standby can be promoted to a master in simple steps in
this recipe.

Getting ready...

We must ensure that at least one standby has been set up for replication to perform a promotion or a failover. In the event of a failover, when the primary/master is lost, any transaction committed on the master that was not already synced/applied to the standby may be lost. Either the application should be designed to handle such situations and apply any lost transactions or we must wait until the recovery is completed, when the required WALs containing those transactions are already shipped to the standby.

Synchronous replication minimizes the possibility of losing transactions on the standby upon failover. We shall discuss synchronous replication in the following recipes.

How to do it...

We will do so using the following steps:

1. Check the replication lag:

   ```
   $ psql -c "select usename, client_addr, write_lag, replay_lag from
   pg_stat_replication"
   ```

2. Switch a WAL segment and check the lag:

   ```
   $ psql -c "select pg_switch_wal()"
   $ psql -c "select usename, client_addr, write_lag, replay_lag from
   pg_stat_replication"
   ```

3. Use any of the following methods to perform the promotion:

   - **Method 1**: Promoting a standby using `pg_ctl`:

     ```
     $ pg_ctl -D $PGDATA promote
     ```

   - **Method 2:** Promoting a standby by creating a trigger file:

     ```
     $ touch <<trigger_file>>
     ```

4. Verify the recovery status:

   ```
   $ psql -c "select pg_is_in_recovery()"
   ```

How it works...

If it is a switchover, where the standby is being promoted by gracefully shutting down the application, we can use Step 1 to check the lag between the master and the standby as the first step, otherwise proceeding directly to Step 3. When we check the replication lag using the command mentioned in Step 1, it displays the write and replay lag. This command needs to be executed on the master. To be safe, we can use Step 2 to switch a WAL offset/segment on the master and check the lag again. Once the lag is zero, we can then proceed to Step 3.

`pg_ctl` can be used to start or stop a PostgreSQL cluster. Similarly, we could also use `pg_ctl` to promote a standby to a master. However, it is not the only approach, as we can see in Step 3. There are two methods. Method 1 is using `pg_ctl`. This needs to be executed on the standby for it to be promoted to a Postgres user.

Method 2 can be used for scripting purposes, as it does not require a Postgres user to perform failover. We can set a parameter, `trigger_file`, in the `postgresql.auto.conf` file with a filename that does not exist, for example:

```
echo "trigger_file = '/tmp/promote'" >> $PGDATA/postgresql.auto.conf
```

The preceding parameter should be added to the `recovery.conf` file. As it is one of the recovery settings, it requires a restart of the PostgreSQL server to take effect.

If we notice the preceding command, we are setting `trigger_file` as `/tmp/promote`. So, if we manually touch/create this file, the standby automatically promotes itself as a master. Depending on the permissions needed to create this file in the specified directory, an external custom script can be used to manage failover as well.

Once the standby is promoted, we could use the command in Step 4 to validate whether the Postgres cluster is in recovery or not. If the command returns false, it means the Postgres cluster is no longer in recovery, so it should be the master.

Adding a cascaded streaming replica

One of the beauties of PostgreSQL is that it supports cascaded replication. There is no limit to the number of cascaded replicas you could add. For example, consider a master M1 replicating to standby S2, and standby S2 replicating to standby S3, and standby S3 replicating to standby S4, and so on until standby N where N has no limit. In this recipe, we shall see how cascaded replica can be added to an existing streaming replication setup.

Getting ready...

In order to add a cascaded replica, we need an existing master-standby replication setup. The recipe *Setting up streaming replication in PostgreSQL 13*, can be used to create such a setup. Once the setup is completed, we need to provision a server with PostgreSQL 13 installed.

How to do it ...

We will add the replica using the following steps:

1. Allow replication connections from the new standby to its master/upstream. Let's say `192.168.90.70` is the new standby:

   ```
   $ echo "host replication replicator 192.168.90.70/32 md5" >>
   $PGDATA/pg_hba.conf
   ```

2. Make the changes take effect through a reload:

   ```
   $ psql -c "select pg_reload_conf()"
   ```

3. Use `pg_basebackup` to make a consistent backup of the data directory of the master or existing standby:

   ```
   $ pg_basebackup -h 192.168.90.70 -U replicator -p 5432 -D $PGDATA -
   Fp -Xs -P -R
   ```

4. Modify the parameter on standby servers with its upstream IP (or hostname):

   ```
   primary_conninfo = 'user=replicator password=secret
   host=192.168.90.50 port=5432'
   ```

5. Start the newly added cascaded replica:

   ```
   $ pg_ctl -D $PGDATA start
   ```

How it works...

In order to add a cascaded slave/standby, we should ensure that the new server can connect to the upstream standby and also the master using port `5432` or any other port (if modified). Enabling connections to the master helps when an upstream server is unavailable and the cascaded standby should start replicating changes from the master.

As seen in Step 1, we should add the entry that allows replication connections from the new server to both the master and the upstream standby servers. For that, we could append the line seen in Step 1 to the `pg_hba.conf` files. In this step, we should modify the IP address to the IP or hostname of the new cascaded standby. Now, to make the change made to the `pg_hba.conf` file take effect, a reload of the configuration is necessary. That can be done using the command seen in Step 2.

Once the reload is completed, we could proceed with taking a consistent file-system-level backup of the data directory of the upstream standby (preferred) or the master, as seen in Step 3. This step can be remotely performed from the new standby so the copying of data files can happen over the network without the need to store them locally. As discussed in the previous recipe, *Setting up streaming replication in PostgreSQL 12*, we could use `-R` to create the replication-specific parameters and files. However, it is important to change the IP or hostname to the appropriate Postgres server from where we are taking the backup.

Once the backup is completed, we could proceed to Step 4, to modify the IP address or the hostname of the upstream standby, if necessary. This is only required when we took a backup from a different server other than the upstream in Step 3. If not, as we have used `-R` while taking the backup, `primary_conninfo` will be automatically updated with the hostname or IP of the upstream. This parameter can be modified in the `postgresql.auto.conf` file.

Upon modifying the parameter, we can now start the new server as a cascaded standby using the command specified in Step 5.

Promoting a standby in a replication cluster with multiple standby servers

In the recipe *Promoting a standby to a master*, we saw the steps involved in promoting a standby server. But, the procedure would be slightly different when we need to promote a specific standby in a replication cluster that consists of more than one standby server. This is because, upon the promotion of one of the standbys, the other standby servers should follow the newly promoted primary.

In this recipe, we shall discuss how to promote a standby when there exists a PostgreSQL replication cluster with multiple standby servers. To understand the steps better, we shall consider a PostgreSQL cluster with the following setup:

Master (M1) replicating to standby (S1) and standby (S2). Additionally, a cascaded standby (S3) replicating from standby (S2).

Getting ready...

In order to proceed with the procedure being illustrated here, we must have an existing PostgreSQL replication cluster that consists of a master and more than one standby server in replication using streaming replication.

How to do it...

We will now promote the standby using the following steps:

1. Identify the target standby server that needs to be promoted:

   ```
   $ psql -c "select usename, client_addr, write_lag, replay_lag from
   pg_stat_replication"
   ```

2. Shut down/demote the current master:

   ```
   $ pg_ctl -D $PGDATA stop -mf
   ```

3. Promote the new standby – let's say S1:

   ```
   $ pg_ctl -D $PGDATA promote
   ```

4. Make standby S2 follow the new master (S1):

   ```
   primary_conninfo = 'user=replicator password=secret
   host=192.168.90.60 port=5432'
   ```

5. Restart standby S2:

   ```
   $ pg_ctl -D $PGDATA restart -mf
   ```

How it works...

This recipe is quite interesting and a similar requirement is seen in the majority of PostgreSQL environments. In this setup, we have three standby servers and one master. One of the standby servers follows another standby server. Now, to perform a switchover (manually), we must identify the standby server that suits the right candidate. For that purpose, we could run the query in Step 1, on the existing master. This should help us determine the standby server with no lag. If for any reason, we are unable to run the command in Step 1 on the master, we must try to choose the server that is set up as a synchronous standby, if setup. If synchronous replication was not enabled, we may go with the manual verification of data or the recent WAL applied on all standby servers.

Once we have chosen the standby server that needs to be promoted, it is important to validate whether the old master is unreachable and not available for reads/writes. Otherwise, it may cause split-brain problems. For that reason, we may use the command in Step 2 to shut down Postgres on the old master that needs to be demoted.

Once Step 2 is completed, we could run the `promote` command as seen in Step 3, on the standby server that needs to be promoted. This may take a second or a few seconds. Let's say that the standby server that got promoted is standby (S1). Now, we have another standby (S2) that initially followed the old master (M1). In order to make the second standby (S2) follow the new master (S1), we could modify the `primary_conninfo` parameter in the `postgresql.auto.conf` file of standby (S2). As seen in Step 4, the `primary_conninfo` parameter can be edited with the IP or the hostname of the new master of standby (S2). Once the change has been performed, we could proceed to restart the standby (S2) using the command specified in Step 5.

As the cascaded standby (S3) was following standby (S2), we need not make any changes or restart the standby (S3) Postgres server. It should automatically replicate all the changes from standby (S2) like before.

Using pg_rewind to re-synchronize a demoted master

In the previous recipe, *Promoting a standby in a replication cluster with multiple standby servers*, and also in the recipe *Promoting a standby to a master*, we discussed how a standby server can be promoted in the event of failover for disaster recovery. In this recipe, we shall discuss how the old master that has diverged from the replication cluster can be added back to the cluster as a standby, without rebuilding it from scratch.

Getting ready...

This works for a replication cluster on which a failover has been performed. Additionally, it only works when either the parameter `wal_log_hints` or `data_checksums` is enabled. Setting both these parameters may add some performance penalty, however, with `wal_log_hints` incurring less overhead.

`wal_log_hints`: When this parameter is active, the PostgreSQL server writes the entire content of each disk page to WAL during the first modification of that page after a checkpoint, even for non-critical modifications of so-called hint bits.

Changing this parameter requires RESTART of the PostgreSQL cluster. The following must be performed on all the PostgreSQL servers in replication:

```
$ psql -c "ALTER SYSTEM SET wal_log_hints TO 'ON'"
$ pg_ctl -D $PGDATA restart -mf
```

Additionally, all the WAL segments since failover must be available for the rewind to complete.

How to do it...

We will do this using the following steps:

1. Shut down PostgreSQL on the old master manually, if required:

   ```
   $ pg_ctl -D $PGDATA stop -mf
   ```

2. Run `pg_rewind`:

   ```
   $ pg_rewind -D /var/lib/pgsql/12/data --source-
   server="host=<new_master_IP> port=5432 user=postgres
   dbname=postgres password=secret"
   ```

3. Add the `primary_conninfo` setting and the `standby.signal` file:

   ```
   $ echo "primary_conninfo = 'user=replicator password=secret
   host=<new_master_IP> port=5432 sslmode=prefer sslcompression=0
   gssencmode=prefer krbsrvname=postgres target_session_attrs=any'" >>
   $PGDATA/postgresql.auto.conf

   $ echo "standby_mode = 'ON'" >> $PGDATA/postgresql.auto.conf
   $ touch $PGDATA/standby.signal
   ```

4. Start the standby (M1):

   ```
   $ pg_ctl -D $PGDATA start
   ```

How it works...

In some of the previous recipes, we have seen how a failover can be done manually using `pg_ctl` with the flag `promote`. Once the promotion has been issued, the timeline on the new master changes and is not the same as the old master. At this point, we could use `pg_rewind` to resynchronize the old master using the new master. This way, we could add the old master as a standby to the new master without rebuilding it. In order to achieve that, we make sure that the old master is not accepting writes and is shut down upon a failover. Otherwise, we could use the command used in Step 1 to manually shut down Postgres running on the old master (M1).

Once the old master is shut down, we could use `pg_rewind` as seen in Step 2 to rewind the master to the point from where the replication should start from the new master. In the command, the only change required is the host, which needs to be either the IP or the hostname of the new master. Additionally, you should be modifying the user and passwords appropriately.

The time taken to perform `pg_rewind` varies. It may be faster or slower depending on the changes that happened upon the failover. After finishing Step 2, we should have the appropriate parameters and files in a place that says that the old master is a standby. We could refer to Step 3, which tells how the two parameters `primary_conninfo` and `standby_mode` can be set in the `postgresql.auto.conf` file of the old master (M1). Upon adding the parameters, we could create an empty file, `standby.signal`, as seen in Step 3. And then, we could simply start the PostgreSQL cluster on server M1.

Enabling synchronous streaming replication

Streaming replication in PostgreSQL is asynchronous by default. In order to avoid data loss upon failover, it is important to have synchronous streaming replication. A synchronous replication gives a success message to the client only when the change has been confirmed by at least one of the standby servers specified. This way, the change is never lost but it may come with a performance penalty. In this recipe, we shall look at how synchronous replication can be enabled.

Getting ready...

To avoid a huge performance overhead, you may have at least one standby sitting in the same data center as the master. This way, the change will be confirmed as received faster. We could also enable synchronous replication at the session level. It allows a user to configure which changes need to be synchronous and which don't.

It is important to set `application_name` appropriately on all the standby servers when setting up replication. For your reference, `application_name` is set in the `primary_conninfo` setting. A standby server is identified using the `application_name` set in the `primary_conninfo` parameter in the `postgresql.auto.conf` file.

For example, the following value set to `primary_conninfo` indicates that the `application_name` value set to the standby server is `standby100`:

```
primary_conninfo = 'user=replicator password=replicator application_name =
standby100 host=192.168.0.11 port=5432'
```

This recipe requires you to have an existing master-standby replication using streaming replication.

How to do it...

Let's get started using the following steps:

1. Enable the required parameters:

    ```
    $ psql -c "ALTER SYSTEM synchronous_commit = 'ON'"
    $ psql -c "synchronous_standby_names = 'standby1, standby2'"
    ```

2. Perform a reload or SIGHUP:

    ```
    $ psql -c "select pg_reload_conf()"
    ```

3. Validate that replication has been enabled using the following step:

    ```
    $ psql -c "select usename, application_name, client_addr,
    client_hostname, sync_priority, sync_state from
    pg_stat_replication"
    ```

How it works...

It is very easy to enable synchronous replication on top of an existing master-standby replication cluster. As seen in Step 1, there are two parameters that need to be modified to enable synchronous replication. `synchronous_commit` can either be set to `ON` or `remote_apply` or `remote_write`.

When `synchronous_commit` is set to `remote_write`, it will cause each commit on the master to wait until the standby confirms that the record has been received and written to the operating system. But, when `synchronous_commit` is set to `remote_apply`, a commit will wait until the standby confirms that the transaction has been replayed and made visible to users. This ensures consistency with a noticeable performance hit, at times. So, `remote_write` may have less of an overhead.

Once we set `synchronous_commit`, we can then proceed to `synchronous_standby_names`. This needs to be set with the `application_name` of one or more standby servers in replication. Adding more than one `application_name` gives the master the flexibility to consider a commit as a success when at least one of the standby servers sent the acknowledgment of the commit record.

To make the changes to parameters take effect, we must perform a reload or a SIGHUP as seen in Step 2. Upon reload, we could validate the synchronous replication by running the command specified in Step 3.

Setting up logical replication in PostgreSQL 13

Built-in logical replication and logical decoding were introduced in PostgreSQL 10. Over a period of time, more and more features are being implemented within logical replication. It is helpful when a selected list of tables needs to be replicated from multiple OLTP databases to a single OLAP database for reporting and analysis.

Logical replication is also helpful to perform replication between two major PostgreSQL versions to perform rolling-fashion upgrades. In this recipe, we shall discuss the steps involved in setting up logical replication between two PostgreSQL servers.

Getting ready...

Logical replication uses a publish and subscribe model. The node that sends the changes becomes a publisher. And the node that subscribes to those changes becomes a subscriber. There can be one or more subscriptions to a publication. We could choose what to replicate – INSERT or DELETE or UPDATE or ALL. By default, it is ALL.

It is always recommended to enable logical replication for tables with primary keys or a column with unique and not null values. Such columns can be set as a replica identity. A replica identity will be used to uniquely identify a record in the event of updates or deletions especially. If that requirement is not met, we may use a replica identity of FULL. This means an entire record will be used as a key, but it may be inefficient.

How to do it...

We will initiate logical replication using the following steps:

1. Enable the required parameters:

   ```
   $ psql -c "ALTER SYSTEM SET wal_level TO 'logical'"
   ```

2. Restart PostgreSQL:

   ```
   $ pg_ctl -D $PGDATA restart -mf
   ```

3. Add all or one tables for replication:

   ```
   $ psql -d percona -c "CREATE PUBLICATION percpub FOR ALL TABLES"
   Or
   $ psql -d percona -c "CREATE PUBLICATION percpub FOR TABLE
   scott.employee scott.departments"
   ```

4. Copy the schema from the publisher to the subscriber:

   ```
   $ pg_dump -h publisher_server_ip -p 5432 -d percona -Fc -s -U
   postgres | pg_restore -d percona -h subscriber_node_ip -p 5432 -U
   postgres
   ```

5. Create the subscription:

   ```
   $ psql -d percona -c "CREATE SUBSCRIPTION percsub CONNECTION
   'host=publisher_server_ip dbname=percona user=postgres
   password=secret port=5432' PUBLICATION percpub"

   # To avoid copying pre-existing data :
   ```

```
$ psql -d percona -c "CREATE SUBSCRIPTION percsub CONNECTION
'host=publisher_server_ip dbname=percona user=postgres
password=oracle port=5432' PUBLICATION percpub WITH (copy_data =
false)"
```

How it works...

Setting up logical replication is as simple as setting up streaming replication but with a couple of additional steps or validations (sometimes). As seen in Step 1, we must ensure that both the PostgreSQL servers have `wal_level` set to logical. If it's required to change it, a restart is required, which may be performed using the command seen in Step 2.

Once the change to `wal_level` is in effect, we could then create a publication on the master aka publisher. If you carefully observe Step 3, the first command shows how all the tables in the database `percona` can be enabled for replication. However, if you need to add one or more tables, you could use the next command seen in the same step.

Once we have created the publication on the master, we will need to copy the schema of the tables that need to be replicated to the subscriber or the standby. This can be achieved using the command seen in Step 4. This command performs `pg_dump` using `-s`, which copies only the schema over PIPE to the subscriber. This can be executed on the publisher or the subscriber.

Once the schema is copied, we can simply create the subscription that will do all the work for us. When we create the subscription, we specify the name of the subscription along with the connection string of the publisher and the name of the publication.

As seen in Step 5, there are two ways to create the subscription. The first one helps us by copying all the pre-existing data and starts replication upon copying all the data. The second avoids copying the pre-existing data and starts replication from the point when the subscription was created.

The second approach is useful when we want to use multiple processes to copy and dump pre-existing data from the publisher to the subscriber manually. However, it involves some downtime as the data copy needs to be consistent. The first approach may not require any downtime as it takes care of both data copying and starting the replication appropriately, but they cannot be performed in parallel. So, the first approach may be recommended but may be slower for large Postgres instances. Once Step 5 is performed, the logical replication setup is complete between the publisher and the subscriber.

5
High Availability and Automatic Failover

The first step toward making a database highly available is setting up replication to another server, which could either be within the same or a different data center. While it is fairly difficult to see such replication methods included for free with some of the commercial databases that are available, you do not have to pay any license fees to set up replication with PostgreSQL. The community PostgreSQL software includes it by default. You may refer to Chapter 4, *Advanced Replication Techniques* to learn how to set up replication in PostgreSQL.

Now that we have replication set up, how do we ensure that we can avoid downtime for an application by letting a failover happen automatically? Are there any open source tools that can be highly trusted, and how do we configure them the right way? All these questions will be answered in this chapter.

In this chapter, we shall discuss one of the most heavily adopted open source HA tools available, called Patroni. This can be used to set up automatic failover. We shall learn how it can be configured and also discuss the advantages and disadvantages of it while using it for HA. It is highly recommended that you use streaming replication for the purpose of HA and automatic failover in PostgreSQL.

In this chapter, we will cover the following recipes:

- Enabling distributed consensus using etcd
- Avoiding split-brain using Watchdog/softdog
- Installing Patroni along with its Python dependencies
- Creating a Patroni configuration file

- Starting Patroni as a service using systemd
- Initializing a PostgreSQL primary database using Patroni
- Adding a standby to a Patroni cluster
- Performing a manual switchover using Patroni

Let's get started!

Technical requirements

The following recipes will require that you have at least two database servers with internet connectivity for the purpose of testing. The commands that will be discussed in these recipes should work on the CentOS/Red Hat/OEL and Ubuntu/Debian family of operating systems. All the recipes in this chapter will be using the following hostnames and corresponding IP addresses. We need to replace the appropriate hostname and IP address that matches our PostgreSQL cluster:

```
pg1 192.168.10.1 (Primary or Master)
pg2 192.168.10.1 (Standby or Replica)
pg3 192.168.10.1 (Second Standby in some recipes)
```

Additionally, it's recommended that the hostnames and their IPs are set in the `/etc/hosts` file as the root user:

```
echo "192.168.10.1 pg1" >> /etc/hosts
echo "192.168.10.2 pg2" >> /etc/hosts
echo "192.168.10.3 pg3" >> /etc/hosts
```

Let's get started!

Automatic failover using Patroni

Patroni originated as a fork of Governor (`https://github.com/compose/governor`), the project from Compose. Patroni is robust and one of the most heavily discussed high availability tools in the open source community. It is also one of the most widely adopted tools because of its rich feature set. It may be slightly complicated to set it up, but the recipes in this chapter should help us understand how to set up a Patroni HA cluster.

Enabling distributed consensus using etcd

etcd was built by CoreOS to initially manage server updates in a round-robin fashion rather than all at once. This was to avoid downtime occurring during updates. Over a period of time, the project has been developed with a lot of features and made it a base for storing cluster configuration in Kubernetes.

etcd is a distributed consensus key-value store that uses the industry-standard RAFT algorithm to elect a leader between a cluster of nodes. There is always one leader in a cluster of nodes, with the rest of the nodes being its followers. When a leader dies, the followers participate in leader election and become candidates. Only one of the followers can win as a leader as the leader election is implemented using the RAFT algorithm.

Patroni can write data into etcd and can also read data from etcd. When an application writes directly into the leader node, the application is only said to be successful when the majority of the follower nodes reply with a success message. When the application on a follower node writes data, the follower node sends that write request to the leader node. The leader node gets into consensus on the write with the other node and the local node replies with a success message to the application, based on the feedback from the leader node. This will be used to determine the cluster's health. This can be depicted with the following diagram:

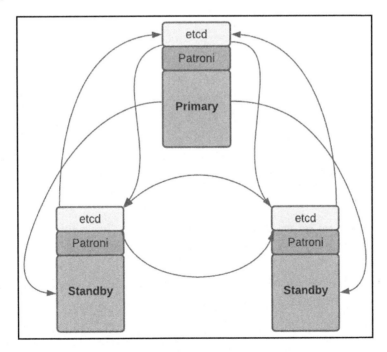

Patroni also stores cluster configuration in etcd. This will be used to maintain the same configuration parameters (`postgresql.conf` or `postgresql.auto.conf`, `pg_hba.conf`, and so on) and keeps all the database nodes identical. In this recipe, we shall discuss how etcd can be installed and configured on database servers for the purpose of setting up high availability using Patroni.

Getting ready

For this recipe, we should have at least two Linux servers that are part of an etcd cluster.

How to do it...

Follow these steps to work with the etcd cluster:

1. Install `wget` to download the latest `.tar` bundle for etcd:

```
$ sudo dnf install wget -y
OR
$ sudo yum install wget -y
```

2. Create a temporary directory where the .tar bundle can be downloaded and switch to that location:

```
$ mkdir -p /tmp/etcd-tmp
$ cd /tmp/etcd-tmp
```

3. Grep for the latest .tar bundle for etcd using `curl` and download it using `wget`, as follows:

```
$ curl -s https://api.github.com/repos/etcd-io/etcd/releases/latest \
| grep -E 'browser_download_url.*linux-amd64' \
| cut -d '"' -f 4 \
| wget -qi -
```

4. Unpack the .tar bundle:

```
$ tar xvf *.tar.gz
```

5. Get the extracted software bundle using the following command and move the binaries to the default binaries location:

```
$ cd /tmp/etcd-tmp/etcd-*/
$ sudo mv etcd* /usr/bin/
```

6. Remove the temporary directory we created in *Step 2*:

```
$ cd ~
$ rm -rf /tmp/etcd-tmp
```

7. Validate the `etcd` and `etcdctl` versions upon installation for validation:

```
$ etcd --version
$ etcdctl --version
```

8. Create a user and a group named `etcd`:

```
$ sudo groupadd --system etcd
$ sudo useradd -s /sbin/nologin --system -g etcd etcd
```

9. Create the directory for storing the `etcd` configuration file and the etcd data directory. Give ownership to the etcd system user and group for the newly created directories:

```
$ sudo mkdir /etc/etcd
$ sudo mkdir -p /var/lib/etcd/
$ sudo chown -R etcd:etcd /var/lib/etcd/
```

10. Create the following service file so that etcd can be managed as a service. Ensure that you create and enable this service on all the nodes that are part of the etcd cluster:

```
# vi /usr/lib/systemd/system/etcd.service
Append the following lines to the preceding service file:
[Unit]
Description=Etcd Server
After=network.target
After=network-online.target
Wants=network-online.target

[Service]
Type=notify
WorkingDirectory=/var/lib/etcd/
EnvironmentFile=-/etc/etcd/etcd.conf
User=etcd
# set GOMAXPROCS to number of processors
ExecStart=/bin/bash -c "GOMAXPROCS=$(nproc) /usr/bin/etcd --
name=\"${ETCD_NAME}\" --data-dir=\"${ETCD_DATA_DIR}\" --listen-
client-urls=\"${ETCD_LISTEN_CLIENT_URLS}\""
Restart=on-failure
LimitNOFILE=65536
```

```
[Install]
WantedBy=multi-user.target
```

11. Enable the newly added etcd service so that etcd can auto-start upon a crash or a restart.

    Verify whether the newly created service appears among the list of services using the following command:

    ```
    # systemctl list-unit-files | grep etcd
    etcd.service disabled
    ```

    Enable the etcd service using the following command:

    ```
    # systemctl enable etcd
    ```

12. Create configuration files for etcd for the first server.

    The following configuration treats the hostname as pg1 and the IP address as 192.168.10.1. Replace it with the appropriate details as needed:

    ```
    # vi /etc/etcd/etcd.conf
    ```

    Add the following entries to the preceding configuration file:

    ```
    ETCD_NAME=pg1
    ETCD_INITIAL_CLUSTER="pg1=http://192.168.10.1:2380"
    ETCD_INITIAL_CLUSTER_TOKEN="patroni-token"
    ETCD_INITIAL_CLUSTER_STATE="new"
    ETCD_INITIAL_ADVERTISE_PEER_URLS="http://192.168.10.1:2380"
    ETCD_DATA_DIR="/var/lib/etcd/postgres.etcd"
    ETCD_LISTEN_PEER_URLS="http://192.168.10.1:2380"
    ETCD_LISTEN_CLIENT_URLS="http://192.168.10.1:2379,http://localhost:
    2379"
    ETCD_ADVERTISE_CLIENT_URLS="http://192.168.10.1:2379"
    ```

    Start the etcd service after adding these entries to the configuration file:

    ```
    # sudo systemctl start etcd
    ```

    Verify whether the service has successfully started using the following command:

    ```
    # sudo systemctl status etcd | grep active
    ```

The output will be as follows:

```
# sudo systemctl status etcd | grep active
 Active: active (running) since Mon 2020-09-21 01:12:16 UTC; 1min
13s ago

# etcdctl member list
8cd4ee6d9fb06fd7: name=pg1 peerURLs=http://192.168.10.1:2380
clientURLs=http://192.168.10.1:2379 isLeader=true
```

13. Add the second node or server to the etcd cluster.

    Add the second node as a member of the existing etcd cluster using the following
    command. Replace the hostname and IP address appropriately:

    ```
    # etcdctl member add pg2 http://192.168.10.2:2380
    ```

14. Create the `etcd.conf` configuration file and start the service on the second
    server:

    ```
    # vi /etc/etcd/etcd.conf
    ```

    Add the following entries to the preceding configuration file:

    ```
    ETCD_NAME=pg2
    ETCD_INITIAL_CLUSTER="pg1=http://192.168.10.1:2380,pg2=http://192.1
    68.10.2:2380"
    ETCD_INITIAL_CLUSTER_TOKEN="patroni-token"
    ETCD_INITIAL_CLUSTER_STATE="existing"
    ETCD_INITIAL_ADVERTISE_PEER_URLS="http://192.168.10.2:2380"
    ETCD_DATA_DIR="/var/lib/etcd/postgres.etcd"
    ETCD_LISTEN_PEER_URLS="http://192.168.10.2:2380"
    ETCD_LISTEN_CLIENT_URLS="http://192.168.10.2:2379,http://localhost:
    2379"
    ETCD_ADVERTISE_CLIENT_URLS="http://192.168.10.2:2379"
    ```

    Start the etcd service after adding the entries to the configuration file:

    ```
    # sudo systemctl start etcd
    ```

    Verify whether the service has successfully started using the following command:

    ```
    # sudo systemctl status etcd | grep active
     Active: active (running) since Mon 2020-09-21 01:12:16 UTC; 9s ago
    ```

The output will be as follows when you list the members of the etcd cluster:

```
# etcdctl member list
8cd4ee6d9fb06fd7: name=pg1 peerURLs=http://192.168.10.1:2380
clientURLs=http://192.168.10.1:2379 isLeader=true
dc48310f919895fd: name=pg2 peerURLs=http://192.168.10.2:2380
clientURLs=http://192.168.10.2:2379 isLeader=false
```

Steps 13 and *14* can be repeated for the third or more servers that need to be part of the etcd cluster.

How it works...

Patroni is an HA template that relies on a distributed consensus store for storing cluster-wide configuration and choosing a leader among a cluster of nodes. DCS can be either etcd, ZooKeeper, or Consul. In this chapter, we considered the widely used etcd as a store that uses the RAFT algorithm for performing leader election. In *Steps 1, 2,* and *3*, we installed wget and created a temporary directory where the etcd .tar bundle can be downloaded. In *Step 4*, we saw the .tar bundle being extracted and then the etcd-specific files being copied to the bin directory in *Step 5*. The temporary directory can then be removed and the etcd version can be validated to ensure that the installation is successful, as shown in *Steps 6* and *7*.

After successfully installing etcd, an etcd-specific group and user can be added and the directories that store the etcd configuration file and the etcd database can be created with appropriate ownership, as shown in *Steps 8* and *9*. To ensure that the etcd service is started upon a crash occurring of a server restarting automatically, we must create a service file, as shown in *Step 10*. The etcd service can be enabled using the steps shown in *Step 11*.

In order to start etcd as a service, it needs a configuration file. This configuration file stores information about the name of the etcd server, its initial cluster state (if it's new or existing), and the location of the data directory for etcd. All the relevant configuration parameters for etcd can be seen in *Step 12*. In the same step, we can see the commands for starting etcd and validating the same.

Now that the etcd cluster has been started with the first server, the second server can be added to the existing cluster using *Steps 13* and *14*. Similarly, another node or server can be added to make it a quorum of three servers, which is recommended in an etcd cluster for a leader election to happen.

Avoiding split-brain using Watchdog/softdog

In order to avoid split-brain, Patroni should ensure that the PostgreSQL primary/master node does not accept any writes when the leader key of the node is expired in the **Distributed Consensus Store (DCS)**. For our use case, DCS is etcd. This can be done by letting Patroni shut down PostgreSQL. But what if Patroni itself is hung or killed? In this case, the PostgreSQL node can still take writes. This could cause a split-brain problem, where there could be multiple nodes accepting writes from the application.

To avoid such exceptions that could cause a split-brain, Patroni uses Watchdog. A software watchdog, also known as a softdog, should receive a timer reset request before making a decision about a node restart. Patroni activates the watchdog timer before starting any PostgreSQL node as a primary node. If watchdog activation cannot happen, then Patroni will not be able to start the PostgreSQL node as a primary, nor would it attempt to promote that node in the event of a failover. In this recipe, we shall discuss how softdog can be configured and made ready for activation, as needed by Patroni.

Getting ready

If the watchdog is not installed on your Linux machine already, you can use the following commands:

On CentOS/RedHat, we can run the following command:

```
$ sudo yum install watchdog
```

On Ubuntu/Debian, we can run the following command:

```
$ sudo apt install watchdog
```

Patroni activates the watchdog so that it expires 5 seconds before the **Time To Live (TTL)** expires. In the default setup, `loop_wait` is set to `10`, `ttl` is set to `30`, and `safety_margin` is set to `5`. So, an HA loop has 15 seconds (`ttl` − `loop_wait` − `safety_margin`) before it goes for a forced reset. To avoid a delay in triggering the watchdog when a Patroni process is suspended and to make sure that the watchdog will trigger under all circumstances, we can set `safety_margin` to `−1`. This makes the watchdog trigger at ttl/2.

How to do it...

Follow these steps to enable softdog (a software watchdog) on Linux:

1. Enable softdog using the following command:

   ```
   $ sudo modprobe softdog
   ```

2. Patroni uses a default location for softdogs. Ensure that it can be accessed by the user that started Patroni:

   ```
   $ sudo chown postgres /dev/watchdog
   ```

   The following steps are optional as they are only needed if they are not part of the Patroni service file. The recipes in this chapter covers the service file that takes care of both watchdog/softdog and Patroni.

3. To enable softdog on server reboot, add the following entry to `rc.modules`:

   ```
   $ sudo sh -c 'echo "modprobe softdog" >> /etc/rc.modules'
   $ sudo chmod +x /etc/rc.modules
   ```

4. To ensure that the users have read and write access to set a timer, add a rule to udev that automatically grants access when a watchdog is detected:

   ```
   $ sudo sh -c 'echo "KERNEL==\"watchdog\", MODE=\"0666\"" >> /etc/udev/rules.d/61-watchdog.rules'
   ```

With that, we have enabled a watchdog for Patroni.

How it works...

Once watchdog has been installed, it needs to be enabled using the command shown in *Step 1*. At this point, the ownership of the file being used by Patroni for the watchdog should be owned by the user who started Patroni, as shown in *Step 2*. As a database server can be restarted for various reasons, the softdog shouldn't be enabled automatically upon restart. by adding the entry shown in *Step 3*. Finally, a rule can be added to udev to ensure that access is always available upon watchdog detection, as shown in *Step 4*. All these steps should make setting up softdog robust.

Installing Patroni along with its Python dependencies

Patroni is coded using Python. Considering the fact that Python 2 is obsolete, it may be tricky to get Patroni installed using Python3 unless the dependencies are known. This recipe should help us understand the steps involved in installing Patroni using Python3.

Getting ready...

To complete this recipe, we must make sure that our servers can connect to the repositories that have Python3 and other dependent modules for installing Patroni. These steps assume that `python3` and `pip3` are installed.

How to do it...

Follow these steps to set up Patroni:

1. Install the necessary Python dependencies so that you can install Patroni:

```
CentOS 8.x
 # dnf install python3-devel -y

OR

CentOS 7.x
 # yum install python3-devel -y
```

2. Install the `gcc` compiler to compile Patroni:

```
CentOS 8.x
 # dnf install gcc -y

Or

CentOS 7.x
 # yum install gcc -y
```

3. Install the `psycopg2` module for PostgreSQL to solve the dependency with Patroni:

```
CentOS 8.x
 # dnf install python3-psycopg2 -y
```

```
Or

CentOS 7.x
 # yum install python3-psycopg2 -y
```

4. Install Patroni using `pip3`. Make sure that you also include `etcd3`, as shown in the following command, to let `pip` install the dependencies specific to `etcd3` for `patroni`:

```
# pip3 install patroni[etcd3]
```

Thus, we have installed Patroni using Python!

How it works...

In this recipe, we learned how to install Patroni using Python 3. To ensure that the steps work properly, we must have `python3` and `python3-devel` installed already in the database servers, as shown in *Step 1*. To install `patroni`, we need `psycopg2`, which can be installed using the commands shown in *Step 3*. Once all the dependencies have been installed, we can install `patroni`, along with its `etcd3` dependencies, using `pip3`, as shown in *Step 4*.

Creating a Patroni configuration file

Now that etcd has been configured and watchdog/softdog has been enabled, we are done with all the prerequisites required for configuring Patroni for high availability and automatic failover. Patroni's setup entirely depends on its configuration file. Once the configuration file is in place, it is just a matter of bootstrapping a PostgreSQL node (primary) using Partroni and adding more nodes to the Patroni cluster to complete the HA setup. In this recipe, we shall discuss how to build the Patroni configuration file correctly.

Getting ready...

There are some PostgreSQL parameters that must be same across the master and the standby/replica servers. Setting such values in the local configuration file has no effect. The following is a list of those parameters and their default values:

```
max_connections: 100
max_locks_per_transaction: 64
max_worker_processes: 8
```

```
max_prepared_transactions: 0
wal_level: hot_standby
wal_log_hints: on
track_commit_timestamp: off
```

All these parameters can only be modified in the shared configuration in the DCS.

Also, the following Patroni configuration options can only be changed dynamically:

```
ttl: 30
loop_wait: 10
retry_timeouts: 10
maximum_lag_on_failover: 1048576
max_timelines_history: 0
check_timeline: false
postgresql.use_slots: true
```

How to do it...

Patroni's configuration file is a YAML file that has several sub-sections for every category. To avoid complexity in discussing each of the parameters, we shall see the sections involved and the parameters that can be set in those sections. Let's get started:

1. Create a directory that will store the Patroni configuration file:

```
$ sudo mkdir -p /etc/patroni
$ sudo touch /etc/patroni/pg.yml
$ sudo chown -R postgres:postgres /etc/patroni
$ sudo chmod -R 755 /etc/patroni
```

In the following steps, we shall see various sections of the configurations that need to be added to the /etc/patroni/pg1.yml file.

The following sections need to be part of the Patroni configuration file. We'll look at all the parameters that belong to the following six sections later in this recipe. All these sections and their parameters make a combined Patroni configuration file:

- REST API
- etcd or etcd3
- Bootstrap
- PostgreSQL
- Watchdog
- Tags

2. Set a name for the Patroni cluster and mention the name of the host that the configuration file is being created on:

```
scope: percona_hacluster
name: pg1
```

3. Add the necessary IP and port in order to access Patroni's RESTAPIs. Optionally, we may add user credentials and certificates to protect them from unsafe REST API endpoints:

```
restapi:
  listen: pg1:8008
  connect_address: pg1:8008
  # cafile: <ca file>
  # certfile: /etc/ssl/certs/ssl-cert-percona.pem
  # keyfile: /etc/ssl/private/ssl-cert-percona.key
authentication:
  username: api_user
  password: secret
```

4. Considering that the DCS that's being used is ectd, provide information about the ectd in the configuration file:

```
etcd:
  #Provide host to do the initial discovery of the cluster
topology:
  host: pg1:2379
```

5. Add some bootstrap configuration that consists of the following:

   - Global dynamic configuration parameters for the cluster under the `dcs` section.
   - `initdb` options under the `initdb` section.
   - Entries to be added to the `pg_hba.conf` file.
   - The user (or admin user) that needs to be created with a password and some roles assigned to it.

The dynamic configuration settings can be found at the following link: `https://patroni.readthedocs.io/en/latest/SETTINGS.html#dynamic-configuration-settings`:

```
bootstrap:
  # this section will be written into
Etcd:/<namespace>/<scope>/config after     initializing new cluster
  # and all other cluster members will use it as a `global
configuration`
```

```
dcs:
  ttl: 30
  loop_wait: 10
  retry_timeout: 10
  maximum_lag_on_failover: 1048576
  # master_start_timeout: 300
  # synchronous_mode: false
#
# some desired options for 'initdb'
initdb:
  - encoding: UTF8
  - locale: en_US.UTF-8
  # - data-checksums
#
# some example entries you wish to maintain in pg_hba.conf for
replication
# and application connections
pg_hba:
  host replication replicator 192.168.10.0/24 md5
  host all all 0.0.0.0/0 md5
  # hostssl all all 0.0.0.0/0 md5
#
# Some additional users users which needs to be created after
initializing new    cluster
users:
  admin:
  password: secret
    options:
      createrole
      createdb
```

6. Set all the configuration parameters and users needed for the PostgreSQL cluster under the postgresql section:

```
postgresql:
  listen: *:5432
  connect_address: pg1:5432
  bin_dir: /usr/pgsql-13/bin
  config_dir: /var/lib/pgsql/13/data
  data_dir: /var/lib/pgsql/13/data
  pgpass: /var/lib/pgsql/.pgpass
  # pre_promote: /path/to/pre_promote.sh
  # use_slots: true
  use_pg_rewind: true
  authentication:
    superuser:
    username: postgres
    password: secret
```

```
        replication:
        username: replicator
        password: secret
        rewind:
          username: rewind_user
          password: secret
        parameters:
          shared_buffers: "128MB"
          work_mem: "4MB"
          wal_level: hot_standby
          hot_standby: "on"
          wal_keep_segments: 8
          max_wal_senders: 10
          max_replication_slots: 10
          wal_log_hints: "on"
          archive_mode: "on"
          archive_timeout: 1800s
          archive_command: mkdir -p ../wal_archive && test ! -f
../wal_archive/%f && cp %p ../wal_archive/%f
          restore_command: cp ../wal_archive/%f %p
```

7. Add the `watchdog` details if watchdog is being used by Patroni to avoid split-brain syndrome:

```
watchdog:
  mode: automatic # Allowed values: off, automatic, required
  device: /dev/watchdog
  #safety_margin: 5
```

8. Add tags that specify whether a failover should be automatic and specify if the replication needs to be synchronous, along with some other tags:

```
tags:
  nofailover: false
  noloadbalance: false
  clonefrom: false
  nosync: false
```

9. The final configuration file for Patroni may look as follows. This configuration file will be used throughout all the recipes related to Patroni in this chapter:

```
scope: percona_hacluster
name: pg1
restapi:
  listen: pg1:8008
  connect_address: pg1:8008
  # cafile: <ca file>
  # certfile: /etc/ssl/certs/ssl-cert-percona.pem
```

```
    # keyfile: /etc/ssl/private/ssl-cert-percona.key
authentication:
  username: api_user
  password: secret
etcd:
  host: pg1:2379
bootstrap:
  dcs:
    ttl: 30
    loop_wait: 10
    retry_timeout: 10
    maximum_lag_on_failover: 1048576
  initdb:
    - encoding: UTF8
    - locale: en_US.UTF-8
    # - data-checksums
  pg_hba:
    - host replication replicator 192.168.10.0/24 md5
    - host all all 0.0.0.0/0 md5
  users:
    admin:
    password: secret
    options:
      - createrole
      - createdb
  postgresql:
    listen: localhost,192.168.10.1:5432
    connect_address: pg1:5432
    bin_dir: /usr/pgsql-13/bin
    config_dir: /var/lib/pgsql/13/data
    data_dir: /var/lib/pgsql/13/data
    pgpass: /var/lib/pgsql/.pgpass
    use_pg_rewind: true
    authentication:
      superuser:
        username: postgres
        password: secret
      replication:
        username: replicator
        password: secret
      rewind:
        username: rewind_user
        password: secret
    parameters:
      shared_buffers: "128MB"
      work_mem: "4MB"
      wal_level: hot_standby
      hot_standby: "on"
```

```
        wal_keep_segments: 8
        max_wal_senders: 10
        max_replication_slots: 10
        wal_log_hints: "on"
        archive_mode: "on"
        archive_timeout: 1800s
        archive_command: /bin/true
        # restore_command: cp ../wal_archive/%f %p
    watchdog:
      mode: automatic
      device: /dev/watchdog
    tags:
      nofailover: false
      noloadbalance: false
```

How it works...

To set up a Patroni cluster, one of the important components is the Patroni configuration file. This file contains the configuration needed to bootstrap an existing cluster from scratch. We need to create appropriate directories to store the Patroni configuration file, as shown in *Step 1*. This configuration file starts with the scope and name, as shown in *Step 2*, where the scope is the name of the cluster and the name is the hostname of the local server where the configuration file is being created.

Patroni exposes REST APIs to allow applications to get the state of a node. For example, if HAProxy-like TCP packet routers or load balancers are used between the application and the database, the HAProxy could probe for the role of all the servers in the list using the Patroni REST API. It could then be configured to redirect the connection to a server that reports the role as master for automatically redirecting writes to a master upon a failover. This helps in enabling a transparent application failover. The port and IP that the REST API accepts connections on, along with optional user credentials, can be added under the `restapi` section, as shown in *Step 3*.

We can then proceed to *Step 4*, where we add the etcd-specific configuration information. All we need to do is provide the hostname or IP address of the local server and the port that the etcd cluster is accepting read or write requests on by an application. Once the etcd configuration has been added, we can then move on to the bootstrap section, as shown in *Step 5*. In this section, we specify the parameters that need to be part of the DCS to configure the requirements of when a failover should happen. This section also includes the `initdb`-specific parameters for setting up a cluster (if they don't already exist) and the content that needs to be added to the `pg_hba.conf` file. Optionally, we could also have a few users being created by Patroni during the bootstrap.

All the PostgreSQL-specific parameters, along with the location of the bin and data directories, the port that the Postgres cluster should run on, and the parameters that the database cluster should be started with should all be listed under the PostgreSQL section, as shown in *Step 6*. In order to avoid a split-brain occurring due to a failover, we need to add watchdog-specific information under the watchdog section, as shown in *Step 7*. Then we can deal with the configuration file's setup by adding tags to it, as shown in *Step 8*. Tags contain the options to specify whether an automatic failover should be enabled and if the replication type should be synchronous or asynchronous. *Step 9* includes the final configuration file that is built using all the sections we discussed until *Step 8* for the example setup. This configuration file will be used throughout all the recipes for the HA setup using Patroni.

Starting Patroni as a service using systemd

A server crash or a restart requires that we start Patroni manually. This may cause additional downtime for the application. For this purpose, a systemd service that auto-starts Patroni upon a crash or restart is needed. In this recipe, we shall look at the Patroni service file that can be enabled to manage Patroni using services.

Getting ready...

The systemd service we will be discussing in this recipe works for almost all the latest Linux operating systems where systemd works. Creating or managing services requires root access.

How to do it...

We will start Patroni using `systemd`. Let's get started:

1. Create a `patroni.service` file in the usual `systemd` service files location with the following text:

    ```
    # vi /usr/lib/systemd/system/patroni.service
    ```

    - Append the following text to the preceding file:

    ```
    # This is an example systemd config file for Patroni
    # You can copy it to "/usr/lib/systemd/system/patroni.service"
    [Unit]
    Description=Runners to orchestrate a high-availability PostgreSQL
    ```

```
After=syslog.target network.target
[Service]
 Type=simple
User=postgres
 Group=postgres
# Read in configuration file if it exists, otherwise proceed
 EnvironmentFile=-/etc/patroni_env.conf
# the default is the user's home directory, and if you want to
change it, you must provide an absolute path.
# WorkingDirectory=/home/sameuser
# Where to send early-startup messages from the server
 # This is normally controlled by the global default set by systemd
 #StandardOutput=syslog
# Pre-commands to start watchdog device
 # Uncomment if watchdog is part of your patroni setup
 ExecStartPre=-/usr/bin/sudo /sbin/modprobe softdog
 ExecStartPre=-/usr/bin/sudo /bin/chown postgres /dev/watchdog
# Start the patroni process
 ExecStart=/usr/local/bin/patroni /etc/patroni/patroni.yml
# Send HUP to reload from patroni.yml
 ExecReload=/bin/kill -s HUP $MAINPID
# only kill the patroni process, not it's children, so it will
gracefully stop postgres
 KillMode=process
# Give a reasonable amount of time for the server to start up/shut
down
 TimeoutSec=30
# Do not restart the service if it crashes, we want to manually
inspect database on failure
 Restart=no
[Install]
 WantedBy=multi-user.target
```

2. Validate and enable the `patroni` service using the following commands:

    - The service will usually be disabled by default. It can be validated using the following command:

    ```
    # systemctl list-unit-files | grep patroni
     patroni.service disabled
    ```

    - The service can be enabled using the following command:

    ```
    # systemctl enable patroni
    ```

How it works...

To ensure that the Patroni cluster auto-starts upon a crash or a restart, a service for Patroni is needed. We need to use the commands shown in *Step 1* to create the service file. Once the file has been created, the Patroni service can be enabled using the command shown in *Step 2*.

Initializing a PostgreSQL primary database using Patroni

In the past few recipes, we have seen how a DCS can be set up using etcd and how a watchdog/softdog can be configured to avoid split-brain upon failover. More importantly, in the previous two recipes, we learned how a Patroni configuration file can be created and how a Patroni service can be enabled. In this recipe, we shall discuss how a PostgreSQL primary cluster can be initialized using Patroni.

Getting ready...

You must complete the previous four recipes before you attempt this recipe. The Patroni configuration file being referenced in this recipe is same as the configuration file shown in Step 9 of the *How to do it...* section of the *Creating a Patroni configuration file* recipe.

The following steps are being performed on the primary database only.

How to do it...

Let's initialize the database, as follows:

1. Start the Patroni service using `systemctl`, as shown in the following command:

   ```
   $ sudo systemctl start patroni
   ```

2. See if any errors have occurred using the `status` command:

   ```
   $ sudo systemctl status patroni
   ```

3. Use `patronictl` to see if the Patroni cluster has been initialized, along with a new PostgreSQL cluster, on the primary database server:

```
$ patronictl -c /etc/patroni/patroni.yml list percona_hacluster
```

The output will be as follows:

```
$ patronictl -c /etc/patroni/patroni.yml list percona_hacluster
+ Cluster: percona_hacluster (6879907124853122699) --+
| Member | Host | Role | State | TL | Lag in MB |
+--------+------+---------+---------+----+-----------+
| pg1 | pg1 | Leader | running | 1 | |
+--------+------+---------+---------+----+-----------+
```

How it works...

Once all the previous recipes have been successfully completed, initializing the Patroni cluster is as simple as starting the Patroni service, as shown in *Step 1*. Its status can be confirmed using the command shown in *Step 2*. We can use `patronictl` to list the status of the cluster that has been initialized using the primary server, as shown in *Step 3*.

Adding a standby to a Patroni cluster

Once the Primary cluster has been initialized using Patroni, the next step is to add the standby servers to the cluster for the purpose of a quorum and high availability. In this recipe, we shall discuss the steps involved in adding one or more standby servers to an existing Patroni cluster.

Getting ready...

You need to have completed the previous recipe before you attempt this one. The steps in this recipe can be performed on one or more standby servers that are also part of the same etcd cluster with watchdog/softdog configured.

In this recipe, the IP address of the example standby server is 192.168.10.2 and the primary's IP is 192.168.10.1.

How to do it...

Follow these steps to complete this recipe:

1. Copy the `patroni.yml` service file from the primary server to the standby server, if it does not already exist:

   ```
   # scp /usr/lib/systemd/system/patroni.service
   vagrant@192.168.10.2:/usr/lib/systemd/system/patroni.service
   ```

2. Enable `patroni` so that it auto-starts if the server crashes or automatically restarts:

   ```
   # sudo systemctl enable patroni
   ```

3. Copy the Patroni configuration file from the primary server to the standby server:

   ```
   # scp /etc/patroni/patroni.yml vagrant@192.168.10.2:/tmp
   ```

4. Replace the primary hostname with the standby hostname and the primary IP address with the standby IP address in the Patroni configuration file. Copy the file to an appropriate location where the service expects the configuration file to be:

   ```
   # sed 's/pg1/pg2/g' /tmp/patroni.yml > /etc/patroni/patroni.yml
   ```

   Additionally, if you have used any hard-coded IP addresses for nodes, replace them with the appropriate node IP address:

   ```
   # sed -i 's/192.168.10.1/192.168.10.2/g' /etc/patroni/patroni.yml
   ```

5. Start the Patroni server to let Patroni run `pg_basebackup`. This will set up the standby and make it part of the Patroni cluster automatically:

   ```
   # sudo systemctl start patroni
   ```

6. Perform validation using the following command to check whether the standby has made itself part of the existing Patroni cluster:

   - Replace `percona_hacluster` with the exact cluster name, as mentioned in the Patroni configuration file:

     ```
     $ patronictl -c /etc/patroni/patroni.yml list percona_hacluster
     ```

This will result in the following output:

```
$ patronictl -c /etc/patroni/patroni.yml list percona_hacluster
+ Cluster: percona_hacluster (6879907124853122699) --+
| Member | Host | Role | State | TL | Lag in MB |
+--------+------+---------+---------+----+-----------+
| pg1 | pg1 | Leader | running | 1 | |
| pg2 | pg2 | Replica | running | 1 | 0 |
+--------+------+---------+---------+----+-----------+
```

How it works...

To add a new standby server to an existing Patroni cluster, we need to ensure that we have completed the recipes where we must make the server part of the etcd cluster with watchdog enabled. Once we've done that, it is very simple to add a standby by copying the Patroni configuration file and the Patroni service from the primary server to the standby server, as shown in *Steps 1* and *2*, using `scp`. Once the files have been copied, the Patroni service can be enabled using the command shown in *Step 3*. The Patroni configuration file that was copied from the primary server should have the hostname and IP address of the standby server. This can be achieved by using the commands shown in *Step 4*. Upon making the minor changes discussed in *Step 4*, we can simply start the `patroni` service using `systemctl`, as shown in *Step 5*. We can validate the cluster's health using the command shown in *Step 6* to validate whether the new standby has been added to the existing Patroni cluster.

Performing a manual switchover using Patroni

The recipes we've discussed so far should help with setting up a Patroni cluster with multiple servers. In this recipe, we shall discuss how a manual switchover can be performed using Patroni.

Getting ready...

To perform a failover, we must have a Patroni cluster running without any errors reported alongside the configuration. You must have completed all the recipes in this chapter to ensure a switchover can occur with Patroni.

How to do it...

Follow these steps to complete this recipe:

1. Validate the status of the Patroni cluster using the `list` command:

```
$ patronictl -c /etc/patroni/patroni.yml list percona_hacluster
+ Cluster: percona_hacluster (6879907124853122699) --+
| Member | Host | Role | State | TL | Lag in MB |
+---------+------+---------+---------+----+-----------+
| pg1 | pg1 | Leader | running | 7 | |
| pg2 | pg2 | Replica | running | 7 | 0 |
+---------+------+---------+---------+----+-----------+
```

2. Run the `switchover` command to perform a manual switchover:

```
$ patronictl -c /etc/patroni/patroni.yml switchover
percona_hacluster
```

The output will look as follows:

```
$ patronictl -c /etc/patroni/patroni.yml switchover
percona_hacluster
 Master [pg1]:
```

3. The previous step asks you to enter the hostname of the existing Master/Primary. We can either enter the same host or just ignore this and hit *Enter* if the host appearing as the master is the actual master:

```
$ patronictl -c /etc/patroni/patroni.yml switchover
percona_hacluster
 Master [pg1]:
 Candidate ['pg2'] []:
```

4. When we hit *Enter,* Patroni asks us to choose the candidate that the failover should be performed for. We may see more than one candidate if there are more servers in the Patroni cluster. We should enter the host that needs to become the primary:

```
$ patronictl -c /etc/patroni/patroni.yml switchover
percona_hacluster
 Master [pg1]:
 Candidate ['pg2'] []: pg2
 When should the switchover take place (e.g. 2020-10-05T01:59 )
[now]:
```

5. Once we've entered the name of the host as a candidate for primary, Patroni will ask us to choose when the switchover should take place. If we need to schedule the switchover at a later date, we could enter the datetime and hit *Enter*. To let the switchover happen immediately, we can hit now, which acts as the default value:

```
$ patronictl -c /etc/patroni/patroni.yml switchover
percona_hacluster
 Master [pg1]:
 Candidate ['pg2'] []: pg2
 When should the switchover take place (e.g. 2020-10-05T01:59 )
[now]:
 Current cluster topology
 + Cluster: percona_hacluster (6879907124853122699) --+
 | Member | Host | Role | State | TL | Lag in MB |
 +--------+------+---------+---------+----+-----------+
 | pg1 | pg1 | Leader | running | 7 | |
 | pg2 | pg2 | Replica | running | 7 | 0 |
 +--------+------+---------+---------+----+-----------+
 Are you sure you want to switchover cluster percona_hacluster,
demoting current master pg1? [y/N]:
```

6. Once we hit *Enter*, we will be asked to confirm this once more and let the switchover continue. We could hit y to let the switchover happen. Upon hitting *Enter*, we should see the following output:

```
$ patronictl -c /etc/patroni/patroni.yml switchover
percona_hacluster
 Master [pg1]:
 Candidate ['pg2'] []: pg2
 When should the switchover take place (e.g. 2020-10-05T01:59 )
[now]:
 Current cluster topology
 + Cluster: percona_hacluster (6879907124853122699) --+
 | Member | Host | Role | State | TL | Lag in MB |
 +--------+------+---------+---------+----+-----------+
 | pg1 | pg1 | Leader | running | 7 | |
 | pg2 | pg2 | Replica | running | 7 | 0 |
 +--------+------+---------+---------+----+-----------+
 Are you sure you want to switchover cluster percona_hacluster,
demoting current master pg1? [y/N]: y
 2020-10-05 01:03:10.34992 Successfully switched over to "pg2"
 + Cluster: percona_hacluster (6879907124853122699) --+
 | Member | Host | Role | State | TL | Lag in MB |
 +--------+------+---------+---------+----+-----------+
```

```
| pg1 | pg1 | Replica | stopped | | unknown |
| pg2 | pg2 | Leader  | running | 7 | |
+--------+------+---------+---------+----+----------+
```

7. Wait for a few seconds and then view the status of the server. Here, we can see that the old master server has become a replica and that the old standby server has become a leader/primary:

```
$ patronictl -c /etc/patroni/patroni.yml list percona_hacluster
+ Cluster: percona_hacluster (6879907124853122699) --+
| Member | Host | Role | State | TL | Lag in MB |
+--------+------+---------+---------+----+----------+
| pg1 | pg1 | Replica | running | 8 | 0 |
| pg2 | pg2 | Leader  | running | 8 | |
+--------+------+---------+---------+----+----------+
```

How it works...

Performing a manual switchover is very simple and user-friendly. Upon validating the cluster's health using the command shown in *Step 1*, we can run the command in *Step 2* to initiate a switchover. As shown in *Steps 3* to *6*, the switchover command asks for confirmation regarding whether the primary host is correct as displayed and whether the standby needs to be chosen as a candidate for the primary. Once the existing primary and the proposed primary hostnames have been entered, Patroni asks for confirmation regarding whether the switchover should happen immediately or at a later date. Upon confirmation, the switchover will be initiated appropriately. The cluster's health can be validated, as shown in *Step 7*. This shows that the old primary will be automatically added as a standby once you've promoted the candidate as a new primary.

6
Connection Pooling and Load Balancing

When a client attempts a connection to a PostgreSQL database, the postmaster acknowledges the connections and forks a backend process. Thus, each client connection in Postgres is a process in the operating system. The postmaster performs a `fork()` system call, which creates an address space, file descriptors, and a copy of the memory segments as of the postmaster process. And once the client disconnects, the child process gets terminated.

In a general workload, benchmarks have proven that PostgreSQL performs well up to 350 transactions per second, without a connection pooler. However, when we expect more transactions that could create hundreds or thousands of processes, it is important to maintain a connection pooler.

A connection pooler will help to maintain persistent connections to the database server. This avoids creating and terminating connections each time a client connects or disconnects. This enables a PostgreSQL server to maintain a stable performance throughout.

Usually, a native application connection pooler is preferred if it does its job well. However, if there are a number of application servers with independent connection poolers, we could see a lot of idle connections on the database servers. Sometimes, you may see the number of idle connections going up to 100 or 1,000 or more. This may cause a problem when the pre-cached memory that includes the execution plans created within a transaction or session and hash tables are not cleaned up. We may estimate each of the idle connections consuming up to 10 MB or more of memory and creating a memory crunch. In such a situation, an external connection pooler, specially built for PostgreSQL, should help. Such an external pooler can stay in a dedicated server to which all the application servers could connect. This external pooler would then redirect the connections to the database server.

The following are two well-known external connection poolers for PostgreSQL:

- pgBouncer
- pgPool-II

In this chapter, we are going to discuss pgBouncer, which is one of the widely implemented lightweight external poolers.

While connection poolers help in avoiding degraded performance, load balancers play a great role in scalability. In a general use case, load balancers help in distributing the load across multiple servers. A standby in PostgreSQL can act as a hot standby, which means that it can accept reads. Thus, a load balancer could help in distributing the reads across multiple Postgres servers to utilize the computing power of standby servers.

In this chapter, we shall consider talking about one of the widely implemented open source connection poolers and a load balancer, through the following recipes:

- Installing pgBouncer on a Linux server
- Creating a pgBouncer configuration file
- Configuring the pool settings on pgBouncer
- Starting and stopping the pgBouncer service
- Installing HAProxy on Linux servers
- Using xinetd to detect a primary or a standby
- Creating an HaProxy configuration file
- Starting and stopping the HAProxy service
- Building a robust HA cluster using Patroni, pgBouncer, and HAProxy

Technical requirements

For this chapter, you must have a PostgreSQL server with at least two CPUs and 2 GB RAM and access to download RPMs over the internet from the PGDG repository and from GitHub.

Installing pgBouncer on a Linux server

pgBouncer is a thread-based pooler (spawns a thread for each connection), designed and built for PostgreSQL. It receives a connection, puts it in the pool, then redirects the connection to a persistent process on the database. It understands the PostgreSQL protocol very well. pgBouncer can be implemented using the following three modes:

- **Session Mode**: When `pool_mode` is set as `session`, the connection given by pgBouncer to the client stays until the client disconnects. The client could either run one transaction or more transactions through one session at a time. This is the safest method when we are not sure whether the application uses prepared statements or some of the features that are not supported by the other pool modes.
- **Transaction Mode**: pgBouncer is said to perform the best when `pool_mode` is set as `transaction`. In this mode, a client connection is active until the transaction is active. Once the transaction is completed, the client is disconnected and the connection is sent back to the pool. However, the transaction mode does not work when prepared statements are used. In such cases, a session mode is preferred.
- **Statement Mode**: This is one of the modes that is very rarely used. In statement mode, a client stays connected only for the duration of a statement. Once the statement is completed, the client is disconnected and the connection is sent back to the pool.

In this recipe, we shall discuss the steps involved in installing pgBouncer.

Getting ready...

pgBouncer can be installed on an application server or an external server between the application and a database server. If it is installed on an external server, we may need to have an active and a passive pgBouncer server to avoid a single point of failure. In addition to that, we may need a server with a very high configuration. A server with 2 GB RAM and 4 CPUs may be extremely helpful for a heavy load of more than 5,000 transactions per second. However, it is always recommended to benchmark before deciding the specifications.

How to do it...

Following are two sections demonstrating the steps to install pgBouncer on Red Hat/Centos and Ubuntu/Debian operating systems.

Section A: To install pgBouncer on the Red Hat or CentOS family of operating systems, we may use the following steps:

1. Install the PGDG repository RPM:

    ```
    $ sudo yum install -y
    https://download.postgresql.org/pub/repos/yum/reporpms/EL-7-x86_64/
    pgdg-redhat-repo-latest.noarch.rpm
    ```

2. Install pgBouncer using the following command:

    ```
    $ sudo yum install pgbouncer -y
    ```

3. We may install the Postgres client package to connect to the local `pgbouncer` database using `psql`:

    ```
    $ sudo yum install postgresql13 -y
    ```

Section B: To install pgBouncer on Debian or Ubuntu operating systems, we may use the following steps:

1. Create the PGDG repository configuration file using the following command:

    ```
    $ sudo sh -c 'echo "deb http://apt.postgresql.org/pub/repos/apt
    $(lsb_release -cs)-pgdg main" > /etc/apt/sources.list.d/pgdg.list'
    ```

2. Import the signing key for the repository:

    ```
    $ wget --quiet -O -
    https://www.postgresql.org/media/keys/ACCC4CF8.asc | sudo apt-key
    add -
    ```

3. Update the package lists using the following command:

    ```
    $ sudo apt-get update
    ```

4. Install the latest version of pgBouncer:

```
$ sudo apt get pgbouncer -y
```

5. We may install the Postgres client package to connect to the local `pgbouncer` database using `psql`:

```
$ sudo apt-get install postgresql-client-13
```

How it works...

pgBouncer can be installed on the Red Hat/CentOS family of operating systems or Ubuntu and Debian operating systems. In the preceding section, we saw the steps to install pgbouncer on all these operating systems.

The common steps in both sections are the setup of the PGDG repository. The steps to set up the repository vary between Red Hat and Ubuntu operating systems, as seen in Section A and Section B. Once the PGDG repository has been set up, we could install pgBouncer using step 2 of Section A on Red Hat/CentOS and step 4 of Section B on Ubuntu/Debian. To connect to the local pgbouncer database for admin and monitoring purposes, we could use step 3 of Section A and step 5 of Section B based on the operating systems.

Creating a pgBouncer configuration file

Upon installation of pgBouncer, we should be able to see a default pgBouncer configuration file in the `/etc/pgbouncer` directory (`/etc/pgbouncer/pgbouncer.ini`).

This default file would not serve the purpose in a real scenario. In this recipe, we shall discuss the parameters that need to be appropriately set to have a successful pgBouncer setup.

Getting ready...

In order to proceed further with the steps in this recipe, we must have already installed pgBouncer in the first recipe *Installing pgBouncer on a Linux server*.

How to do it...

The following are the list of parameters that need to be appropriately configured in the configuration file `/etc/pgbouncer/pgbouncer.ini`:

1. Under the `[databases]` section, add a database name and the corresponding `libpq` style connection string in a key-value pair format, as seen in the following example. The name specified in the key is considered as a database alias name that redirects a connection to the appropriate database specified in the value:

    ```
    [databases]
    primary = host=primary_server_ip port=5432 dbname=migops
    standby = host=standby_server_ip port=5432 dbname=migops
    ```

2. We can have as many entries as we can for different databases in a PostgreSQL server, as seen in the following example:

    ```
    [databases]
    primary_1 = host=primary_server_ip port=5432 dbname=migops_1
    standby_1 = host=standby_server_ip port=5432 dbname=migops_1
    primary_2 = host=primary_server_ip port=5432 dbname=migops_2
    standby_2 = host=standby_server_ip port=5432 dbname=migops_2
    ```

3. Add the pgBouncer IP to `pg_hba.conf` for both the primary and standby and any other database servers to which pgBouncer is supposed to connect. The following is an example entry that allows all connections from a pgBouncer server to any database as any user upon password authentication:

    ```
    host all all pgBouncer_IP/32 md5
    ```

4. Append the username and MD5 passwords to the `userlist.txt` file located in the `/etc/pgbouncer` directory. The following command needs to run on the database server to which `pgbouncer` is expected to connect:

    ```
    $ psql -Aqt -c "select '\"'||usename||'\" \"'||passwd||'\"' from
    pg_shadow"
    "postgres" "md553f48b7c4b76a86ce72276c5755f217d"
    "migops_user" "md51176b388537b6f28fd4a98362062bf6d"
    "migops_admin" "md5735aa9a418b5d55c126ab90c8b6463a2"
    ```

    Add the output from the preceding command to the `/etc/pgbouncer/userlist.txt` file on the pgBouncer server.

5. Set the `auth_type` parameter to md5 or any of the supported authentication methods in the `pgbouncer.ini` file (`/etc/pgbouncer/pgbouncer.ini`). pgBouncer supports almost all the authentication methods supported by PostgreSQL. Ensure to provide the location of the `userlist.txt` file that contains the MD5 passwords:

```
$ sudo vi /etc/pgbouncer/pgbouncer.ini
...
auth_type = md5
auth_file = /etc/pgbouncer/userlist.txt
```

6. Optionally, we may create an `hba.conf` file on the pgBouncer server in addition to the `hba.conf` file on the PostgreSQL server or trust the connections from pgBouncer to PostgreSQL database server with an `hba.conf` file on the pgBouncer server:

```
$ sudo vi /etc/pgbouncer/pgbouncer.ini
...
auth_hba_file = /etc/pgbouncer/auth_hba.conf
```

The preceding `auth_hba.conf` file could act as a firewall similar to the original `pg_hba.conf` on the PostgreSQL server.

7. Finally, set the `listen_addr` and `port` parameters appropriately. We need to set `listen_addr` to `'*'` if we need to allow connections through all IP interfaces. The port can be modified from the default pgBouncer port of `6432`:

```
$ sudo vi /etc/pgbouncer/pgbouncer.ini
...
listen_addr = '*'
port = 6432
```

How it works...

A pgBouncer configuration file consists of many parameters that need to be set correctly. It starts with the `[databases]` section as seen in *step 1*. This section must contain the entries in a key-value format, where the key is the database alias name used by the application to connect to a target database specified in the value part. The database alias name specified in the key may not be the same as the actual database name to which the application is supposed to connect.

As seen in *step 2*, we can have as many entries as possible with different combinations, as long as the same key and name do not repeat. Once the databases have been added, we should ensure to allow connections from the pgBouncer server to the database server by adding an appropriate entry as seen in *step 3*. After adding the entry, we could proceed to create a `userlist.txt` file that contains the user and the MD5 hash password with the same format as seen in *step 4*. We could then proceed to enable password authentication at the `pgBouncer` layer by specifying the authentication mode to the `auth_type` parameter as seen in *step 5*. As mentioned in *step 5*, we may optionally create another pgBouncer specific `hba.conf` file to restrict or allow connections from a certain IP address or to allow a connection only when the entry in `auth_hba.conf` matches.

Finally, as seen in *step 7*, we must set `listen_addr` to `'*'` to enable connections over all IP interfaces and the default port can be changed from `6432` to any other port if the default does not solve the purpose for any reason.

Configuring the pool settings on pgBouncer

In the previous recipe, *Creating a pgBouncer configuration file*, we saw some of the mandatory settings for pgBouncer to start. However, the importance of pgBouncer is seen when some of the connection pool-specific settings are set correctly. In this recipe, we shall discuss the best ways of configuring the pool-specific parameters.

Getting ready...

In order to proceed further with the steps in this recipe, we must have already installed pgBouncer using the first recipe *Installing pgBouncer on a Linux server*, and also configured the mandatory settings as specified in the recipe *Creating a pgBouncer configuration file*.

How to do it...

The following is the list of parameters that we should configure to set the pool settings correctly:

1. If the nature of the connections from the client supports the transaction mode, set `pool_mode` to `transaction`. Otherwise, leave it as the session mode, which is the default:

   ```
   $ sudo vi /etc/pgbouncer/pgbouncer.ini
   ...
   ```

```
pool_mode = session
```

2. Set `default_pool_size` to the maximum client connections we wish to establish to the database server through each pool:

```
$ sudo vi /etc/pgbouncer/pgbouncer.ini
...
default_pool_size = 20
```

 It is not wise to have `default_pool_size` set to more than double the number of CPUs in a database server, considering only one pool.

Please note that a pool is created for every unique combination of a user and database.

3. Set `min_pool_size`, `max_db_connections`, and `max_user_connections` appropriately:

```
$ sudo vi /etc/pgbouncer/pgbouncer.ini
...
min_pool_size=2
max_db_connections=200
max_user_connections=200
```

The parameters seen here can be described as follows:

- `min_pool_size` is the minimum number of server connections to keep in a pool.
- `max_db_connections` is the maximum number of server connections allowed to a database.
- `max_user_connections` is the maximum number of server connections allowed by a user.

4. Set the `max_client_conn` parameter to the total number of clients that can connect to pgBouncer. If the preceding settings limit pgBouncer from creating additional connections to the database server, then the remaining connections wait on pgBouncer. A wait on pgBouncer is less costly than a CPU wait on the database server:

```
$ sudo vi /etc/pgbouncer/pgbouncer.ini
...
max_client_conn=1000
```

How it works...

To begin with the advanced settings of pgBouncer, `pool_mode` has to be set appropriately as seen in *step 1*. pgBouncer must be carefully set to allow only a limited number of persistent connections through a pool. This can be configured using the `default_pool_size` parameter as seen in *step 2*. We can then proceed to *step 3* to set the `min_pool_size` to always allow so many connections to remain at any time. Additionally, we can also limit the number of connections to a database and through a user using the `max_db_connections` and `max_user_connections` parameters. Finally, as seen in *step 4*, we could set the parameter `max_client_conn` to the number of client connections up to which pgBouncer can create a wait queue. The wait queue will be equal to `max_client_conn` minus the total number of connections that have been established until the maximum limits.

Starting and stopping the pgBouncer service

In the last three recipes of this chapter, we have seen how to install pgBouncer and the parameters that need to be configured appropriately. In this recipe, we shall see some of the simple commands to start, stop, and reload pgBouncer manually and through services.

Getting ready...

To start or stop pgBouncer successfully, we must install pgBouncer and set all the parameters correctly. So, the prerequisite is to ensure that the three previously discussed recipes are successfully implemented.

How to do it...

Here are the steps to start, stop, and reload a pgBouncer instance:

1. The following command can be used to start pgBouncer using a service:

```
$ sudo systemctl start pgbouncer
```

2. The following command can be used to start pgBouncer manually. The command-line argument –d would daemonize pgBouncer:

```
$ su - pgbouncer
$ /usr/bin/pgbouncer -d /etc/pgbouncer/pgbouncer.ini
```

3. The following command can be used to stop pgBouncer using a service:

```
$ sudo systemctl stop pgbouncer
```

4. The following command can be used to reload pgBouncer using a service:

```
$ sudo systemctl reload pgbouncer
```

5. The following command can be used to reload pgBouncer manually:

```
$ kill -HUP <pgbouncer_pid>
```

<pgbouncer_pid> in the preceding command must be substituted by the process ID of pgBouncer.

How it works...

When pgBouncer is installed using RPMs or packages, a service file is automatically created. The same service can be used to start pgBouncer as seen in *step 1*. However, we must ensure that the location of the pgBouncer configuration file stays the same as the file in the service file. To manually start pgBouncer, we could use the command seen in *step 2*. We must substitute the configuration file location appropriately. pgBouncer can be stopped using the service seen in *step 3*.

If any of the configuration parameters have been modified, pgBouncer needs to be reloaded. This can be done using the command seen in *step 4* or by manually performing a SIGHUP using the pgBouncer process ID as seen in *step 5*.

Installing HAProxy on Linux servers

HaProxy is one of the widely implemented lightweight load balancers. It can be used to load balance reads using round-robin or least connection count algorithms between multiple database servers. In this recipe, we shall see the steps involved in installing HAProxy on a Linux server.

Getting ready...

HAProxy is generally available through the default repositories of both Red Hat/Centos or Ubuntu/Debian operating systems. All it needs is internet connectivity to download the packages from a remote repository.

How to do it...

HAProxy can be installed on RedHat/CentOS and Ubuntu/Debian using the following steps:

1. We can use the following command to install HAProxy on Red Hat/Centos:

   ```
   $ sudo yum install haproxy -y
   ```

2. We can use the following command to install HAProxy on Ubuntu/Debian:

   ```
   $ sudo apt-get install haproxy -y
   ```

How it works...

Installing HaProxy is a simple one-line command as seen in the preceding section. It can be installed using YUM on the Red Hat/CentOS family and using APT on Ubuntu/Debian operating systems.

Using xinetd to detect a primary or a standby

HAProxy can be used to load balance the connections or even route the connections to a specific host that passes a check. This check can be performed using Xinetd (Extended Internet Service Daemon). The Xinetd daemon can listen to requests on any custom port. It executes custom logic to serve the request. We could then send unique status codes based on the server to which it has connected. For example, if the server is the primary, the status code should be 200. If the server is a standby, the status code can be 300.

In this recipe, we shall see how HAProxy can rely on xinetd for transparent application failover.

Getting ready...

Performing checks using xinetd may be time-consuming if a connection could not be established to a database server while performing the checks. This needs to be well tested before implementing it in production.

How to do it...

The following are the steps to enable consistency checks using xinetd:

1. Create a script locally in the database that can be executed by the xinetd daemon to check the status of the server. The following is a sample script. We may create the script with the name /opt/pgsqlchk:

```
#!/bin/bash
#
PGBIN=/usr/pgsql-13/bin
PGSQL_HOST="migops_server"
PGSQL_PORT="5432"
PGSQL_DATABASE="migops"
PGSQL_USERNAME="migops_user"
export PGPASSWORD="migops"
TMP_FILE="/tmp/pgsqlchk.out"
ERR_FILE="/tmp/pgsqlchk.err"

# Following query will be executed against the database server.

VALUE=`/usr/pgsql-13/bin/psql -t -h localhost -U postgres -p 5432 -
c "select pg_is_in_recovery()" 2> /dev/null`
# If output is not null, then do something.
if [ $VALUE == "t" ]
then
    /bin/echo -e "HTTP/1.1 300 OK\r\n"
    /bin/echo -e "Content-Type: Content-Type: text/plain\r\n"
    /bin/echo -e "\r\n"
    /bin/echo "Standby"
    /bin/echo -e "\r\n"
elif [ $VALUE == "f" ]
then
    /bin/echo -e "HTTP/1.1 200 OK\r\n"
    /bin/echo -e "Content-Type: Content-Type: text/plain\r\n"
    /bin/echo -e "\r\n"
    /bin/echo "Primary"
    /bin/echo -e "\r\n"
else
```

```
/bin/echo -e "HTTP/1.1 400 Service Unavailable\r\n"
/bin/echo -e "Content-Type: Content-Type: text/plain\r\n"
/bin/echo -e "\r\n"
/bin/echo "DB down"
/bin/echo -e "\r\n"
fi
#
```

2. Give execute permission to the script created in the previous step:

```
$ sudo chmod 755 /opt/pgsqlchk
```

3. Install xinetd on the database server:

```
$ sudo yum install -y xinetd
```

4. Create an xinetd configuration file that specifies the port on which the service is running and the script that should be executed:

```
$ sudo vi /etc/xinetd.d/pgsqlchk
## Add the following entries to the file
service pgsqlchk
{
 flags = REUSE
 socket_type = stream
 port = 23267
 wait = no
 user = nobody
 server = /opt/pgsqlchk
 log_on_failure += USERID
 disable = no
 only_from = 0.0.0.0/0
 per_source = UNLIMITED
}
```

5. Now that the service file is created under /etc/xinetd.d, add the service to /etc/services so that it is always up and running on port 23267:

```
$ sudo bash -c 'echo "pgsqlchk 23267/tcp # pgsqlchk" >>
/etc/services'
```

6. Start the xinetd service using systemctl:

```
$ sudo systemctl start xinetd
```

How it works...

Xinetd is a daemon that can listen to requests on a port and can execute a script for each request. This can be used as an advantage to perform a check to determine whether a database server is a primary or standby. This helps in redirecting connections from HAProxy to a primary or a standby only. A sample script to print an HTTP header with a status code based on the output of the `psql` command can be seen in *step 1*.

We could then give execute privileges to the script so that it can be successfully executed. If not installed already, `xinetd` can be installed using the command seen in *step 3*. Once it has been installed, we could create a service as seen in *step 4*. This service runs on a specific port – `23267` is the port in our example. This service would execute the script created in *step 1* when a request is received.

To ensure that the service is monitored and always running, we could add an entry similar to what we saw in *step 5*. Once the entry has been made to `/etc/services`, we could start the `xinetd` service.

Creating an HAProxy configuration file

There are four sections that play a key role in creating an HAProxy configuration file. Unless all the sections are configured correctly, we may not achieve good performance. The sections are as follows:

- global
- defaults
- frontend
- backend

In this recipe, we shall discuss how the preceding four sections can be configured appropriately and understand what is needed to build a configuration file.

Getting ready...

HAProxy should preferably be installed on the application server as it is lightweight. This avoids the need to have an active-passive HAProxy server when it is hosted on an external server between the application and the database server.

We must have already installed HAProxy to successfully execute the steps in this recipe.

Please note that the default location of an HAProxy configuration file is `/etc/haproxy/haproxy.cfg`.

How to do it...

The following is the minimal list of settings for each section. These can be added to an HAProxy configuration file.

This section contains the list of settings under the `global` section:

1. Set the maximum number of connections that can be accepted by HAProxy through the `maxconn` parameter:

   ```
   $ sudo vi /etc/haproxy/haproxy.cfg

   global
       maxconn 10000
   ```

2. Add the log directory to which warnings can be written. Additionally, we can set a syslog facility, `local0`:

   ```
   $ sudo vi /etc/haproxy/haproxy.cfg

   global
       maxconn 10000
       log /dev/log local0
   ```

3. Add the operating system-level user and group to avoid HAProxy from keeping root privileges.

   Without the user and group lines in the `global` section, we see `haproxy` started by the root user as seen in the following log:

   ```
   # systemctl start haproxy
   # ps -eaf | grep haproxy
   root 15042 1 0 02:03 ? 00:00:00 /usr/sbin/haproxy-systemd-wrapper -
   f /etc/haproxy/haproxy.cfg -p /run/haproxy.pid
   root 15044 15042 0 02:03 ? 00:00:00 /usr/sbin/haproxy -f
   /etc/haproxy/haproxy.cfg -p /run/haproxy.pid -Ds
   root 15045 15044 0 02:03 ? 00:00:00 /usr/sbin/haproxy -f
   /etc/haproxy/haproxy.cfg -p /run/haproxy.pid -Ds
   ```

We can add the user and group as `haproxy` as seen in the following block:

```
global
    maxconn 10000
    log /dev/log local0
    user haproxy
    group haproxy
```

4. We can finally specify the number of processes and threads using which HAProxy should be spawned upon startup. This can be done using `nbproc` for processes and `nbthread` for threads, as seen in the following block:

```
global
    maxconn 10000
    log /dev/log local0
    user haproxy
    group haproxy
    nbproc 2
    nbthread 4
```

This section contains all the TCP settings that will be applicable to the next sections, the frontend and backend:

1. Add the following timeout parameters to the configuration file under the `defaults` section:

- `timeout_connect`: This is the amount of time HAProxy will wait to connect to a backend server before it hits a timeout.
- `timeout_client`: This is the amount of time that the client may be inactive before sending TCP segments to the server.
- `timeout_server`: This is the amount of time the backend server is expected to stay inactive while performing an activity on the server.

After adding the aforementioned timeout settings, the `defaults` section may look like the following:

```
defaults
    timeout connect 10s
    timeout client 30m
    timeout server 30m
```

2. Set the mode as either TCP or HTTP. If HAProxy is expected to inspect the HTTP messages of the incoming traffic, then we may set it to HTTP. However, it performs better when the mode is set to TCP. If the frontend or backend is expected to operate in a different mode, it can be set in further sections too. If not specified, the setting in the `defaults` section is applicable.

Once the mode has been added, the `defaults` section looks like the following:

```
defaults
    timeout connect 10s
    timeout client 30m
    timeout server 30m
    mode tcp
```

We can replace the frontend and backend sections with a single `listen` section. The frontend section determines the IP addresses and the ports to which the clients can connect, whereas the backend section lists the servers to which the client requests can be assigned or load balanced. We can combine both sections into a single `listen` section.

1. Add the following settings to see the stats of HAProxy:

```
listen stats
    bind *:7000
    stats enable
    stats uri /migops
    stats refresh 5s
```

2. In the previous recipe, *Using xinetd to detect a primary or a standby*, we saw how xinetdb can be used to determine whether the server is a primary or a standby. We could now create a `listen` section specifically for writes. All the connections that are intended to perform writes to a database must connect to the port specified in the following block:

```
listen writes
    bind *:5000
    option httpchk
    http-check expect status 200
    default-server inter 3s fall 3 rise 2 on-marked-down shutdown-
sessions
    server primary_IP primary_IP:5432 maxconn 100 check port 23267
    server standby_IP standby_IP:5432 maxconn 100 check port 23267
```

The preceding block is performing an `http-check` to check which among the two listed backends returns the status code as 200. As there is only one primary, only one of the servers succeeds. When an application to port 5000 of the HAProxy, the connections are redirected to the primary always.

3. Similarly, we could add another `listen` section for reads as seen in the following section:

```
listen reads
    bind *:5001
    option httpchk
    http-check expect status 300
    default-server inter 3s fall 3 rise 2 on-marked-down shutdown-
sessions
        server primary_IP primary_IP:5432 maxconn 100 check port 23267
        server standby_IP standby_IP:5432 maxconn 100 check port 23267
```

The preceding block is performing an `http-check` to see which of the two servers returns 300 as a status code. This way, the connections to port 5001 of the HAProxy server will be sent to a server that returns the status code as 300.

How it works...

The HAProxy configuration file is subdivided into four sections. We would start with creating the first section, which is Globals. This is a section that adds the global settings that serve well for all the further sections. Some of the settings discussed in *steps 1, 2, 3, 4,* and *5* are `maxconn`, `log`, `user`, `group`, `nbproc`, and `nbthread`.

Once the globals section is added, we can then proceed to the `defaults` section, which includes the timeout settings and the mode through which the backend connections are created, as seen in *steps 1* and *2* of this section.

We could then move the Frontend and the Backend sections. However, we could always replace these two sections with a `listen` section. As seen in *step 1*, we could see the HaProxy statistics on port 7000 of the HAProxy server. We could then move to *step 2* to create another `listen` section for write connections. This helps applications to perform a seamless application failover without modifying a lot of connection settings in several application servers. The application connects to port 5000 of the HAProxy and the connection is redirected to a primary database that returns the status code as 200.

Similarly, applications can connect to port 5001 of the HAProxy server to connect to a standby only, using the settings seen in *step 3*. Upon successfully configuring all these settings, an HAProxy configuration file may look like the following:

```
$ vi /etc/haproxy/haproxy.cfg

global
    maxconn 10000
    log /dev/log local0
    user haproxy
    group haproxy
    nbproc 2
    nbthread 4

defaults
    timeout connect 10s
    timeout client 30m
    timeout server 30m
    mode tcp

listen stats
    bind *:7000
    stats enable
    stats uri /migops
    stats refresh 5s

listen writes
    bind *:5000
    option httpchk
    http-check expect status 200
    default-server inter 3s fall 3 rise 2 on-marked-down shutdown-sessions
    server primary_IP primary_IP:5432 maxconn 100 check port 23267
    server standby_IP standby_IP:5432 maxconn 100 check port 23267

listen reads
    bind *:5001
    option httpchk
    http-check expect status 300
    default-server inter 3s fall 3 rise 2 on-marked-down shutdown-sessions
    server primary_IP primary_IP:5432 maxconn 100 check port 23267
    server standby_IP standby_IP:5432 maxconn 100 check port 23267
```

Starting and stopping the HAProxy service

HAProxy can either be started manually or using a service managed by systemctl. In this recipe, we shall we how the starting and stopping of the HAProxy service can be managed.

Getting ready...

In order to start or stop HAProxy, we should have already performed the steps in the following two recipes that have already been discussed earlier in this chapter:

- Installing HAProxy on Linux servers
- Creating an HaProxy configuration file

How to do it...

The following are the steps to start and stop the HAProxy service:

1. To start the HAProxy service using `systemctl`, we could simply run the following command:

   ```
   $ sudo systemctl start haproxy
   ```

2. To ensure that the HAProxy service automatically starts upon a server reboot, we could enable the auto start for the HAProxy service using the following command:

   ```
   $ sudo systemctl enable haproxy
   ```

3. To start HAProxy manually, we could use the following command:

   ```
   $ haproxy -f /etc/haproxy/haproxy.cfg -p /run/haproxy.pid -D
   ```

4. The following command can be used to stop HAProxy using `systemctl`:

   ```
   $ sudo systemctl stop haproxy
   ```

How it works...

Starting and stopping any service is usually recommended to be managed by systemctl. As seen in *step 1*, we could start HAProxy with a simple command using systemctl. To enable auto-start upon a server crash or a reboot, we could use the command seen in *step 2*. For emergency purposes, we may need to know how to start it manually. We can see the command to start HAProxy manually in *step 3*. Finally, to stop HAProxy, we could use the command specified in *step 4*.

Building a robust HA cluster using Patroni, pgBouncer, and HAProxy

In this chapter, we have seen how pgBouncer can be used for the purpose of connection pooling and HAProxy for the purpose of load balancing. We have also discussed how xinetd can be used to perform a seamless application failover. However, to build a robust high-availability architecture, we could combine pgBouncer and HAProxy with Patroni as seen in the following diagram:

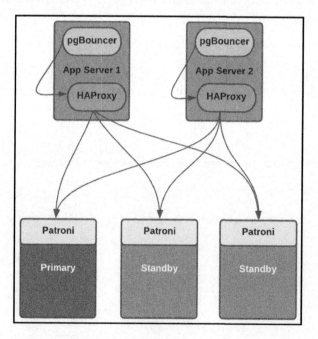

We have already discussed Patroni and how it helps in performing an automatic failover in Chapter 5, *High Availability and Automatic Failover*. In this recipe, we shall see the high-level architecture involved in achieving the best HA setup using a combination of three majorly used open source tools.

Getting ready...

In order to proceed further with this recipe, you must have already set up a Patroni cluster using the recipes discussed in Chapter 5, *High Availability and Automatic Failover*.

How to do it...

Patroni exposes REST APIs to let external applications determine the role of the server. As seen in the following log, we can see whether the server is a master or a replica:

```
$ curl -s 'http://192.168.80.10:8008' | python -c "import sys, json; print
json.load(sys.stdin)['role']"
master
$ curl -s 'http://192.168.80.20:8008' | python -c "import sys, json; print
json.load(sys.stdin)['role']"
replica
```

The following are the steps to enable high availability and seamless application failover using Patroni, HAProxy, and pgBouncer.

1. Under the listen section of the HAProxy configuration file, add entries similar to the following:

```
# Redirect Write Connections to port 5000 of HAProxy from
Application
listen Primary
    bind *:5000
    option tcp-check
    tcp-check send GET\ / HTTP/1.0\r\n
    tcp-check send HOST\r\n
    tcp-check send \r\n
    tcp-check expect string "role":\ "master"
    default-server inter 3s fall 3 rise 2 on-marked-down shutdown-
sessions
    server pg1 pg1:5432 maxconn 100 check port 8008
    server pg2 pg2:5432 maxconn 100 check port 8008
    server pg3 pg3:5432 maxconn 100 check port 8008
```

```
# Redirect Read Connections to port 5001 of HAProxy from
Application
listen Standby
    bind *:5001
    option tcp-check
    tcp-check send GET\ / HTTP/1.0\r\n
    tcp-check send HOST\r\n
    tcp-check send \r\n
    tcp-check expect string "role":\ "replica"
    default-server inter 3s fall 3 rise 2 on-marked-down shutdown-
sessions
    server pg1 pg1:5432 maxconn 100 check port 8008
    server pg2 pg2:5432 maxconn 100 check port 8008
    server pg3 pg3:5432 maxconn 100 check port 8008
```

The preceding configuration would call the Patroni REST APIs to determine the role of the server. Based on the preceding settings, when an application connects to port 5000, the connection is redirected to a server whose role is master. Similarly, when an application connects to port 5001, the connections are redirected to all the servers whose role is a replica, using either round-robin or any algorithm as specified.

2. Replace the entries in the [databases] section with the HAProxy server details in the pgbouncer.ini configuration file. For example, if the HAProxy server is running on 192.168.90.10, then the [databases] section may look like the following:

```
[databases]
writes = host=192.168.90.10 port=5000 dbname=migops
reads = host=192.168.90.10 port=5001 dbname=migops
```

3. Restart the HAProxy and pgBouncer services:

```
$ sudo systemctl restart haproxy
$ sudo systemctl restart pgbouncer
```

How it works...

In order to enable such a robust setup that enables a seamless application failover using a combination of Patroni, pgBouncer, and HAProxy, we must first set up a Patroni cluster using at least three database servers. This setup requires a slight change in the way we deploy pgBouncer. We should have pgBouncer deployed on the application server locally. pgBouncer will then redirect the connections to a local HAProxy load balancer.

HAProxy determines whether the server to which it is connecting is a master or replica using the Patroni REST APIs as seen in *step 1*. To perform writes, as seen in *step 2*, pgBouncer can redirect the connections to the HAProxy port that connects to a server with the role of master. Similarly, pgBouncer could connect to the port that redirects connections to a server whole role is a replica, for read-only connections.

When such a change is made to pgBouncer and HAProxy configurations, it requires a restart of both services using the commands seen in *step 3*. Once the services are restarted, we should be able to achieve a robust HA setup that helps achieve several nines of availability.

7
Securing through Authentication

In this chapter, you will learn how to secure PostgreSQL encryption through authentication,
authorization, and auditing. You will also see how to encrypt connections over the wire and also at rest using SSL. We will also look at some extensions for performing auditing in PostgreSQL. By the end of this chapter, you should know how to audit your PostgreSQL server and make it highly secure.

The following recipes will be covered in this chapter:

- Securing client connections using the `pg_hba.conf` file
- Performing authorization using roles and privileges
- Setting up row-level security
- Configuring encryption of data over the wire using SSL
- Enabling certificate authentication using SSL
- Auditing PostgreSQL through logging
- Auditing PostgreSQL using `pgaudit`
- Setting up object-level auditing using `pgaudit`

Technical requirements

To practice the steps discussed in these recipes, you will need a virtual machine either from the CentOS/Red Hat or Debian/Ubuntu family of operating systems. If you have already got a server with PostgreSQL 13 installed, then all the commands discussed in the chapter should work for you.

Securing client connections using the pg_hba.conf file

PostgreSQL uses the `pg_hba.conf` file as a built-in firewall to manage authorization. **HBA** in `pg_hba.conf` stands for **host-based authentication**. This file is appended with entries that serve the purpose of enabling and disabling user connections based on a combination of five categories, as follows:

- Connection type
- Database name
- Username
- IP address
- Authentication method

The entries in the `pg_hba.conf` file determine whether a user connecting from a remote server is allowed to connect to a database using a specific username with the specified authentication method.

Categories in the pg_hba.conf file

Let's look into the five categories in detail and we shall then proceed to learn how the `pg_hba` file can be modified through this recipe:

- **Connection type**: A connection type can be of four types:
    - `local`: A connection from the local Unix socket, for example, connections to `localhost`
    - `host`: A connection from a remote host
    - `hostssl`: Enables SSL for remote connections from the specified remote hosts
    - `hostnossl`: Allows connections without SSL when SSL is enabled in PostgreSQL
- **Database**: Database(s) to which connections are either accepted or not accepted. Possible values are as follows:
    - **All**: Allow/disallow connections to all databases.
    - **Comma-separated list of databases**: Allow connections to one or more databases in the list.
    - **Replication**: Specified to allow replication connections.

- **User**: Usernames with which connections are either allowed or disallowed. Possible values are as follows:
    - **All**: Allow/disallow connections from all users to the database specified from the specified host.
    - **Comma-separated list of users**: Specify one or more usernames that are allowed to connect.
- **IP address**: One or a range of IP addresses from which connections can either be allowed or disallowed. For example, setting this to `192.168.1.0/24` allows/disallows connections from a range of IPs that are equal to or between `192.168.1.0` and `192.168.1.255`.

  To set it to a specific IP, we may set it to `192.168.1.24/32` where `192.168.1.24` is the IP address.

- **Authentication method**: We could use several authentication methods, as follows, for each entry:
    - **Peer**: Allows local connections with the same operating system name as the database user to connect. Allows mapping an operating system user with a database user.
    - **Trust**: Allows connections without password authentication.
    - **Certification**: Used to allow authentications using SSL client certificates.
    - **Password authentication MD5**: When you specify MD5, the client must always supply an MD5-encrypted password for authentication.
    - **Password**: Allows clients to supply a plain-text or unencrypted password for authentication.
    - **scram-sha-256**: Performs SCRAM-SHA-256 authentication as described in RFC 7677. This method prevents password sniffing and supports storing passwords on the server in a cryptographically hashed form.
    - **GSS**: Used for secured authentications using GSSAPI with Kerboros authentication. When using GSSAPI, only authentication is secured and not the data sent over the connection. You may use SSL to encrypt data in motion.
    - **SSPI**: Used for secured authentications in Windows environment. Both the client and server must be using Windows. Works the same way as GSSAPI when using Kerboros authentication.
    - **BSD**: To use BSD authentication that validates a user/password pair.

- **Ident**: Obtain the client operating system username and validate whether it is the same as the database username. This works well for TCP/IP connections. Local connections use a peer authentication method.
- **LDAP**: To use LDAP authentication for connections to the database.
- **RADIUS**: To use password authentication using RADIUS.
- **PAM**: To use the authentication mechanism that uses a **Pluggable Authentication Module (PAM)**.

In this recipe, we shall see how to enable or disable connections to a database from local or remote hosts using the `pg_hba.conf` file.

Getting ready

Adding appropriate entries to the `pg_hba.conf` file can allow or disallow connections to a Postgres database. However, just adding the entries may not serve the whole purpose. If any firewall rules are enabled on the database server, it must have appropriate rules to allow connections to the Postgres port from the specific remote server from where connections are to be allowed.

How to do it...

Let's get started by using the following steps:

1. Allow the `perc_user` user through MD5 password authentication from host `10.112.120.96` to connect to the `percona` database.

   The following entry should be added to the `pg_hba.conf` file:

   ```
   host percona perc_user 10.112.120.96/32 md5
   ```

2. Allow the `perc_user` user through MD5 password authentication from host `10.112.120.96` to connect to any database in the Postgres server:

   ```
   host all perc_user 10.112.120.96/32 md5
   ```

3. Allow any database user through MD5 password authentication from host `10.112.120.96` to connect to any database in the Postgres server:

   ```
   host all all 10.112.120.96/32 md5
   ```

4. Allow any database user through MD5 password authentication from any host using SSL encryption to connect to any database in the server:

```
hostssl all all 0.0.0.0/0 md5
```

5. Allow password-less streaming replication from host `10.112.120.96` using the user named `replicator`:

```
host replication replicator 10.112.120.96/32 trust
```

How it works...

In the examples listed in these steps, we could see how the `pg_hba.conf` file can be appended with entries to allow connections. It is important to note that the sequence with which the entries are added to the `pg_hba.conf` file makes a lot of difference.

For example, let's see the following two lines taken from the `pg_hba.conf` file:

```
host all all 10.112.120.0/24 md5
host all all 10.112.120.132/32 reject
```

In the preceding two lines, we are allowing connections from `10.112.120.*` in the first entry. The second entry says that any connection from IP `10.112.120.132` must be rejected. However, PostgreSQL would read the lines in this file sequentially. After reading the first line, it assumes that IP `10.112.120.132` is allowed to connect. This means the line that is read and matched first is always taken into consideration.

In order to avoid this, have the sequence written appropriately, as we see in the following example:

```
host all all 10.112.120.132/32 reject
host all all 10.112.120.0/24 md5
```

Now, if someone tries to connect from `10.112.120.132`, we will see an error indicating that the connections from this host are rejected:

```
$ psql -h 10.112.120.132 -p 5432 -U perc_user -d percdb
psql: FATAL: pg_hba.conf rejects connection for host "10.112.120.132", user
"perc_user", database "percdb", SSL on
FATAL: pg_hba.conf rejects connection for host "10.112.120.132", user
"perc_user", database "percdb", SSL off
```

Performing authorization using roles and privileges

It is quite common to see a user being given more than the required privileges in a database. Sometimes, the default `postgres` user is used as an application user and a backup user. This can be dangerous as the superuser has the highest level of privileges. A user with a superuser role can drop a database along with its data. At the same time, it may be difficult to grant privileges on each database object to every user. For this purpose, we could use the concept of roles and privileges. In this recipe, we shall discuss how roles and privileges can be used to perform a better authorization mechanism in PostgreSQL.

Getting ready

Before attempting to segregate privileges using roles and privileges, it is important to distinguish the access control you wish to implement in your database. For example, if the database is serving two application modules that connect to different schemas or tables, it is better to have two or multiple roles that serve the purpose of granting read or write access to each of the schemas or each set of objects serving an application module. This way, we may grant `read_only` access to a user that only grants read access to objects serving a specific application module but not all.

How to do it...

We can tweak authorization privileges by using the following steps:

1. Create a `read_only` and `read_write` role that has the `NOLOGIN` privilege by default:

   ```
   $ psql -d percdb "CREATE ROLE scott_read_only"
   $ psql -d percdb "CREATE ROLE scott_read_write"
   ```

2. Grant read access on all tables to the `read_only` role and write access on all tables to the `read_write` role:

   ```
   $ psql -d percdb "GRANT USAGE, SELECT ON ALL TABLES IN SCHEMA scott
   TO scott_readonly"

   $ psql -d percdb "GRANT USAGE, SELECT, INSERT, UPDATE, DELETE ON
   ALL TABLES IN SCHEMA scott
   TO scott_readwrite"
   ```

3. Now, grant the `read_only` role to the developer and the `read_write` role to the application user:

```
$ psql -d "GRANT scott_read_only TO dev_user"
$ psql -d "GRANT scott_read_write TO app_user"
```

How it works...

In the steps discussed in this recipe, we are assuming that the objects being accessed by the application are all in the `scott` schema. To properly segregate read and write access, we see the commands using which two roles are created in *step 1*. Once the roles are created, the roles can be granted read and write access appropriately as seen in *step 2*. Once the privileges are granted, the `read_only` role can be assigned to a user needing read-only access (developer) and the `read_write` access can be granted to the user who should have both read and write access, as seen in *step 3*.

Setting up row-level security

Row-level security is one of the advanced features in PostgreSQL to limit access to a subset of records of a table using policies. For example, a manager can be allowed to read or modify only the records of the employees to which they are a manager. In this recipe, we shall discuss the steps involved in enabling row-level security.

Getting ready

The policies for enabling row-level security must be created by a superuser who has access to create policies.

How to do it...

In the following steps, we are creating a table and inserting some sample records to demonstrate how row-level security can be enabled:

1. Create an `employee` table and insert three records that have two different managers:

```
CREATE TABLE employee (id INT, first_name varchar(20), last_name
varchar(20), manager varchar(20));
```

```
INSERT INTO employee VALUES (1,'avi','kumar','john');
INSERT INTO employee VALUES (2,'naga','vallarapu','steven');
INSERT INTO employee VALUES (3,'sammy','vallarapu','john');
```

2. Create the users using which both managers could connect to the database:

```
CREATE USER john WITH ENCRYPTED PASSWORD 'secret';
 CREATE USER steven WITH ENCRYPTED PASSWORD 'secret';
```

3. Create a role to which read and write access to the employee table is granted. Grant the read/write role to both the managers:

```
CREATE ROLE managers;
GRANT SELECT, INSERT, UPDATE, DELETE ON employee TO managers;
GRANT USAGE ON SCHEMA public TO managers;

GRANT managers TO john, steven;
```

4. Enable row-level security on the employee table:

```
ALTER TABLE employee ENABLE ROW LEVEL SECURITY;
```

5. Create a policy to which a condition to limit the visibility of records can be added:

```
CREATE POLICY employee_managers ON employee TO managers USING
(manager = current_user);
```

6. Validate by selecting all records using one of the managers as a user:

```
$ psql -d percona -U john
 psql (13.1)
 Type "help" for help.
percona=> select * from employee ;
 id | first_name | last_name | manager
----+------------+-----------+---------
  1 | avi        | kumar     | john
  3 | sammy      | vallarapu | john
 (2 rows)
```

How it works...

In order to implement row-level security, we should have a role on which a policy has to be created. In the steps discussed, we are creating an employee table and inserting three records into it, as seen in *step 1*. Our end goal in this example is to let a manager only read/modify the records of employees of whom they are a manager. So, we go ahead and create the users that are the same as the values in the `manager` column of the employee table, as seen in *step 2*.

Now, we shall create a role that has both read and write access to all the records of the employee table, as seen in *step 3*. To enable row-level security, we should explicitly run an `ALTER TABLE` command as seen in the command in *step 4*. The final step is to create a policy, as seen in *step 5*, to restrict the role to display only the records matching the condition for the employee table. The condition in the example says that the values in the `manager` column should be equal to the user using which the table is being accessed. As seen in the validation performed in *step 6*, when manager `john` queries the employee table, he could only see the two employee records of which he is a manager but not all.

Configuring encryption of data over the wire using SSL

It may be one of the most important requirements to enable encryption of communication between the client and the server when dealing with critical financial databases and also to satisfy certain compliances. PostgreSQL satisfies this requirement by allowing connections to use SSL. In this recipe, we shall discuss the steps involved in setting up the encryption of data moving over the wire.

Getting ready

In order to enable SSL, we must have the server and client certification files that are signed by a **Certification Authority (CA)**. This is usually performed by the security teams in most organizations. Admins could use OpenSSL to generate the certificates. Once they are created, we should set the following parameters in PostgreSQL:

- `ssl_ca_file`: Specifies the name of the file containing the SSL server CA
- `ssl_cert_file`: Specifies the name of the file containing the SSL server certificate

- `ssl_key_file`: Specifies the name of the file containing the SSL server private key

We must also have OpenSSL installed on the server:

```
$ sudo yum install openssl
```

How to do it...

Let's get started by using the following steps:

1. Ensure that the permissions set to the files are appropriate. Grant read access to the `postgres` user only:

   ```
   $ cd $PGDATA
   $ chmod 0400 server.crt server.key rootCA.crt
   ```

2. Enable SSL-related parameters in PostgreSQL:

   ```
   $ psql -c "ALTER SYSTEM SET ssl TO 'ON'"
   $ psql -c "ALTER SYSTEM SET ssl_ca_file TO 'rootCA.crt'"
   $ psql -c "ALTER SYSTEM SET ssl_cert_file TO 'server.crt'"
   $ psql -c "ALTER SYSTEM SET ssl_key_file TO 'server.key'"
   ```

3. Perform a reload to get the changes into effect:

   ```
   $ psql -c "select pg_reload_conf()"
   ```

4. Validate by enabling SSL for connections over a socket. Add the following entry to the `pg_hba.conf` file. Make sure to add it to the top to avoid the already existing entries to get it into effect:

   ```
   $ vi $PGDATA/pg_hba.conf
    hostssl all all 127.0.0.1/32 trust
   ```

   Perform a reload to get the changes into effect:

   ```
   $ psql -c "select pg_reload_conf()"
   ```

Validate using `psql`:

```
$ psql -h localhost
 psql (13.1)
 SSL connection (protocol: TLSv1.2, cipher: ECDHE-RSA-AES256-GCM-
SHA384, bits: 256, compression: off)
 Type "help" for help.
postgres=# \q
```

5. For enabling SSL for remote connections, add the IP of the remote host to the `pg_hba.conf` file and specify `hostssl`. In this example, `192.168.130.70` is the IP of the database server and `192.168.130.1` is the IP of a remote server.

   Add the following entry to the `pg_hba.conf` file:

   ```
   $ vi $PGDATA/pg_hba.conf
    hostssl postgres postgres 192.168.130.1 md5
   ```

   Perform a reload to get the changes into effect:

   ```
   $ psql -c "select pg_reload_conf()"
   ```

   Validate from the remote host:

   ```
   $ psql -h 192.168.130.70 -d postgres -U postgres
    Password for user postgres:
    psql (13.1 (Ubuntu 13.1-1.pgdg18.04+1))
    SSL connection (protocol: TLSv1.2, cipher: ECDHE-RSA-AES256-GCM-
   SHA384, bits: 256, compression: off)
    Type "help" for help.
   postgres=# \q
   ```

How it works...

As seen in the preceding steps, the server and client certification files that are signed by a CA are a must to enable SSL. Once they are in place, they need to be copied to a location that is accessible by the `postgres` user and only readable by the `postgres` user. Once they are made available, we could set the parameters that are seen in *step 2* to set SSL to `ON` and also to set the location of the certificates. It requires a reload but not a restart to get the changes into effect. So, SSL mode can be enabled on an existing database server without the need for a restart.

To validate SSL, as seen in *steps 4* and *5*, we could add `hostssl` as a prefix instead of `host` in the `pg_hba.conf` file. We need to add the appropriate IP from where the communications to the database should be encrypted over SSL.

By default, all the connections are sent over SSL when it is enabled. To avoid establishing communication over SSL for a certain instance, use `hostnossl` instead of `hostssl` as a prefix, as seen in the following log:

```
hostnossl postgres postgres 192.168.130.1 md5
```

Enabling certificate authentication using SSL

As additional security, you may wish to enable certificate authentication using SSL certificates. When it is enabled, every client connection will be authenticated through an additional certificate exchange. For this purpose, a client certificate must be used for identifying the client. The client certificates must be copied to the remote server (or an application server) to use this method. In this recipe, we shall discuss the steps involved in enabling certificate authentication using SSL.

Getting ready

In order to enable SSL, we must have the server and client certification files that are signed by a CA. This is usually performed by the security teams in most organizations. Admins could use OpenSSL to generate the certificates.

How to do it...

We will enable certificate authentication using the following steps:

1. Copy the client certificate signed by the CA to the remote server:

   ```
   $ scp postgresql.crt postgresql.key rootCA.crt
   postgres@192.168.130.1:/var/lib/postgresql
   ```

   On the remote server, modify the permissions of the certificates:

   ```
   $ chmod 0400 postgresql.crt postgresql.key rootCA.crt
   ```

2. Modify the authentication method in the `pg_hba.conf` file of the database server to enable certification authentication:

   ```
   $ vi $PGDATA/pg_hba.conf
    hostssl postgres postgres 192.168.130.1 cert clientcert=1
   ```

3. Perform a reload to get the changes into effect:

```
$ psql -c "select pg_reload_conf()"
```

4. Validate the connection from the remote host using the client certificates:

```
$ psql "host=192.168.130.70 user=postgres port=5432
sslcert=postgresql.crt sslkey=postgresql.key
sslrootcert=rootCA.crt"
```

This results in the following output:

```
$ psql "host=192.168.130.70 user=postgres port=5432
sslcert=postgresql.crt sslkey=postgresql.key
sslrootcert=rootCA.crt"
 Password for user postgres:
 psql (12.4 (Ubuntu 12.4-1.pgdg18.04+1))
 Type "help" for help.
postgres=#
```

How it works...

To enable certificate authentication using SSL, the additional requirement is that the client certificates need to be copied to the remote server or the application server from where the connections are considered to be using this authentication mode. Once copied, the only change to the pg_hba.conf file, as seen in *step 2*, is that the authentication mode must be replaced with cert clientcert=1. Once this is done, we could issue a reload to get the changes into effect and validate the connection from the remote server. As you see in *step 4*, we must now add sslcert, sslkey, and sslrootcert to the psql connection URI. These certificates are used to perform the authentication between the databases. It does not mean that the password is no longer needed. The server should supply the password set to that user for a successful connection.

Auditing PostgreSQL through logging

One of the important security features of PostgreSQL is to perform logging of a certain activity. When a certain modification is done to a Postgres table or when a table has been dropped, it is important to know whether that was intended to be a requirement or was performed illegally by misusing the access to the database. In this recipe, we shall discuss the steps required to log certain types of activity required for auditing in PostgreSQL.

Getting ready

It is always important to know that logging additional information to PostgreSQL logs causes more disk writes and uses a lot of disk space. For this reason, it is important to monitor the disk usage and the IOPS increase when any extensive logging has been enabled. It is also important to segregate logs and data across different disks. This way, none of the logging-specific writes cause any I/O saturation for a data directory that contains database objects.

How to do it...

We will log data using the following steps:

1. Set `log_line_prefix` to log more details, such as the username, IP address, timestamp, and application name, as an example:

   ```
   $ psql -c "ALTER SYSTEM SET log_line_prefix TO '%t [%p]: [%l-1]
   host=%r,user=%u,db=%d,app=%a'"
   ```

2. Set `log_statement` to the type of activity that needs to be logged. As CREATE, ALTER, and DROP are vital to be monitored, we could use the following setting:

   ```
   $ psql -c "ALTER SYSTEM SET log_statement TO 'ddl'"
   ```

3. Reload the server to get the changes into effect:

   ```
   $ psql -c "select pg_reload_conf()"
   ```

How it works...

Most of the damages to a database through security breaches may happen in the form of DDLs. Thus, we could use the `log_statement` setting to log the DDLs, such as CREATE, ALTER, and DROP statements, to a log file as seen in *step 2*. In order to capture maximum information for future analysis, it is important to modify `log_line_prefix` to provide more information regarding the connection. Information such as the remote host IP address, port number, application name, user, and database name would help in trying to identify the source from where a breach has happened so that action can be taken accordingly. Modifications to both of the parameters discussed in this recipe require a reload, as seen in *step 3*, to come into effect.

Auditing PostgreSQL using pgaudit

pgaudit is an extension in PostgreSQL to enable extensive auditing that satisfies several security compliances. The advantage of pgaudit over logging through Postgres parameters is that the latter is more general and does not handle the logging of SQL injections well. Additionally, pgaudit provides fine-grained control over what sessions or objects need to be monitored. In this recipe, we shall discuss the steps required to install pgaudit as an extension.

Getting ready

In order to install and use pgaudit as an extension, we must have the contrib module installed in the PostgreSQL server: the postgresql-contrib-12 package on Ubuntu/Debian or the postgresql12-contrib package on CentOS/Red Hat.

Additionally, pgaudit is available on the PGDG repository. So, if the repository has been configured in the database server, installing pgaudit is very easy.

 Only a superuser can modify user-level settings for pgaudit.

How to do it...

We will do this using the following steps:

1. Install pgaudit using yum or apt.

   For CentOS/Red Hat, use the following command:

   ```
   -- CentOS/RedHat
   $ sudo yum install pgaudit14_12
   ```

   For Ubuntu/Debian, use the following command:

   ```
   $ sudo apt install postgresql-12-pgaudit
   ```

2. Load the extension using shared_preload_libraries:

   ```
   $ psql -c "ALTER SYSTEM SET shared_preload_libraries TO pgaudit";
   ```

Alternatively, you can use the following command:

```
-- Use the following command to load pgaudit along with some of the
libraries already loaded.

$ psql -c "ALTER SYSTEM SET shared_preload_libraries TO pgaudit,
auto_explain, pg_stat_statements, pg_repack"
```

3. Restart PostgreSQL to get the changes to `shared_preload_libraries` to come into effect:

```
$ pg_ctl -D $PGDATA restart -mf
```

4. Create the extension in the database that needs to be audited:

```
$ psql -d percdb -c "CREATE EXTENSION pgaudit"
```

5. We can perform auditing of the read and write activities performed by a specific user, `perc_user`, as follows:

```
ALTER USER perc_user SET pgaudit.log TO 'read, write';
```

How it works...

Installing the `pgaudit` extension is straightforward when the PGDG repository has been set up in the PostgreSQL server. We could install `pgaudit` using `yum` or `apt` as seen in *step 1*. After a successful installation, `shared_preload_libraries` can be used to load `pgaudit` followed by a restart of PostgreSQL as seen in *steps 2* and *3*. After the restart, `pgaudit` needs to be created in the database that needs to be audited. In *step 5*, we see an example syntax to enable auditing of both reads and writes by the `perc_user` user.

Setting up object-level auditing using pgaudit

`pgaudit` can be used to enable the logging of `SELECT`, `INSERT`, `UPDATE`, and `DELETE` commands for a specific relation (or a table). This is finer-grained when compared to the global logging of every statement. In this recipe, we shall discuss the steps involved in enabling object-level logging using `pgaudit`.

Getting ready

In order to enable object-level logging using `pgaudit`, we must have the extension downloaded and loaded to `shared_preload_libraries` and created in the database that needs to be enabled for object-level auditing.

How to do it...

Let's do this using the following steps:

1. Create a role that does not have the `LOGIN` role:

```
$ psql -c "CREATE ROLE auditor"
```

2. Set the newly created role as the master role:

```
$ psql -c "ALTER SYSTEM SET pgaudit.role TO 'auditor'"

-- Reload to get the parameter changes into effect.
$ psql -c "SELECT pg_reload_conf()"
```

3. Enable audit of selects on a specific table by granting `SELECT` on that table to the auditor role:

```
$ psql -d percdb -c "GRANT SELECT ON employee TO auditor"
```

4. To enable auditing of only specific columns of a table, grant access on that column to the auditor role:

```
$ psql -d percdb -c "GRANT SELECT (id, name) ON employee TO
auditor"
$ psql -d percdb -c "GRANT INSERT,UPDATE(name),DELETE ON employee
TO auditor"
```

How it works...

Object-level logging relies on a master role. To enable object-level auditing, we need to start by creating a role that can be assigned as a master role for auditing, as seen in *steps 1* and *2*. In order to simply enable auditing of selects on a specific table, we could grant `SELECT` on the table to the new master role as seen in *step 3*. Similarly, to audit selects and updates involving a specific column(s) of a table along with `INSERT` and `DELETE`, we could use the commands as seen in *step 4*.

8
Logging and Analyzing PostgreSQL Servers

This chapter introduces you to logging and analyzing in PostgreSQL. Most of the important information related to locks, deadlocks, query executions, errors, or warnings are all logged to a PostgreSQL log file. It may be difficult for admins to tune a PostgreSQL database when such information is not logged. It is also important to see whether a query is generating temp and fetching pages from disk or memory. Even when all the information is available in logs, it may be difficult for someone to parse through the logs, whose size may range from several MBs to GBs.

For this purpose, this chapter has been designed to let admins know of the available options in PostgreSQL to enable the logging of certain important activities and to help admins/developers get familiar with some views, extensions, and tools to analyze live and historic activity in Postgres catalogs and log files.

The following are the recipes that will be covered in this chapter:

- Setting up slow query logging in PostgreSQL
- Logging runtime execution plans in PostgreSQL using `auto_explain`
- Logging locks, waits, and temp in PostgreSQL
- Logging autovacuum and analyzing activity in PostgreSQL
- Generating a `pgBadger` report
- Configuring `pg_stat_statements` as an extension
- Query analysis using `pg_stat_statements`
- Getting the kernel-level statistics of a query using `pg_stat_kcache`

Technical requirements

To practice the steps discussed in these recipes, you will need a virtual machine with either the CentOS/RedHat or Debian/Ubuntu family of operating systems. If you have already got a server with PostgreSQL 13 installed, then all the commands discussed in the chapter should work for you.

Setting up slow query logging in PostgreSQL

PostgreSQL allows configuring the settings of log queries that are running for more than a certain duration using some parameters. This helps admins in understanding the queries that need to be optimized to improve the overall application performance. In this recipe, we shall discuss the steps involved in enabling the logging of time-consuming queries in PostgreSQL.

Getting ready

It is always important to know that logging additional information to PostgreSQL logs causes more disk writes and uses a lot of disk space. For this reason, it is important to monitor the disk usage and the IOPS increase when any extensive logging has been enabled. It is also important to segregate logs and data across different disks. This way, none of the logging-specific writes cause any I/O saturation for the data directory that contains the database objects.

How to do it...

We will initiate the logging process using the following steps:

1. Ensure that `logging_collector` is set to `ON` to enable logging in PostgreSQL. The following steps can be used to set `logging_collector` to `ON`:

```
$ psql -c "show logging_collector"
$ psql -c "ALTER SYSTEM SET logging_collector TO 'ON'"
```

It is definitely wise to isolate the database logs from the syslogs so that it is easy to differentiate kernel-level messages and PostgreSQL-level events. So, we should set the `log_destination` parameter to `'stderr'` instead of `'syslog'`.

2. Set `log_line_prefix` appropriately so that enough information is visible in each line of the log file:

```
$ psql -c "ALTER SYSTEM SET log_line_prefix TO '%t [%p]: [%l-1]
user=%u,db=%d'"
```

3. Set `log_min_duration_statement` to the time after which a query is said to be time-consuming. We will check out various examples for specific time ranges as follows:

   - The following command can be used to log all queries running for more than 10 milliseconds:

     ```
     -- To log all the queries running for more than 10 milliseconds
     $ psql -c "ALTER SYSTEM SET log_min_duration_statement TO
     '10ms'"
     ```

   - The following command can be used to log all queries running for more than 15 seconds:

     ```
     $ psql -c "ALTER SYSTEM SET log_min_duration_statement TO
     '15s'"
     ```

   - The following command can be used to log all queries running for more than 20 minutes:

     ```
     $ psql -c "ALTER SYSTEM SET log_min_duration_statement TO
     '20min'"
     ```

   - The following command can be used to log all queries running for more than 1 hour:

     ```
     $ psql -c "ALTER SYSTEM SET log_min_duration_statement TO '1h'"
     ```

4. Restart or reload to get the changes into effect. Changes to `logging_collector` require a restart:

   - The following command may be used to perform a restart:

   ```
   $ pg_ctl -D $PGDATA restart -mf
   ```

   - The following command may be used to perform a reload:

   ```
   $ pg_ctl -D $PGDATA reload
   ```

Thus, we have learned how to start logging data.

How it works...

There is only one type of log file in PostgreSQL. What this means is, there is no separate log file for recording errors or warnings and no separate log file to log slow queries. For this reason, to log errors or slow queries, `logging_collector` must be set to `ON`. Otherwise, we would not see any information logged to logs. Once this has been confirmed as enabled, it is important to make sure that all the details, such as the application or user running SQL, are also visible. For this purpose, we could use the `log_line_prefix` parameter. This can be set to the value seen in *step 2* or using the runtime configs for logging as seen in *step 2*.

To enable the logging of slow queries, we must set `log_min_duration_statement` to a time after which a SQL query is said to be performing slow. This is a global setting. As seen in the examples in *step 3*, it can be set to a few milliseconds, seconds, minutes, or a few hours. If it's just `log_min_duration_statement` or `log_line_prefix` that have been changed, we can just perform a reload as seen in *step 4*.

There's more...

Some more logging parameters we may want to look into are the following:

- `log_connections`: Every new connection (received and authorized) is logged to PostgreSQL logs.
- `log_disconnections`: Every disconnection of a PostgreSQL connection is logged to logs.
- `log_duration`: Enable logging of the duration of every query running in the database server.

Logging runtime execution plans in PostgreSQL using auto_explain

One fact that not many people know about PostgreSQL is that it does hard parsing for every SQL statement that hits the database. It doesn't matter if the same query has millions of repeated executions. Except when using prepared statements, the lowest cost-based execution plan is chosen each time a SQL query is executed. It does not matter if it is the same SQL query that has already been executed several times. This is because there is no such plan table that stores execution plans and is reusable. This may bring some challenges at times. While it is great that PostgreSQL finds it optimal to prepare a plan each time, a plan may change if statistics are not intact and there is no way to keep track of such abnormal changes.

For this reason, PostgreSQL provides a module called `auto_explain` that helps to log execution plans of a query that runs for more than a certain time. In this recipe, we shall discuss `auto_explain` and how to enable the session-level and global-level logging of execution plans of queries to log files.

Getting ready

We must ensure that there is enough disk space to enable the logging of execution plans. Make sure to also install the `contrib` module if not installed already to load this extension.

How to do it...

`auto_explain` can be used to enable both the global and session levels. We shall see how both the global- and session-level settings can be set in the following steps.

Global level

Let's check out `auto_explain` using the following steps:

1. For the global-level logging of execution plans, add `auto_explain` to the list of libraries in `shared_preload_libraries`, as seen in the following code:

   ```
   $ psql -c "ALTER SYSTEM SET shared_preload_libraries TO
   auto_explain"
   ```

Add `auto_explain` to the list of libraries if one or more extensions are already loaded to `shared_preload_libraries`:

```
$ psql -c "ALTER SYSTEM SET shared_preload_libraries TO
auto_explain, pg_stat_statements, pg_repack"
```

2. Changes to `shared_preload_libraries` require a PostgreSQL restart:

```
$ pg_ctl -D $PGDATA restart -mf
```

3. Set `auto_explain`-specific global parameters to log execution plans to the log files:

- `auto_explain.log_min_duration`: Minimum duration upon which a statement's execution plan must be logged:

```
$ psql -c "ALTER SYSTEM SET auto_explain.log_min_duration to '10s'"
```

- `auto_explain.log_analyze`: Log output similar to what is logged by EXPLAIN ANALYZE:

```
$ psql -c "ALTER SYSTEM SET auto_explain.log_analyze to 'ON'"
```

- `auto_explain.log_buffers`: Log output similar to what is logged by EXPLAIN (ANALYZE, BUFFERS):

```
$ psql -c "ALTER SYSTEM SET auto_explain.log_buffers to 'ON'"
```

- `auto_explain.log_timing`: Log per-plan node timing information:

```
$ psql -c "ALTER SYSTEM SET auto_explain.log_timing to 'ON'"
```

- `auto_explain.log_triggers` Log trigger execution statistics:

```
$ psql -c "ALTER SYSTEM SET auto_explain.log_triggers to 'ON'"
```

- `auto_explain.log_verbose`: Log output similar to EXPLAIN VERBOSE:

```
$ psql -c "ALTER SYSTEM SET auto_explain.log_verbose to 'ON'"
```

- `auto_explain.log_settings`: Log modified configuration parameters applicable to the statement:

```
$ psql -c "ALTER SYSTEM SET auto_explain.log_settings to 'ON'"
```

- auto_explain.log_format: Helpful to choose the output format of the execution plan from text, xml, json, and yaml:

```
$ psql -c "ALTER SYSTEM SET auto_explain.log_format to 'text'"
```

- auto_explain.log_level: Enable any of the DEBUG5, DEBUG4, DEBUG3, DEBUG2, DEBUG1, INFO, NOTICE, WARNING, and LOG information for statements being logged:

```
$ psql -c "ALTER SYSTEM SET auto_explain.log_level to 'LOG'"
```

- auto_explain.log_nested_statements: Log statements executed within a function:

```
$ psql -c "ALTER SYSTEM SET auto_explain.log_nested_statements to 'ON'"
```

- auto_explain.sample_rate: Choose the sample rate of statements to be logged:

```
$ psql -c "ALTER SYSTEM SET auto_explain.sample_rate to '1'"
```

4. Perform a reload to get the parameter changes into effect:

```
$ pg_ctl -D $PGDATA reload
Or
$ psql -c "select pg_reload_conf()"
```

We'll now check out how to use auto_explain at the session level.

Session level

In order to set session-level auto_explain parameters, auto_explain does not need to be set to shared_reload_libraries. So, this does not require a restart of PostgreSQL.

Within the transaction block, load auto_explain and set auto_explain-specific parameters. Then, continue to run the statements:

```
$ psql -d percdb
percdb=# LOAD 'auto_explain';
LOAD
percdb=# SET auto_explain.log_min_duration to '0';
SET
percdb=# SET auto_explain.log_analyze to 'ON';
SET
```

```
percdb=# select ......
percdb=# UPDATE ......
percdb=# END;
```

How it works...

In this recipe, we discussed how `auto_explain` can be used to log execution plans of a time-consuming SQL query. This module can be used for both global- and session-level logging. In order to enable global-level logging (statements that are executed by all the sessions), we must add `auto_explain` to the list of libraries being loaded by `shared_preload_libraries` using the command seen in *step 1*, followed by a restart of PostgreSQL as seen in *step 2*.

Once restarted, we could set a list of parameters that change the behavior of the extent and verbosity at which the logging should be enabled. For example, we see a list of 10 parameters that are available for `auto_explain`-specific functionality:

- `auto_explain.log_min_duration`: Log execution plans for queries that run for more than this duration. Defaults to −1.
- `auto_explain.log_analyze`: When this parameter is set to ON, it produces the EXPLAIN OUTPUT output of the SQL executed. This may impact the performance adversely. So, it is only recommended when an admin or a developer wishes to find some information temporarily.
- `auto_explain.log_buffers`: When this parameter is set to ON, it prints the information that is printed when the BUFFERS option is used with EXPLAIN, for example, EXPLAIN (ANALYZE, BUFFERS). It prints all the buffer usage statistics per plan node. This parameter is only valid when `auto_explain.log_analyze` is set to ON.
- `auto_explain.log_timing`: For each execution plan that has been logged, per-node timing information is printed. This may cause performance issues and thus it is just recommended for temporary usage. This parameter is only valid when `auto_explain.log_analyze` is set to ON.
- `auto_explain.log_triggers`: Trigger execution statistics are logged when this parameter is set to ON. For example, if there is a trigger that performs an action upon each INSERT, the execution statistics for that trigger are logged to log files.

- `auto_explain.log_verbose`: This is equivalent to the VERBOSE option of EXPLAIN. When set to ON, verbose information is printed for each execution plan being logged.
- `auto_explain.log_settings`: When set to ON, any modified configuration parameters such as changes to `work_mem` or `statement_timeout` at the session level are logged when they are applicable to the execution plan being logged.
- `auto_explain.log_format`: This parameter is to set the output format of the execution plan. Defaults to text and the accepted formats are text, xml, json, and yaml.
- `auto_explain.log_level`: Sets the log level at which execution plans are logged to the log file. Defaults to LOG. Also accepts DEBUG5, DEBUG4, DEBUG3, DEBUG2, DEBUG1, INFO, NOTICE, WARNING, and LOG.
- `auto_explain.log_nested_statements`: To log all the statements executed within a function, this parameter can be set to ON.
- `auto_explain.sample_rate`: Defaults to 1, which means it logs execution plans for all the SQL queries in each session. Valid values are between 0 and 1. 0.5 means 50%.

The same functionality is also applicable for session-level logging using `auto_explain`. The advantage is that a developer could use this method to open a session and load `auto_explain` and set session-level settings for `auto_explain` parameters. With this method, any statement or some statements specific to that session will be logged, which thus avoids writing a lot of information to the log files.

Logging locks, waits, and temp in PostgreSQL

In order to satisfy *concurrency* in the ACID properties, every relational database implements locking. This locking may cause one or more sessions to wait until the lock has been released by a session holding the lock. Much of this information may be available to see in real time by querying the `pg_locks` view, but it would not produce an accurate view. For this purpose, we could use the facility available within PostgreSQL to log all the SQL statements that are waiting due to a lock acquired by another SQL. Similar to locks, we could also log when multiple sessions are involved in a deadlock. In this recipe, we shall discuss the steps to enable logging of such waits due to locking and deadlocks in PostgreSQL.

Getting ready

Locks are logged for SQL that has been waiting for more than `deadlock_timeout` amount of time. `deadlock_timeout` is set to 1 second by default. Increasing this to larger amounts may make the deadlock checks less expensive for a query when it waits for this duration. However, having a higher value set for `deadlock_timeout` may not log much information about lock waits. This is because lock waits are only logged when they are waiting for longer than this duration.

How to do it...

Let's get started with the following steps:

1. Set `log_lock_waits` to `ON` to log a message when a session waits for a longer duration than `deadlock_timeout`:

   ```
   $ psql -c "ALTER SYSTEM SET log_lock_waits to 'ON'"

   -- reload to get the change into effect.
   $ psql -c "select pg_reload_conf()"
   ```

2. Set `log_temp_files` to log a message including the statement when `temp` reaches this size.

   The following command enables the logging of all SQLs generating more than 100 KB of `temp`:

   ```
   $ psql -c "ALTER SYSTEM SET log_temp_files to '100KB'"
   $ psql -c "select pg_reload_conf()"
   ```

   The following command enables the logging of all SQLs generating more than 100 MB of `temp`:

   ```
   $ psql -c "ALTER SYSTEM SET log_temp_files to '100MB'"
   $ psql -c "select pg_reload_conf()"
   ```

How it works...

In order to start logging waits due to locks, we can use the command seen in *step 1*. When `log_lock_waits` is enabled, upon a reload, every query that is waiting due to locks for more than `deadlock_timeout` amount of time is logged.

Similarly, to log all queries generating more than a certain amount of `temp`, we need to set `log_temp_files` as seen in *step 2*. In the example, we see the commands that can set `log_temp_files` to 100 KB and 100 MB. What this means is that if a query generates 100 KB or 100 MB of `temp`, the statement will be logged to the log file.

Logging autovacuum and analyzing activity in PostgreSQL

As undos and past images are stored within the same table but not in a separate `UNDO` tablespace, it is important to have a cleanup process that removes the undo data. Autovacuum is the process that is responsible for performing this cleanup. At the same time, it is also important to have the statistics updated for the tables periodically based on the DML activity. For this purpose, the same autovacuum takes an additional responsibility of running `ANALYZE` on tables to update the statistics. Tuning autovacuum in PostgreSQL is one of the crucial tasks for an admin as the performance of the database can be impacted if autovacuum does not kick in for the tables at the right time. Sometimes, running autovacuum more adversely may cause performance issues due to a lot of writes or CPU/memory utilization. In this recipe, we shall discuss the steps involved in logging `autovacuum vacuum` and `autovacuum analyze` for analyzing vacuum activity.

Getting ready

It is always important to know that logging additional information to PostgreSQL logs causes more disk writes and uses a lot of disk space. For this reason, it is important to monitor the disk usage and the IOPS increase when any extensive logging has been enabled. It is also important to segregate logs and data across different disks. This way, none of the logging-specific writes cause any I/O saturation for the data directory that contains the database objects.

How to do it...

We will start logging additional information by using the following steps:

1. Set `log_autovacuum_min_duration` to a duration upon which an autovacuum vacuum or autovacuum analysis should be logged.

   The following command can be used to set `log_autovacuum_min_duration` to 1s to log autovacuum on a table that runs for more than 1 second:

   ```
   $ psql -c "ALTER SYSTEM SET log_autovacuum_min_duration TO '1s'"
   $ psql -c "select pg_reload_conf()"
   ```

   Setting the parameter to 0 logs every autovacuum activity:

   ```
   $ psql -c "ALTER SYSTEM SET log_autovacuum_min_duration TO '0'"
   $ psql -c "select pg_reload_conf()"
   ```

2. Perform a reload to get the changes into effect:

   ```
   $ pg_ctl -D $PGDATA reload
   $ psql -c "select pg_reload_conf()"
   ```

How it works...

It is very simple to log autovacuum vacuums and analyses to a PostgreSQL log file. As seen in *step 1*, we could modify the `log_autovacuum_min_duration` parameter to a duration upon which the autovacuum activity should be logged. Once the parameter has been set, it requires a reload, as seen in *step 2*, to get the changes into effect.

Generating a pgBadger report

The PostgreSQL logger process collects any log event (when enabled) that contains queries or errors/messages to just one log file. It is currently not possible to configure separate log files for separate tasks. For example, you cannot have a separate error log and a slow-query log. The logging we may enable using the previous recipes we discussed in this chapter may produce several thousand or millions of lines. It could get difficult for a DBA/developer to parse the log files and get a better view of what is running slow and how many times a query has run.

For this reason, we use `pgBadger`, which can parse log files and generates a rich HTML-based report that can be accessed from a browser. In this recipe, we shall discuss how to analyze Postgres logs and generate a report using `pgBadger`.

A sample `pgBadger` report is visible at the following URL: `http://pgbadger.darold.net/samplev7.html`. The following screenshot shows what the `pgBadger` dashboard looks like:

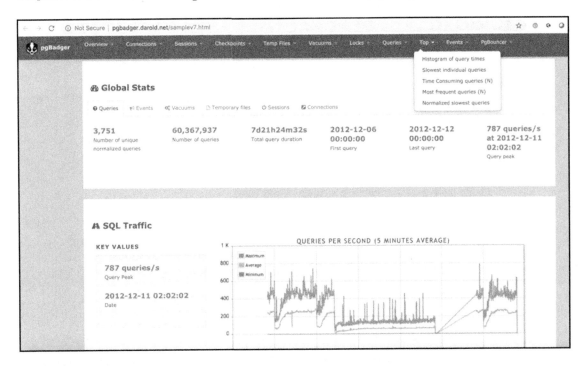

Let's get started!

Getting ready

`pgBadger` can be installed on a database server or a remote server to which Postgres logs have been copied to. Most companies stream Postgres logs of all their databases to a monitoring server where `pgBadger` is installed and scheduled to generate a report hourly or daily. Installing `pgBadger` is very easy. As long as the PGDG repository has been configured in the database server, it is just a matter of using `yum` or `apt` to install `pgBadger` depending on the Linux distribution:

```
-- On RedHat/CentOs
$ sudo yum install pgbadger
```

```
-- On Ubuntu/Debian
$ sudo apt install pgbadger
```

The following steps have been tested on CentOS and should not be any different on Ubuntu/Debian except for the command to install `pgBadger`.

How to do it...

Let's get started with the following steps:

1. Download the PGDG repo for your PostgreSQL version appropriately:

    ```
    $ sudo yum install
    https://yum.postgresql.org/13/redhat/rhel-7.7-x86_64/pgdg-redhat-re
    po-latest.noarch.rpm -y
    ```

2. Install the latest version of `pgBadger`:

    ```
    $ sudo yum install pgbadger
    ```

3. The following syntax can be used to generate a `pgBadger` report. `$PGDATA` in the following command is the full path to the data directory in which the log directory exists by default. If this is different from the actual log directory, we should substitute it with the full path to the log directory:

    ```
    $ pgbadger --prefix '%t [%p]: [%l-1] user=%u,db=%d'
    $PGDATA/log/postgresql-*.log -o pgbadger_report_aug_2020.html
    ```

    The `--prefix` parameter should be substituted with the value set to the `log_line_prefix` parameter in your PostgreSQL server for which the logs are being analyzed.

4. We can generate a `pgBadger` report for a certain time frame in the logs:

    ```
    $ pgbadger -a 1 -b "2020-07-09 13:30:00" -e "2020-07-09 14:00:00" -
    -prefix '%t [%p]: [%l-1] user=%u,db=%d' postgresql-*.log -o
    pgbadger_1330_1400_9thJuly_2020.html
    ```

    In the preceding command, we see the following command-line arguments used:

    - `-a`: The number of minutes to build the average graphs of queries and connections. The default is 5 minutes.
    - `-b`: Start timestamp.
    - `-e`: End timestamp.

5. We can now get to generating a faster `pgBadger` report by making use of multiple CPUs:

```
$ pgbadger -j 8 -J 4 --prefix '%t [%p]: [%l-1] user=%u,db=%d'
postgresql-*.log -o pgbadger_parallel_4thaugust_2020.html
```

In the preceding command, we see the following command-line arguments used:

- `-J`: The number of log files to parse in parallel. The default is 1, run as a single process.
- `-j`: The number of jobs to run at the same time. The default is 1, run as a single process.

How it works...

`pgBadger` parses the log files and produces the following details in an HTML-based report:

- Global statistics throughout the instance, such as the following:
  - The number of sessions
  - Total number of queries executed
  - Prepared statements
  - `READS` and `WRITES` activity plotted on a graph
- Top time-consuming queries
- Most-waited-for queries due to locks
- Top frequent SQLs in the instance with the highest number of executions
- Queries waiting due to locks
- Vacuum and analysis stats
- Locks stats
- Temp file stats and queries generating more temp
- Checkpoint stats
- Queries that were canceled or killed
- Number of errors, warnings, and panic messages
- A few detailed error messages for each type of error

Upon downloading the PGDG repository, we could install `pgBadger` using `yum` as seen in *steps 1* and *2*. Once installed, we could generate a `pgBadger` report by passing the parameters as seen in *step 3*. `--prefix` should be substituted with `log_line_prefix`. Then, we should pass a list of Postgres log files separated by a space or using regex (for example, `postgresql.*.log`). Finally, the naming convention of the report and the log file location can be set using the `-o` parameter. This determines the output filename and also the destination if passed to it.

When a `pgBadger` report needs to be generated within a certain time frame, we should pass it with the beginning and end timestamp as seen in *step 4*. You may see `pgBadger` taking a long time to complete when the source log files have a considerable size. The processing of these files is usually CPU-bound, so you may make use of multiple CPUs for parallel processing using the command seen in *step 5* as an example. If you are planning on running `pgBadger` on the production server, just make sure you do so outside of peak hours. Alternatively, you may want to have the logs sent to an intermediate server or desktop periodically, where you can run `pgBadger` reports without impacting the database server.

Finally, to get to know the full list of pgBadger options, try the following:

```
$ pgbadger --help
```

Configuring pg_stat_statements as an extension

When using an enterprise version in Oracle such as databases, we see historic information such as what query ran through what user at a certain point in time, through some views. Such views may help in identifying the queries that ran some time ago and their overall statistics, such as the total number of times the query ran and the average time consumption. Such information can be visible in PostgreSQL using an extension called `pg_stat_statements`. In this recipe, we shall discuss how `pgBadger` can be configured as an extension.

Getting ready

In order to configure this extension, we must have a PostgreSQL server that has the `contrib` module installed. This extension is part of the `contrib` module and does not involve any complex procedure to install and configure. So, all it requires is the `postgresql-contrib-13` package on Ubuntu or the `postgresql13-contrib` package on CentOS/Red Hat to install this extension.

How to do it...

We will configure the extensions using the following steps:

1. Add `pg_stat_statements` to `shared_preload_libraries`:

   ```
   $ psql -c "ALTER SYSTEM SET shared_preload_libraries TO
   pg_stat_statements"
   ```

   If there are multiple extensions that are to be loaded, we could use a command similar to the following:

   ```
   $ psql -c "ALTER SYSTEM SET shared_preload_libraries TO
   auto_explain, pg_stat_statements, pg_repack"
   ```

2. Restart the PostgreSQL server to get the changes into effect. `$PGDATA` is the path to the data directory:

   ```
   $ pg_ctl -D $PGDATA restart -mf
   ```

3. Create the extension in the database for which query statistics need to be collected:

   ```
   $ psql -d percdb -c "CREATE EXTENSION pg_stat_statements"
   ```

4. Validate by selecting the count from `pg_stat_statements`:

   ```
   $ psql -d percdb -c "select count(*) from pg_stat_statements"
   ```

How it works...

Setting up `pg_stat_statements` is very simple. If the `contrib` module is installed, it is just a matter of loading `pg_stat_statements` libraries through `shared_preload_libraries` as seen in *step 1*.

As any change to `shared_preload_libraries` requires a restart, we have to restart PostgreSQL as seen in *step 2*. Upon restart, we should create the extension using the CREATE EXTENSION statement and we would start looking at the queries we ran immediately through a simple validation as seen in *steps 3 and 4*.

Query analysis using pg_stat_statements

The `pg_stat_statements` extension exposes a lot of query statistics that will be helpful in finding slow queries that need to be optimized. In this recipe, we shall see some example queries to view some information from `pg_stat_statements`.

Getting ready

In order to run the views or queries discussed in this recipe, we should have `pg_stat_statements` successfully configured and created as an extension. Please note that every query for which the statistics are collected by `pg_stat_statements` can be uniquely identified through `queryid`. A hash is generated based on the query text and is visible as `queryid` when we query the `pg_stat_statements` view.

How to do it...

In the following commands, we have used a function to trim the query up to just 40 characters for better visibility. We may use an expanded display using `\x` and avoid truncating the query when viewing the statistics:

1. Find the queries that are writing to `temp` the most:

   ```
   select queryid, left(query,40), calls, temp_blks_read,
   temp_blks_written from pg_stat_statements order by
   temp_blks_written desc;
   ```

2. Find the queries that are reading from `temp` the most:

   ```
   select queryid, left(query,40), calls, temp_blks_read,
   temp_blks_written from pg_stat_statements order by temp_blks_read
   desc;
   ```

3. Find the queries that are reading from disk the most:

```
select queryid, left(query,40), calls, local_blks_read,
local_blks_read/calls as avg_read_per_call from pg_stat_statements
order by local_blks_read desc;
```

4. Find the queries with the highest execution times:

```
select queryid, left(query,40), mean_time, max_time from
pg_stat_statements where calls > 10 order by mean_time desc,
max_time desc;
```

5. Find the queries that are executed the most:

```
select queryid, left(query,40), calls, mean_time from
pg_stat_statements order by calls desc;
```

How it works...

The following is the list of columns available through the pg_stat_statements view. For this view, we could query a lot of information that can be useful for query analysis:

```
percdb=# \d pg_stat_statements
View "public.pg_stat_statements"
Column | Type | Collation | Nullable | Default
--------------------+------------------+-----------+----------+---------
userid | oid | | |
dbid | oid | | |
queryid | bigint | | |
query | text | | |
calls | bigint | | |
total_time | double precision | | |
min_time | double precision | | |
max_time | double precision | | |
mean_time | double precision | | |
stddev_time | double precision | | |
rows | bigint | | |
shared_blks_hit | bigint | | |
shared_blks_read | bigint | | |
shared_blks_dirtied | bigint | | |
shared_blks_written | bigint | | |
local_blks_hit | bigint | | |
local_blks_read | bigint | | |
local_blks_dirtied | bigint | | |
local_blks_written | bigint | | |
temp_blks_read | bigint | | |
```

```
temp_blks_written | bigint | | |
blk_read_time | double precision | | |
blk_write_time | double precision | | |
```

Some of the queries discussed in this recipe serve a specific purpose. However, more such queries can be constructed in several combinations to filter queries going through a certain phase similar to getting a list of the queries that are generating more `temp`, reading from `temp`, and reading from disk but not from memory, highest execution times, and the queries called (executed) the most, as seen in *steps 1* to *5*. At any point in time, all the stats collected can be reset using the following function call:

```
percdb=# select pg_stat_statements_reset();
 pg_stat_statements_reset
---------------------------

(1 row)
```

Getting the kernel-level statistics of a query using pg_stat_kcache

In the previous recipe, we discussed how `pg_stat_statements` can be used for query analysis. However, some information, such as the CPU (system and user) usage and reads and writes on the filesystem layer, are not visible through `pg_stat_statements`. For this purpose, we could use the `pg_stat_kcache` extension, which works in conjunction with `pg_stat_statements`, to display this information. In this recipe, we shall discuss how `pg_stat_kcache` can be installed and used to get kernel-level information of a SQL query.

Getting ready

In order to use `pg_stat_kcache`, we should also the `pg_stat_statements` have the extension installed and created in the database. This extension is available as an open source project on GitHub (`https://github.com/powa-team/pg_stat_kcache`) and also made available on the PGDG repository. Similar to any other extension, `pg_stat_kcache` also has a dependency on the `contrib` module, that is, the `postgresql-contrib-13` package on Ubuntu/Debian or the `postgresql13-contrib` package on CentOS/Red Hat.

How to do it...

We will use the following steps to get the kernel statistics:

1. Install `pg_stat_kcache` using `yum` or `apt`:

   ```
   -- On RedHat/CentOS
   $ sudo yum install pg_stat_kcache13

   -- On Ubuntu/Debian
   $ sudo apt install postgresql-13-pg-stat-kcache
   ```

2. Load `pg_stat_kcache` by adding it to the list of libraries in `shared_preload_libraries`. Make sure that `pg_stat_statements` is the first in the sequence:

   ```
   $ psql -c "ALTER SYSTEM SET shared_preload_libraries TO
   pg_stat_statements, pg_stat_kcache"
   ```

3. Restart PostgreSQL to get the changes to `shared_preload_libraries` into effect. Replace `PGDATA` with the full path to the data directory if the variable is not set already:

   ```
   $ pg_ctl -D $PGDATA restart -mf
   ```

4. Create both the `pg_stat_kcache` and `pg_stat_statements` extensions in the database for which statistics need to be made available:

   ```
   $ psql -d percdb -c "CREATE EXTENSION pg_stat_statements"
   $ psql -d percdb -c "CREATE EXTENSION pg_stat_kcache"
   ```

   We may also just use the following command to create the `pg_stat_kcache` extension, which also creates the `pg_stat_statements` extension automatically:

   ```
   $ psql -d percdb -c "CREATE EXTENSION pg_stat_kcache CASCADE"
   ```

5. Connect to the database and run the following query:

   ```
   SELECT datname,
    queryid,
    Round(total_time::numeric, 2) AS total_time,
    calls,
    Pg_size_pretty((shared_blks_hit+shared_blks_read)*8192 - reads) AS
   memory_hit,
    Pg_size_pretty(reads) AS disk_read,
    Pg_size_pretty(writes) AS disk_write,
    Round(user_time:: numeric, 2) AS cpu_user_time,
   ```

```
Round(system_time::numeric, 2) AS cpu_system_time
FROM pg_stat_statements s
JOIN Pg_stat_kcache() k
using (userid, dbid, queryid)
JOIN pg_database d
ON s.dbid = d.oid
WHERE datname NOT LIKE 'template%'
ORDER BY total_time DESC limit 10;
```

This results in the following output:

```
datname | queryid | total_time | calls | memory_hit | disk_read |
disk_write | cpu_user_time | cpu_system_time
---------+----------------------+------------+------------+----------+------------
-+-----------+------------+----------------+------------------
 percdb | 2082821715455191239 | 165388.31 | 917114 | 25 GB | 256 kB
| 96 kB | 9.09 | 20.93
 percdb | 6330549881103975164 | 36294.97 | 917115 | 27 GB | 240 kB
| 224 kB | 7.23 | 17.69
 percdb | -4269504897428794475 | 29279.73 | 917120 | 36 GB | 677 MB
| 7424 kB | 8.20 | 25.83
 percdb | 4755987678167182604 | 8408.81 | 917120 | 28 GB | 0 bytes
| 0 bytes | 4.35 | 12.05
 percdb | 8817650346475871488 | 7680.02 | 917112 | 7257 MB | 0
bytes | 46 MB | 5.27 | 11.46
 percdb | 1645016356245305504 | 2.20 | 4 | 136 kB | 56 kB | 0 bytes
| 0.00 | 0.00
 percdb | 6313270867072907211 | 0.51 | 100 | 792 kB | 0 bytes |
8192 bytes | 0.00 | 0.00
 percdb | 7112618187697570123 | 0.26 | 4 | 128 kB | 0 bytes | 0
bytes | 0.00 | 0.00
 percdb | 4906396473173435834 | 0.10 | 10 | 72 kB | 0 bytes | 8192
bytes | 0.00 | 0.00
(9 rows)
```

6. We could get the query text by querying pg_stat_statements using queryid, as in the following example:

```
percdb=# select query from pg_stat_statements where queryid =
2082821715455191239;
 query
----------------------------------------------------------------------
---
 UPDATE pgbench_branches SET bbalance = bbalance + $1 WHERE bid =
$2
(1 row)
```

How it works...

pg_stat_kcache can be installed using both yum or apt if the PGDG repository has been configured. Once installed, as seen in *step 1*, we should set shared_preload_libraries to pg_stat_statements and pg_stat_kcache ensuring that pg_stat_statements is first in the sequence. This is because pg_stat_kcache depends on pg_stat_statements. Upon making any modification to shared_preload_libraries, it requires a restart of the PostgreSQL server. Upon restart, the extensions should be created in the database in which the queries should be analyzed. *Step 5* has an example SQL statement that displays a list of SQL queries along with the number of pages hit in memory versus the number of pages fetched from disk or written to disk by the query. Additionally, it only shows the CPU user time and the system time spent by each query.

The pg_stat_kcache view contains several columns using which a lot of information can be retrieved specific to each:

```
percdb=# \d pg_stat_kcache()
View "public.pg_stat_kcache"
Column | Type | Collation | Nullable | Default
-------------+------------------+-----------+----------+---------
datname | name | | |
user_time | double precision | | |
system_time | double precision | | |
minflts | numeric | | |
majflts | numeric | | |
nswaps | numeric | | |
reads | numeric | | |
reads_blks | numeric | | |
writes | numeric | | |
writes_blks | numeric | | |
msgsnds | numeric | | |
msgrcvs | numeric | | |
nsignals | numeric | | |
nvcsws | numeric | | |
nivcsws | numeric | | |
```

If the statistics gathered by pg_stat_kcache need to be reset, there is a function for that, as seen in the following command:

```
$ psql -d percdb -c "select pg_stat_kcache_reset()"
```

Once the statistics have been reset, the counters visible in pg_stat_kcache restart from 0.

Critical Services Monitoring 9

Upon deploying your PostgreSQL databases in production, it is very important to monitor them regularly. We could categorize the monitoring of any database into three types:

- Reactive
- Proactive
- Predictive

To understand the preceding three categories better, let's consider an example of a PostgreSQL database with a size of 100 GB on a disk of size 150 GB:

- **Reactive**: Receive an alert when a database server crashes because it has reached its capacity of storage. This is said to be reactive.
- **Proactive**: You know that the database server is about to reach its threshold and add more space to avoid an outage. The impact may be very little to users if it requires a server reboot or a restart.
- **Predictive**: Based on the data captured over several days, you are able to predict the outage several days or months in advance. In this case, performance and availability are never impacted.

Gone are the days where we used to be reactive or proactive. Today's world requires us to be predictive when looking forward to more nines of availability. Some monitoring tools connect to a PostgreSQL database and alert us when a condition is met. But this may not allow users to be proactive and predictive. Considering this fact, we shall discuss some open source tools that could help us to be predictive and also help us to achieve the monitoring of almost everything we need in PostgreSQL today.

Grafana is a web application that is commonly used for visualizing the trends of a metric. It allows users to analyze data using charts and graphs. This requires a data source that stores the time series data of metrics, which can be Prometheus or several other data sources supported by Grafana. In this chapter, we are going to consider Prometheus, considering its popularity and its user-friendly query language PromQL.

It is Prometheus that pulls diagnostic data from clients. So, we need exporters on the client servers that expose data that can be pulled by Prometheus. To expose kernel-level metrics, we could use Node Exporter, and to expose PostgreSQL database-level information, we will use the Postgres exporter.

The following are the recipes that will be covered to demonstrate how we can set up monitoring using Grafana and Prometheus:

- Installation of Grafana and its dependencies
- Prometheus as a data source on the monitoring server
- Configuring Node Exporter on Postgres servers to monitor operating system metrics
- Adding metrics being collected using `node_exporter` to Prometheus
- Collecting PostgreSQL metrics using `postgres_exporter`
- Adding metrics exposed by `postgres_exporter` to Prometheus
- Importing a dashboard for monitoring Linux metrics
- How to import a dashboard for monitoring Postgres metrics
- Adding custom queries to `postgres_exporter`

Technical requirements

Grafana is very lightweight in terms of system resources. A server with as low as 255 MB RAM and one CPU is needed to start using Grafana. However, if we need to deploy the image rendering and monitoring of 10 servers, it would be wise to have a server allocated with at least 4 GB RAM and two CPUs to start with.

In order to try monitoring using Grafana and Prometheus using the steps discussed in this chapter, you will need two servers (or virtual machines) with a CentOS/Red Hat/Debian/Ubuntu operating system, 2 GB RAM, and two CPU(s). These two servers should have internet connectivity to download and install Grafana, PostgreSQL, and Prometheus.

The steps discussed in the following recipes have been tested against CentOS 7.8 and 8 (and should work on all CentOS 7.x releases).

Installation of Grafana and its dependencies

Grafana can be installed on the Windows, macOS, Debian/Ubuntu, and CentOS/Red Hat family of operating systems. Installing it is very easy and straightforward. We shall discuss the steps involved in installing Grafana on both CentOS and Ubuntu operating systems.

Getting ready

To install Grafana, we should have a server or a virtual machine that has connectivity to the internet. Some of the ports we configure for exposing the metrics should be made available for inbound connections in the firewall settings. For example, in order to access the Grafana dashboards, the port defaults to 3000. However, this can always be modified. Unless the port is open, a client/user cannot see any metrics on the Grafana dashboard.

How to do it...

In this recipe, we shall cover the Debian/Ubuntu and CentOS/Red Hat family of operating systems.

1. Use the following step to add the yum repository to Grafana:

Please refer to
https://grafana.com/docs/grafana/latest/installation/rpm/ for any
changes to the repository.

```
$ sudo bash -c 'cat << EOF > /etc/yum.repos.d/grafana.repo
[grafana]
name=grafana
baseurl=https://packages.grafana.com/oss/rpm
repo_gpgcheck=1
enabled=1
gpgcheck=1
gpgkey=https://packages.grafana.com/gpg.key
sslverify=1
sslcacert=/etc/pki/tls/certs/ca-bundle.crt
EOF'
```

2. Install Grafana using yum:

```
$ sudo yum install grafana -y
```

3. Reload systemd and start Grafana:

```
$ sudo systemctl daemon-reload
$ sudo systemctl start grafana-server
```

Verify the status using the following command:

```
$ sudo systemctl status grafana-server
```

4. To enable the Grafana service to start automatically upon server restart, use the following command:

```
$ sudo systemctl enable grafana-server
```

Installing Grafana on Debian/Ubuntu operating systems

1. Install the dependencies and add the gpg key:

```
$ sudo apt-get install -y apt-transport-https
$ sudo apt-get install -y software-properties-common wget
$ wget -q -O - https://packages.grafana.com/gpg.key | sudo apt-key add
```

2. Add the repository and run apt-get update:

```
$ echo "deb https://packages.grafana.com/oss/deb stable main" |
sudo tee -a /etc/apt/sources.list.d/grafana.list
$ sudo apt-get update
```

3. Install Grafana using apt-get:

```
$ sudo apt-get install grafana
```

4. Check the status of the grafana-server service and start it if not started already:

```
$ sudo service grafana-server start
$ sudo service grafana-server status
```

5. Enable auto start of the grafana-server service upon reboot:

```
$ sudo update-rc.d grafana-server defaults
```

Verification

Once Grafana is started upon successful installation, you can use the following URL in your web browser to see your Grafana home page. The HTTP port that Grafana listens to is 3000 unless configured differently.

The username/password defaults to `admin`. It is advised to change the password immediately:

```
http://192.168.29.10:3000/
# -- Replace 192.168.29.10 with your Grafana server's IP address.
```

A URL similar to the preceding (with the appropriate IP address for the server) can be opened on any browser, as seen in the following screenshot:

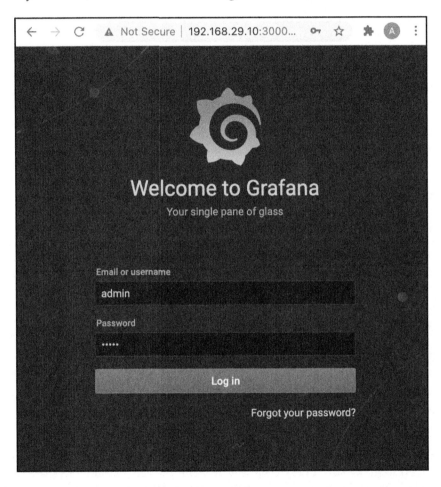

The Grafana installation is successful when we are able to see the welcome screen as in the preceding screenshot.

How it works...

In the preceding section, we saw the simple steps involved in installing Grafana on both CentOS and Ubuntu operating systems.

When installing on CentOS/Red Hat, we must have the appropriate `yum` repository created, as seen in *step 1*. Once the repo is created, we could simply use `yum` to install Grafana, as seen in *step 2*. Using *steps 3* and *4*, we can start the Grafana service using `systemctl` and enable the service for auto restart upon server reboot or crash.

When installing on Ubuntu/Debian, the appropriate `gpg` key and dependencies should be set up as seen in *step 1*. We could then use the commands seen in *step 2* to add the Grafana repository. Once added, it is important to perform `apt-get update` so that the repository is loaded to install Grafana using *step 3*. Upon installing Grafana, we could start the `grafana-server` service using *step 4*. To enable auto start of the `grafana-server` service upon restart of the server or a crash, we could use the command seen in *step 5*.

Prometheus as a data source on the monitoring server

Grafana is used as a visualizer for metrics as graphs, tables, and so on. However, the data that is needed to visualize this information needs to be made available through a data source. This data source should contain all the time series diagnostic data of a PostgreSQL server. In this recipe, we shall discuss Prometheus, which is one of the famous data sources. We can use a simple query language called **PromQL** (**Prometheus Query Language**) to fetch the time series data stored in Prometheus. These queries will be used in panels on a Grafana dashboard to visualize the diagnostic data as graphs. We will now see the steps involved in installing and configuring Prometheus.

Getting ready

Prometheus can be installed on the same server as the Grafana server or another remote server. We need to make sure that we have sufficient storage available to store the time series data of all targets being monitored based on the data retention configured. This can be estimated by observing the growth rate of the Prometheus data directory for a few days.

The latest binaries for Prometheus are available at `https://prometheus.io/download/`. At the time of writing this recipe, the current stable version of Prometheus is 2.19.2. We shall see this version being used in the steps in the following sections.

How to do it...

We will install and run Prometheus using the following steps:

1. Download the latest binaries of Prometheus from GitHub:

   ```
   $ sudo curl -LO
   https://github.com/prometheus/prometheus/releases/download/v2.19.2/
   prometheus-2.19.2.linux-amd64.tar.gz
   ```

2. Extract or unpack the downloaded `.tar` file:

   ```
   $ sudo tar -xzf prometheus-2.19.2.linux-amd64.tar.gz
   ```

3. Create a directory to store the extracted binaries in the new directory for simplicity:

   ```
   $ sudo mkdir ~/prom/
   $ sudo mv prometheus-2.19.2.linux-amd64/* ~/prom/
   ```

4. Verify that the installation is successful:

   ```
   $ ~/prom/prometheus --version
    prometheus, version 2.19.2 (branch: HEAD, revision:
   c448ada63d83002e9c1d2c9f84e09f55a61f0ff7)
    build user: root@dd72efe1549d
    build date: 20200626-09:02:20
    go version: go1.14.4
   ```

5. Create credentials for accessing the Prometheus data source on the Grafana dashboard. The `basic_auth` section can be appended at the end to avoid any errors. This section must usually appear after `job_name` under `scrape_configs`. As it is YAML, the configuration file should have appropriate indentation:

   ```
   $ vi ~/prom/prometheus.yml
   # Add the basic_auth section under already existing scrape_configs
   section.
   scrape_configs:
     - job_name: 'prometheus'
       ...
       ...
       basic_auth:
         username: prom
         password: secret
   ```

6. Start Prometheus by passing the appropriate parameters.

   In the following command, replace `192.168.29.10` with the Prometheus server's IP address:

```
$ sudo ~/prom/prometheus --config.file ~/prom/prometheus.yml --
storage.tsdb.path ~/prom/promdb --web.console.templates
~/prom/consoles --web.console.libraries ~/prom/console_libraries --
web.listen-address 192.168.29.10:9090
```

How it works...

In order to use Prometheus as a data source, its binaries must be installed on the monitoring server or another remote server. The steps used in this recipe incorporate the Prometheus version that was the latest as of July 29, 2020. As seen in *step 1*, you can use `curl` to download a Prometheus `.tar` file from GitHub. Once downloaded, we can extract the `.tar` file using the command in *step 2*.

To avoid passing a long path, we could simply create a directory and move all the binaries to it as seen in *step 3*. Once done, the installation can be verified by probing its version using the command in *step 4*.

There is also a default configuration file, `prometheus.yml`, which will be good for testing purposes:

```
$ cd ~/prom/
$ ls -la prometheus.yml
```

The following link gives a detailed explanation of each of the configuration settings available with Prometheus: `https://prometheus.io/docs/prometheus/latest/configuration/configuration/`.

When Prometheus needs to be added as a data source on the Grafana dashboard, it needs some credentials to access the data source. These credentials can be created by adding the username and password under `scrap_configs` of the `prometheus.yml` file, as seen in *step 5*.

Once the credentials have been added, we can use the command seen in *step 6* to start Prometheus. To let it run as a daemon, we can create a service or use & at the end of the command. In the command, you can see that we are passing the location of the configuration file to --config-file, the location of the Prometheus data directory to --storage.tsdb.path, and the IP and port using which the metrics can be visible on the web using --web.listen-address.

Once started, we shall see a log as seen in the following output:

```
[vagrant@grafana ~]$ sudo ~/prom/prometheus --config.file
~/prom/prometheus.yml --storage.tsdb.path ~/prom/promdb --
web.console.templates ~/prom/consoles --web.console.libraries
~/prom/console_libraries --web.listen-address 192.168.29.10:9090 &
 [1] 30876
  level=info ts=2020-06-30T16:43:40.207Z caller=main.go:302 msg="No time or
size retention was set so using the default time retention" duration=15d
  level=info ts=2020-06-30T16:43:40.207Z caller=main.go:337 msg="Starting
Prometheus" version="(version=2.19.2, branch=HEAD,
revision=c448ada63d83002e9c1d2c9f84e09f55a61f0ff7)"
  level=info ts=2020-06-30T16:43:40.207Z caller=main.go:338
build_context="(go=go1.14.4, user=root@dd72efe1549d,
date=20200626-09:02:20)"
  level=info ts=2020-06-30T16:43:40.207Z caller=main.go:339
host_details="(Linux 3.10.0-1127.el7.x86_64 #1 SMP Tue Mar 31 23:36:51 UTC
2020 x86_64 grafana (none))"
  level=info ts=2020-06-30T16:43:40.207Z caller=main.go:340
fd_limits="(soft=1024, hard=4096)"
  level=info ts=2020-06-30T16:43:40.207Z caller=main.go:341
vm_limits="(soft=unlimited, hard=unlimited)"
  level=info ts=2020-06-30T16:43:40.210Z caller=main.go:678 msg="Starting
TSDB ..."
  level=info ts=2020-06-30T16:43:40.212Z caller=head.go:645 component=tsdb
msg="Replaying WAL and on-disk memory mappable chunks if any, this may take
a while"
  level=info ts=2020-06-30T16:43:40.212Z caller=web.go:524 component=web
msg="Start listening for connections" address=192.168.29.10:9090
  level=info ts=2020-06-30T16:43:40.213Z caller=head.go:706 component=tsdb
msg="WAL segment loaded" segment=0 maxSegment=4
  level=info ts=2020-06-30T16:43:40.215Z caller=head.go:706 component=tsdb
msg="WAL segment loaded" segment=1 maxSegment=4
  level=info ts=2020-06-30T16:43:40.216Z caller=head.go:706 component=tsdb
msg="WAL segment loaded" segment=2 maxSegment=4
  level=info ts=2020-06-30T16:43:40.216Z caller=head.go:706 component=tsdb
msg="WAL segment loaded" segment=3 maxSegment=4
  level=info ts=2020-06-30T16:43:40.217Z caller=head.go:706 component=tsdb
msg="WAL segment loaded" segment=4 maxSegment=4
  level=info ts=2020-06-30T16:43:40.217Z caller=head.go:709 component=tsdb
```

```
msg="WAL replay completed" duration=4.284985ms
 level=info ts=2020-06-30T16:43:40.218Z caller=main.go:694
fs_type=XFS_SUPER_MAGIC
 level=info ts=2020-06-30T16:43:40.218Z caller=main.go:695 msg="TSDB
started"
 level=info ts=2020-06-30T16:43:40.218Z caller=main.go:799 msg="Loading
configuration file" filename=/home/vagrant/prom/prometheus.yml
 level=info ts=2020-06-30T16:43:40.219Z caller=main.go:827 msg="Completed
loading of configuration file" filename=/home/vagrant/prom/prometheus.yml
 level=info ts=2020-06-30T16:43:40.219Z caller=main.go:646 msg="Server is
ready to receive web requests."
```

As we see in the log, default values are considered for most of the parameters, for example, retention.

Configuring Node Exporter on Postgres servers to monitor operating system metrics

In the previous two recipes, we have seen the steps involved in installing Grafana to visualize the metrics and Prometheus to store the metrics. In this recipe, we shall discuss an exporter that can collect some kernel-level diagnostic data from a PostgreSQL server and store it in a Prometheus database.

Node Exporter is an open source exporter that exposes a wide variety of operating system kernel-level metrics, such as CPU, memory, storage, I/O, and so on. It needs to run on each PostgreSQL server being monitored, if interested in operating system-level metrics. In this recipe, we shall see how `node_exporter` can be configured to expose operating system kernel-level information.

Getting ready

In order to use `node_exporter` following the steps discussed in this recipe, we should have a PostgreSQL server running on a Linux operating system. The port being used by Node Exporter to expose the operating system-level metrics should be open for inbound connections from the Prometheus deployed server.

The latest `node_exporter` binaries can always be downloaded from the Prometheus website: `https://prometheus.io/download/`.

How to do it...

We'll configure `node_exporter` using the following steps:

1. Download the latest `node_exporter` binaries `.tar` file from GitHub:

   ```
   $ sudo curl -LO
   https://github.com/prometheus/node_exporter/releases/download/v1.0.
   1/node_exporter-1.0.1.linux-amd64.tar.gz
   ```

2. Extract the `.tar` file and copy the `node_exporter` binary to `/usr/bin/` for simplicity:

   ```
   $ tar -xzf node_exporter-1.0.1.linux-amd64.tar.gz
   $ sudo cp node_exporter-1.0.1.linux-amd64/node_exporter /usr/bin/
   ```

3. Verify that `node_exporter` is working correctly:

   ```
   $ node_exporter --version
    node_exporter, version 1.0.1 (branch: HEAD, revision:
   3715be6ae899f2a9b9dbfd9c39f3e09a7bd4559f)
    build user: root@1f76dbbcfa55
    build date: 20200616-12:44:12
    go version: go1.14.4
   ```

4. Start `node_exporter` on the PostgreSQL server as a daemon:

   ```
   $ node_exporter &
   ```

5. Validate the metrics being collected using `curl`:

   ```
   $ curl http://localhost:9100/metrics
   ```

How it works...

As a first step toward installing `node_exporter`, we use the command seen in *step 1* to download the `node_exporter` TAR file using `curl`. We could then extract the `.tar` file and copy the `node_exporter` file to the `/usr/bin` location, as seen in *step 2*. This way, we do not have to use a full path to run the exporter. Once done, we can verify whether `node_exporter` is working correctly without any dependency issues using the command seen in *step 3*. Upon verification, we can start `node_exporter` as a daemon using the command seen in *step 4*.

Once installed and running, we can validate the metrics being exported using `curl` on the terminal as seen in *step 5*. This should show all the kernel-level metrics being exposed by Node Exporter.

Adding metrics being collected using node_exporter to Prometheus

In the previous recipe, we saw how Node Exporter can expose several Linux metrics. Now, these metrics need to be collected in regular intervals to build dashboards on Grafana. As we are using Prometheus as a data source, we need to add the Postgres node details to the `prometheus.yml` file along with the port using which the metrics exposed by `node_exporter` can be collected. In this recipe, we shall see how we can enable Prometheus to collect these operating system metrics from a Postgres node.

Getting ready

In order to add the collection of metrics exposed by `node_exporter` to Prometheus, we should have `node_exporter` running on the PostgreSQL server. The Prometheus server must also be able to access the metrics exposed over the port used by `node_exporter`.

How to do it...

Let's get started by using the following steps:

1. Add the PostgreSQL server IP and the port used by `node_exporter` to the `prometheus.yml` file on the monitoring server. The IP of the Postgres server in my setup is `192.168.29.20`. Notice the last line, which adds the PostgreSQL server on `192.169.29.20` as a target in the following log, under `static_configs`:

```
scrape_configs:
  - job_name: 'prometheus'
    basic_auth:
      username: prom
      password: secret
```

```
static_configs:
- targets: ['localhost:9090']
- targets: ['192.169.29.20:9100']
```

2. Start Prometheus upon modifying the configuration file:

```
$ sudo ~/prom/prometheus --config.file ~/prom/prometheus.yml --
storage.tsdb.path ~/prom/promdb --web.console.templates
~/prom/consoles --web.console.libraries ~/prom/console_libraries --
web.listen-address 192.168.29.10:9090 &
```

3. Go to the following URL and see whether the new target is visible:

```
http://192.168.29.10:9090/targets
```

We should see a new target as seen in the following screenshot:

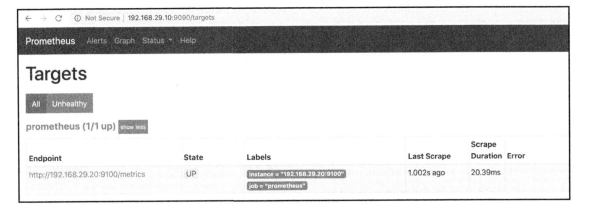

How it works...

In order to let Prometheus collect and store the metrics of node_exporter, we should edit the prometheus.yml configuration file and add the Postgres node IP and port using which metrics are visible under scrape_configs, as seen in *step 1*. Once done, we can terminate the already-running Prometheus daemon using the Linux KILL command and start it back using the originally used command that was discussed in the *Prometheus as a data source on the monitoring server* recipe. Upon starting it, we can use the browser to see whether a new target is visible.

Collecting PostgreSQL metrics using postgres_exporter

Now that we have discussed how to collect operating system-level metrics using `node_exporter` in the previous recipe, we shall discuss how we can collect PostgreSQL metrics using `postgres_exporter` in this recipe. `postgres_exporter` has to be installed on the PostgreSQL server.

Getting ready

In order to expose PostgreSQL metrics using `postgres_exporter`, we should have a database user that is able to connect to the target database being used by the exporter in the connection string. Additionally, the port using which the metrics are visible should be open for the Prometheus data source to access it.

The following is the GitHub URL of `postgres_exporter`: https://github.com/wrouesnel/postgres_exporter.

How to do it...

The `postgres_exporter` installation and setup are done on the PostgreSQL database server only. Thus, all the following steps in this section, unless when explicitly specified, need to be done on the PostgreSQL server:

1. Install all the dependencies for `postgres_exporter` to work:

    ```
    $ sudo yum install epel-release -y
    $ sudo yum install golang -y
    ```

2. As a Postgres user, download the `postgres_exporter` source:

    ```
    $ go get github.com/wrouesnel/postgres_exporter
    ```

3. Install `postgres_exporter` using `go`:

    ```
    $ cd ${GOPATH-$HOME/go}/src/github.com/wrouesnel/postgres_exporter
    $ go run mage.go binary
    ```

4. Verify the installation by checking the version:

```
$ ./postgres_exporter --version
postgres_exporter v0.8.0-7-ge2df41f (built with go1.13.11)
```

5. Add appropriate entries to the `pg_hba.conf` file to allow connections from `postgres_exporter`:

```
$ echo "host all all 192.168.29.20/32 md5" >> $PGDATA/pg_hba.conf
$ pg_ctl -D $PGDATA reload
```

6. Validate by connecting to the database using the connection URI used by the exporter. This validation can be done on the monitoring server. This step is optional and is only for the purpose of validation:

```
$ psql -d
"postgresql://postgres:secret@192.168.29.20:5432/postgres?sslmode=d
isable"
psql (12.3)
Type "help" for help.
postgres=# \q
```

7. Set the environment variable that contains the database connection URI in the legacy format:

```
$ export
DATA_SOURCE_NAME="postgresql://login:password@hostname:port/dbname"
```

For my setup, it looks like the following:

```
$ export
DATA_SOURCE_NAME="postgresql://postgres:secret@192.168.29.20:5432/p
ostgres"

-- If sslmode is disable, use

$ export
DATA_SOURCE_NAME="postgresql://postgres:secret@192.168.29.20:5432/p
ostgres?sslmode=disable"
```

8. Start the Postgres exporter as a daemon:

```
$ ./postgres_exporter &
```

9. Validate using `curl`. `postgres_exporter` exposes metrics being collected over port `9187` by default:

```
$ curl http://192.168.29.20:9187/metrics
```

How it works...

`postgres_exporter` is coded using Golang. For this purpose, we should install Golang using the command seen in *step 1*. Download the `postgres_exporter` source using the commands seen in *step 2* and install it. The build system is based on `mage`. So, run the command seen in *step 3* to install `postgres_exporter`. Once the installation is completed without any errors, we can validate the functionality by probing the version of `postgres_exporter`, as seen in *step 4*.

For `postgres_exporter` to work successfully, the exporter should be able to connect using the credentials passed to it. At the same time, the `pg_hba.conf` file should also have appropriate entries to allow connections from `postgres_exporter`. So, we shall add appropriate entries as necessary as seen in *step 5*. We should replace the IP address used in this command with the actual Postgres server IP address. Once done, we can use the `psql` command as seen in *step 6* to validate whether connectivity is working fine.

Upon validation, we should set the `DATA_SOURCE_NAME` environment variable that is used by `postgres_exporter` as seen in *step 7*. Once completed, we can start `postgres_exporter` as a daemon using the command in *step 8*. The metrics exported by the Postgres exporter can be seen using `curl`. *Step 9* includes the `curl` command; however, we need to replace it with the appropriate IP address of the Postgres node.

Adding metrics exposed by postgres_exporter to Prometheus

Now that we have started `postgres_exporter` on the Postgres server, we should tell Prometheus to collect the metrics and store them on the Prometheus database in regular intervals (defaults to 15 seconds). In this recipe, we shall see how the metrics being exposed by the Postgres exporter are collected by Prometheus on the monitoring server.

Getting ready

In order to add a collection of metrics, `postgres_exporter` must be started in the Postgres server. Additionally, the port on which the metrics are being exposed must be open for the Prometheus server. Else, the metrics cannot be stored or collected in regular intervals by Prometheus.

How to do it...

We will collect and store the metrics as follows:

1. Add the Postgres server and the port used by `postgres_exporter` as a target to the `prometheus.yml` file:

```
- targets: ['192.168.29.20:9187']
```

`scrape_configs`, after adding `node_exporter` and `postgres_exporter`, looks like the following:

```
scrape_configs:
  # The job name is added as a label `job=<job_name>` to any
timeseries scraped from this config.
  - job_name: 'prometheus'
# metrics_path defaults to '/metrics'
  # scheme defaults to 'http'.
static_configs:
  - targets: ['192.168.29.20:9100']
  - targets: ['192.168.29.20:9187']
```

2. Reload using `SIGHUP` or restart Prometheus:

```
$ kill -HUP <pid>

Or

$ sudo ~/prom/prometheus --config.file ~/prom/prometheus.yml --
storage.tsdb.path ~/prom/promdb --web.console.templates
~/prom/consoles --web.console.libraries ~/prom/console_libraries --
web.listen-address 192.168.29.10:9090 &
```

3. Validate the targets using the following URL on the browser:
   `http://192.168.29.10:9090/targets`:

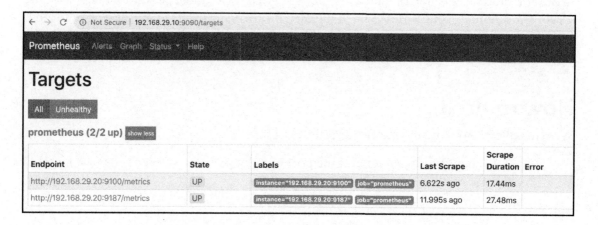

How it works...

In order to add the Postgres exporter metrics collection as a target to the Prometheus data source, we should add the target information such as the IP address of the Postgres server and the port using which the metrics are exposed. This information should be added under `scraper_configs` of the Prometheus configuration file, as seen in *step 1*. Once done, we can kill the Prometheus daemon and start it using the command mentioned in *step 2*. If you wish to avoid a restart, you can perform `SIGHUP` by substituting the PID with the Prometheus daemon's PID. Once *step 2* is completed, we can use the link seen in *step 3* to validate the targets in the browser. The IP address must be substituted with the IP address of the Prometheus server.

Importing a dashboard for monitoring Linux metrics

A dashboard in Grafana is used to plot several metrics as panels for a meaningful visualization. You may wish to observe the CPU and memory utilization trend for the past 2 hours and relate it to the trend of active connections in the past 2 hours. For such a visualization, we can use PromQL, which is a query language used to fetch time series data from Prometheus. This time series data will be used by Grafana to build visualizations.

There are many such dashboards that are built/contributed by users for both Linux and Postgres monitoring. These dashboards are available at https://grafana.com/grafana/dashboards.

In this recipe, we shall discuss how to import one of the most widely used dashboards for Linux metrics that works accurately for the metrics being collected by node_exporter.

Getting ready

In order to import the dashboards discussed in this recipe, you should have already set up monitoring of your PostgreSQL server using node_exporter. Grafana should be up and running on your monitoring server.

How to do it...

The dashboards that are imported using the following steps are the most popular ones for monitoring Linux metrics:

1. Identify the most downloaded and popular dashboard for Linux metrics exposed by node_exporter: https://grafana.com/grafana/dashboards/1860.

   Copy the dashboard ID. Here, it is 1860.

2. Now, go to your Grafana browser and click on **Import**, as seen in the following screenshot:

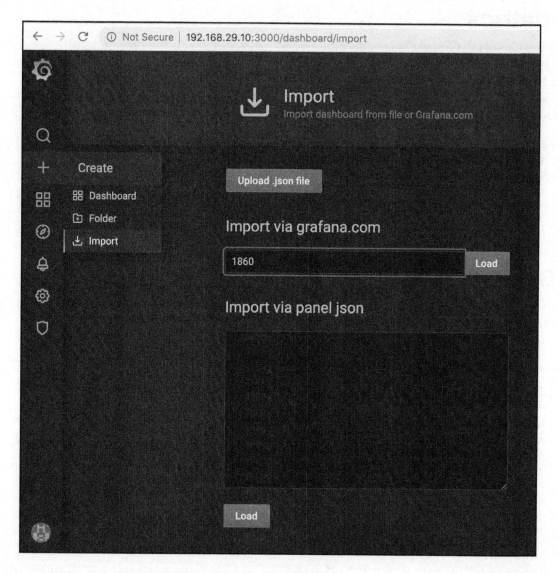

3. Click on **Load** to import the dashboard from the Grafana website:

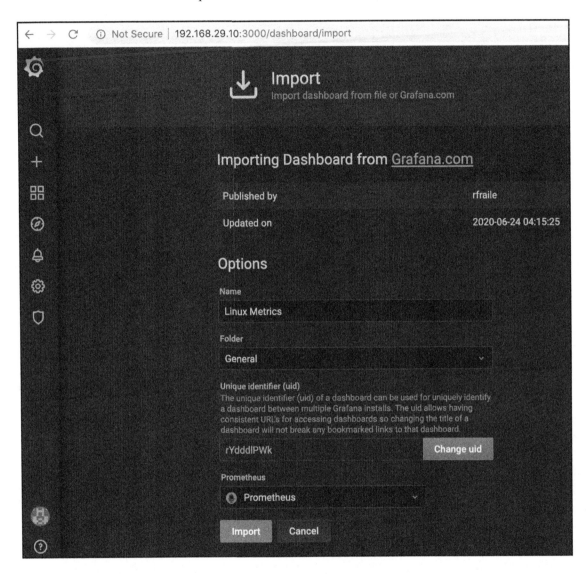

4. Observe the Linux metrics by connecting to the imported dashboard:

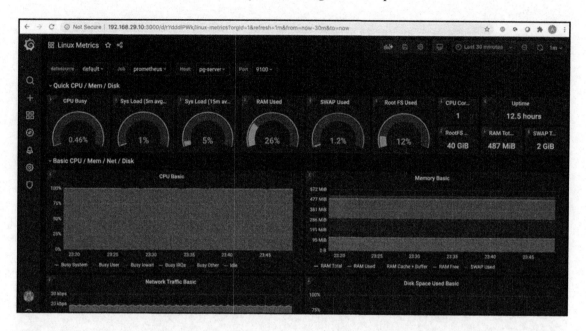

How it works...

When you search for a Node Exporter dashboard on `grafana.com`, the following is the most downloaded and popular with several interesting visualizations: `https://grafana.com/grafana/dashboards/1860`.

Import the dashboard to your Grafana server using just a couple of clicks, as seen in *step 2*. Once done, you could modify the name if you wish to give a different name to this dashboard. Then, choose the name of the Prometheus data source and click on **Import**. Once the dashboard has been imported, you should automatically see the Linux metrics for the Postgres server from where the metrics from `node_exporter` are collected, as seen in *step 4*.

How to import a dashboard for monitoring Postgres metrics

We discussed how to import a dashboard to display Linux metrics in the previous recipe. In this recipe, we shall discuss a popular PostgreSQL dashboard and see how it can be imported to your Grafana server.

Getting ready

In order to import the dashboard discussed in this recipe, you should have already set up monitoring of your PostgreSQL server using `postgres_exporter`. Grafana should be up and running on your monitoring server.

How to do it...

We will import the dashboard as follows:

1. Import a popular dashboard for Postgres built based on the default queries being used by the Postgres exporter: `https://grafana.com/grafana/dashboards/9628`.

2. We can import this dashboard and choose Prometheus as a data source:

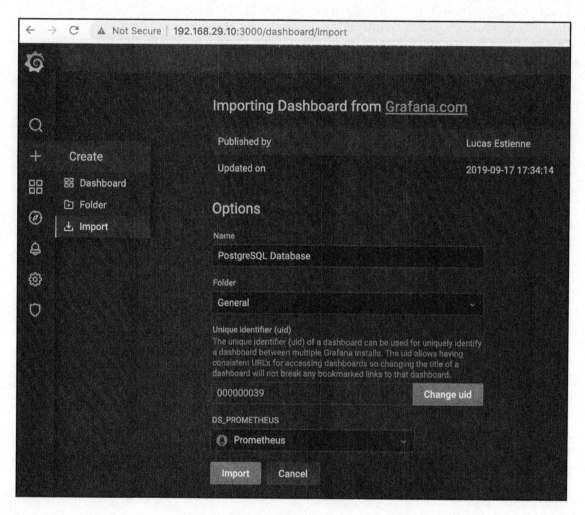

3. Once successfully imported, we will automatically see the metrics for the PostgreSQL server on the dashboard:

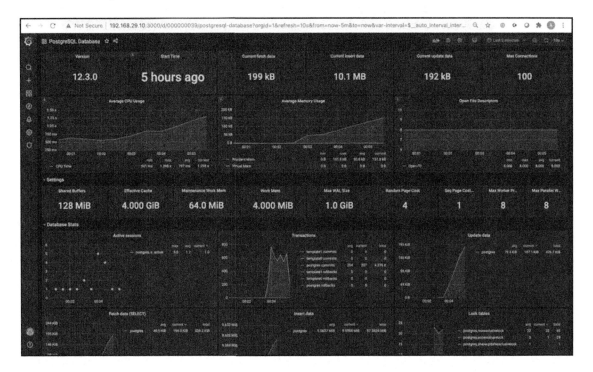

How it works...

The following is one of the popular dashboards available for visualizing PostgreSQL metrics fetched by
`postgres_exporter`: https://grafana.com/grafana/dashboards/9628.

Import this dashboard, `9628`, as seen in *step 2*. As seen in *step 3*, this dashboard visualizes several important metrics, such as connections, tuples information, locks, and transactions, which are already built for you to start with.

Adding custom queries to postgres_exporter

The queries that are run by `postgres_exporter` by default may not be sufficient for a user to visualize a lot of important metrics. For this purpose, we could always create custom queries and ask `postgres_exporter` to expose the output of the custom queries. We shall discuss how this can be achieved through this recipe.

Getting ready

In order to add custom queries to `postgres_exporter`, we should have already set up monitoring of the PostgreSQL server using `postgres_exporter`. Grafana should also be up and running on the monitoring server.

How to do it...

Prepare the list of custom queries and add it to the `custom_queries.yml` file:

1. Add your custom queries to a file as seen in the following example:

```
$ cat
/var/lib/pgsql/go/src/github.com/wrouesnel/postgres_exporter/custom
_queries.yaml

pg_database_age:
 query: "SELECT datname, age(datfrozenxid) age FROM pg_database"
 metrics:
 - datname:
 usage: "LABEL"
 description: "Name of the database"
 - age:
 usage: "COUNTER"
 description: "Age of database"

pg_stat_progress_vacuum:
 query: "SELECT current_database() datname, relid::regclass as
table, phase, heap_blks_total, heap_blks_scanned,
heap_blks_vacuumed, index_vacuum_count, max_dead_tuples,
num_dead_tuples FROM pg_stat_progress_vacuum"
 metrics:
 - datname:
 usage: "LABEL"
```

```
description: "Name of the database"
- table:
usage: "LABEL"
description: "Name or oid of the table"
- phase:
usage: "LABEL"
description: "Phase of the vacuum"
- heap_blks_total:
usage: "COUNTER"
description: "Total number of heap blocks"
- heap_blks_scanned:
usage: "COUNTER"
description: "Scanned heap blocks so far"
- heap_blks_vacuumed:
usage: "COUNTER"
description: "Heap blocks vacuumed"
- index_vacuum_count:
usage: "COUNTER"
description: "Number of completed index vacuum cycles."
- max_dead_tuples:
usage: "COUNTER"
description: "Number of dead tuples that we can store before
needing to perform an index vacuum cycle"
- num_dead_tuples:
usage: "COUNTER"
description: "Number of dead tuples collected since the last index
vacuum cycle."

pg_tables_info:
 query: "select current_database() datname, pn.nspname as
schema_name, pc.relname as table_name, age(pc.relfrozenxid) as
xid_age,(pg_table_size(pc.oid)) as table_size,
pt.seq_scan,pt.idx_scan, pt.n_tup_ins,pt.n_tup_upd,pt.n_tup_del,
pt.n_live_tup,pt.n_dead_tup,pt.vacuum_count,pt.autovacuum_count,pt.
analyze_count,pt.autoanalyze_count FROM pg_class pc JOIN
pg_namespace pn ON pn.oid = pc.relnamespace JOIN
pg_stat_user_tables pt ON pc.oid = pt.relid where pc.relkind = 'r'"
 metrics:
 - datname:
usage: "LABEL"
description: "Name of the database"
- schema_name:
usage: "LABEL"
description: "Name of the schema"
- table_name:
usage: "LABEL"
description: "Name of the schema"
- xid_age:
```

```
usage: "COUNTER"
description: "Age of the table"
- table_size:
usage: "COUNTER"
description: "Size of the table"
- seq_scan:
usage: "COUNTER"
description: "Number of sequence scans of this table"
- idx_scan:
usage: "COUNTER"
description: "Number of index scans of this table"
- n_tup_ins:
usage: "COUNTER"
description: "Number of inserts to this table"
- n_tup_upd:
usage: "COUNTER"
description: "Number of updates on this table"
- n_tup_del:
usage: "COUNTER"
description: "Number of deletes on this table"
- n_live_tup:
usage: "COUNTER"
description: "Number of live tupes in this table"
- n_dead_tup:
usage: "COUNTER"
description: "Number of dead tupes in this table"
- vacuum_count:
usage: "COUNTER"
description: "Number of manual vacuumes on this table"
- autovacuum_count:
usage: "COUNTER"
description: "Number of automatic vacuumes on this table"
- analyze_count:
usage: "COUNTER"
description: "Number of manual analyzes on this table"
- autoanalyze_count:
usage: "COUNTER"
description: "Number of automatic analyzes on this table"
```

2. Start the exporter along with the custom queries:

```
$ export
DATA_SOURCE_NAME="postgresql://postgres:secret@192.168.29.20:5432/p
ostgres"
$ cd /var/lib/pgsql/go/src/github.com/wrouesnel/postgres_exporter
$./postgres_exporter --extend.query-
path=/var/lib/pgsql/go/src/github.com/wrouesnel/postgres_exporter/c
ustom_queries.yaml &
```

How it works...

The default queries used by `postgres_exporter` may not be sufficient to expose several metrics. For example, we may wish to monitor the age of a database or a table so that we can be predictive and proactive about transaction ID wraparound. Similarly, we may want to look into the dead tuples and live tuples information and see whether the tables are being vacuumed. For this purpose, we could some custom queries and ask `postgres_exporter` to also include metrics for these custom queries.

Hence, we could add all the queries using the syntax seen in *step 1* to `custom_queries.yml`, as seen in *step 1*. Once added, we could use the steps as seen in *step 2* to start `postgres_exporter` by adding an additional parameter, `--extend.query-path`, which should be given the filename and path to the custom queries file. Please remember to replace the connection string passed to the `DATA_SOURCE_NAME` variable with the appropriate values that suit your environment.

10
Extensions and Performance Tuning

This chapter is one of the most relevant chapters for admins in terms of their day-to-day lives. Here we will learn what extensions are and examine some of the most commonly used extensions for routine maintenance activities. We will also learn about the concept of using EXPLAIN in PostgreSQL for performance tuning and how to read an execution plan to identify a problematic area in a tree. We will then proceed to learn how to build caches using pg_prewarm. By the end of this chapter, you will be familiar with many great extensions in PostgreSQL and will be confident in managing maintenance activities and the performance tuning of a PostgreSQL cluster.

We will discuss some of the extensions that are helpful in many of the more important activities performed by an administrator or developer.

The following are the recipes that are covered in this chapter:

- Installing and creating pg_repack to rebuild objects online
- Rebuilding a table online using pg_repack
- Rebuilding indexes of a table online using pg_repack
- Moving a table or an index to another tablespace online
- Warming up the cache using pg_prewarm
- Tuning a function or a stored procedure using plprofiler
- Capturing statements that require tuning using pg_stat_statements
- Viewing execution plans using EXPLAIN in PostgreSQL

Technical requirements

For this chapter, you must have a PostgreSQL server with at least two CPUs and 2 GB RAM and access to download RPMs over the internet from the PGDG repository and from GitHub.

Installing and creating pg_repack to rebuild objects online

We discussed in Chapter 1, *Cluster Management Fundamentals*, that there is no separate UNDO storage in PostgreSQL. PostgreSQL stores UNDO records as multiple versions within the same table. UNDO records or dead tuples may be cleaned by autovacuum or manual vacuum, but space may not be reclaimed by the operating system unless the empty pages are at the end of the heap.

Untuned vacuum settings may lead to further damage. For example, a query may have to scan 100 pages instead of 10 pages due to bloat. In this case, the only choice we are left with is to rebuild the table. This can be performed using VACUUM FULL; however, it would put an exclusive lock on the table and does not allow reads and writes on the table. You may always want to avoid this in a production database. For this reason, we have an extension named `pg_repack`, which can do a great job in performing an online rebuild of database objects such as tables and indexes.

`pg_repack` (`https://github.com/reorg/pg_repack`) is an open-source extension that can be helpful for administrators or developers in performing various activities such as the following:

- Rebuilding a table online (online VACUUM FULL)
- Rebuilding the index(es) of a table online
- Relocating a table or an index to another tablespace online
- Online CLUSTER of a table (ordered by a cluster index)

In this recipe, we will discuss the steps involved in installing and creating `pg_repack` as an extension.

Getting ready

In order to use `pg_repack` for the online rebuild of a table, the table must have a primary key or a unique total index (but not a functional index) on a `NOT NULL` column.

The RPM and `deb` for `pg_repack` are available in the PGDG repository and the packages are specific to each PostgreSQL release.

How to do it...

In the following two sections, we shall see the steps required to install `pg_repack` on both CentOS and Ubuntu.

Installing pg_repack on CentOS

We install `pg_repack` on CentOS as follows:

1. Install the PGDG repository, if it does not exist already:

   ```
   $ sudo yum install -y
   https://download.postgresql.org/pub/repos/yum/reporpms/EL-7-x86_64/
   pgdg-redhat-repo-latest.noarch.rpm
   ```

   Visit the following link to find the RPM that suits your Linux distribution:

   ```
   https://www.postgresql.org/download/linux/redhat/
   ```

2. Install `pg_repack` using YUM:

   ```
   $ sudo yum install pg_repack13
   ```

3. Verify the installation using the `version` and `help` options (you should not get any errors):

   ```
   $ pg_repack --version
   $ pg_repack --help
   ```

Installing pg_repack on Ubuntu

We install `pg_repack` on Ubuntu as follows:

1. Install the PGDG repository, if it does not exist already, using the following commands:

   ```
   # The following command would create the repository file
   configuration.
   $ sudo sh -c 'echo "deb http://apt.postgresql.org/pub/repos/apt
   $(lsb_release -cs)-pgdg main" > /etc/apt/sources.list.d/pgdg.list'

   # We could then import the repository signing key and perform an
   apt-get update.
   $ wget --quiet -O -
   https://www.postgresql.org/media/keys/ACCC4CF8.asc | sudo apt-key
   add -
   $ sudo apt-get update
   ```

2. Install `pg_repack` using `apt`:

   ```
   $ apt install postgresql-13-repack
   ```

3. Verify the installation using the `version` and `help` options (you should not get any errors). You may have to use the full path to PostgreSQL binaries, if `PATH` has not been set:

   ```
   $ pg_repack --version
   $ pg_repack --help
   ```

How it works...

This recipe targeted both CentOS/RedHat and Ubuntu/Debian distributions. As such, it was divided into two sections. The first section gave the steps involved in installing `pg_repack` on CentOS and the second one gave the steps for Ubuntu.

To install `pg_repack` on CentOS using `rpm` or Ubuntu using `deb`, we can download and install the latest package from the PGDG repository. *Step 1* in each section showed how to set up the PGDG repository for PostgreSQL 13. Once the PGDG repository is set up, we can use YUM or APT to install `pg_repack` as seen in *Step 2* for both of the sections. Note that the name of the package differs between CentOS and Ubuntu. On CentOS, we install the `pg_repack13` package, while on Ubuntu it's `postgresql-13-repack`.

Once the installation is complete, we can validate the installation using the `version` and `help` command-line options, as seen in *Step 3*. Both commands should return their output successfully.

How to rebuild a table online using pg_repack

In the previous recipe, we saw how `pg_repack` can be installed as an extension. `pg_repack` can be used to perform an online VACUUM FULL of a table. This feature is useful in a production environment where downtime is unacceptable. In this recipe, we will discuss how `pg_repack` can be used to rebuild a table online and look at the steps for using parallelism to finish the rebuild faster.

Getting ready

To use `pg_repack`, this extension must be installed and created in the database to which the table belongs:

```
$ psql -d percdb -c "CREATE EXTENSION pg_repack"
```

The table being rebuilt must have a primary key or a unique index on a NOT NULL column.

> It is always recommended to have a valid full backup, as it's helpful for point-in-time recovery, before performing any maintenance on a database server.

How to do it...

The following are the steps required to rebuild a table online using `pg_repack`:

1. Use `--dry-run` to verify whether the table can be rebuilt using `pg_repack`:

    ```
    $ pg_repack --dry-run -d database_name --table schemaname.tablename
    Output :
    $ pg_repack --dry-run -d percdb --table public.pgbench_accounts
    INFO: Dry run enabled, not executing repack
    INFO: repacking table "public.pgbench_accounts"
    ```

2. Once the dry run is found to be successful, perform `pg_repack` on the table:

```
$ pg_repack -d percdb --table public.pgbench_accounts
Output :
INFO: repacking table "public.pgbench_accounts"
```

3. To run `pg_repack` using parallel processes, use `-j`. The following syntax uses four parallel processes:

```
$ pg_repack -d percdb -j 4 --table public.pgbench_accounts
Output :
NOTICE: Setting up workers.conns
INFO: repacking table "public.pgbench_accounts"
```

How it works...

To rebuild a table online, the prerequisite is that the `pg_repack` extension must be created in the database that contains the table in question. Once it is created, we can perform a dry run to see whether the table is valid for an online rebuild by `pg_repack` using the command seen in *Step 1*. If the dry run is successful, we can run `pg_repack` using just one process, as seen in *Step 2*, or by using multiple processes in parallel using the command in *Step 3* for a faster rebuild. Use as many parallel processes as you like, but make sure to see whether there are many CPUs that are idle in your production server.

How to rebuild indexes of a table online using pg_repack

An index in PostgreSQL may become very bloated if there is no proper vacuuming or regular index maintenance. An index can be created online using the `CONCURRENTLY` option. However, switching the index to its original name or rebuilding a primary key index or a unique index may need to be done with some additional care. All of this can be made easy using `pg_repack`. In this recipe, we shall discuss how an index of all the indexes of a table can be rebuilt online using `pg_repack`.

Getting ready

There are currently no restrictions on what indexes can or cannot be rebuilt. However, it is important to test using a dry run before repacking a specific index or all the indexes of a table using `pg_repack`.

How to do it...

In the following sections, we shall see how to rebuild all the indexes of a table and how to rebuild a specific index of a table.

Rebuilding all the indexes of a table

Let's get started with the following steps:

1. The `-x` parameter is used to rebuild all the indexes of a table. Perform a dry run for validation:

```
$ pg_repack --dry-run -d migops -t public.emp -x
 INFO: Dry run enabled, not executing repack
 INFO: repacking indexes of "public.emp"
 INFO: repacking index "public.idx_1"
 INFO: repacking index "public.idx_2"
 INFO: repacking index "public.idx_3"
 INFO: repacking index "public.idx_4"
```

2. Remove `--dry-run` to perform the indexes rebuild using the following command:

```
$ pg_repack -d migops -t public.emp -x
Output :
 INFO: repacking indexes of "public.emp"
 INFO: repacking index "public.idx_1"
 INFO: repacking index "public.idx_2"
 INFO: repacking index "public.idx_3"
 INFO: repacking index "public.idx_4"
```

Rebuilding a specific index

Let's get started with the following steps:

To rebuild a specific index, use the -i parameter. Specify the index you wish to rebuild using -i. Before proceeding with the rebuild, perform a dry run as seen in the following command:

```
$ pg_repack --dry-run -d migops -i public.pgbench_accounts_pkey
Output :
 INFO: Dry run enabled, not executing repack
 INFO: repacking index "public.pgbench_accounts_pkey"


Once the dry run is successful, we can proceed to perform the index
rebuild using the following command as an example:

$ pg_repack -d migops -i public.pgbench_accounts_pkey
Output :
INFO: repacking index "public.pgbench_accounts_pkey"
```

How it works...

It is very easy to rebuild an index or all the indexes of a table using pg_repack. Here we have seen two demonstrations of this. As seen in the first section, we can rebuild all the indexes of a table by specifying the -x parameter and the name of the table using --table or -t. To rebuild a specific index, we need not pass the table name but just the name of the index, along with the schema prefix, as seen in *Step 1* of the second section. It is always recommended to perform a dry run before performing a rebuild, as seen in *Step 1* of both sections.

Moving a table or an index to another tablespace online

Over a period of time, a table or database may grow to be huge in size. The disk that contains the data directory may become saturated with IOPS. For this reason, we want to scatter selected tables or indexes across different tablespaces on another disk. While this can be done using ALTER TABLE, it is not an online operation. So, we can use pg_repack to move a table or an index online to another tablespace. In this recipe, we will discuss how this can be done in simple steps.

Getting ready

To move a table or an index to another tablespace online using `pg_repack`, we need the `pg_repack` extension created in the database that contains the table or the index. A table cannot be moved online if the table does not have a primary key or a not-null unique key. The target tablespace must be created in advance. `pg_repack` will not create the tablespace.

Create the target tablespace manually, if it does not exist already:

```
$ sudo mkdir -p /tblspc_dir/new_tblspc
$ sudo chown -R postgres:postgres /tblspc_dir/new_tblspc
$ sudo chmod -R 700 /tblspc_dir/new_tblspc
$ psql -c "CREATE TABLESPACE new_tblspc LOCATION '/tblspc_dir/new_tblspc'"
```

How to do it...

Follow these steps:

1. Use the following commands to perform a dry run and then move a table to another tablespace online using `pg_repack`:

   ```
   $ pg_repack --dry-run -d migops -t public.pgbench_accounts --
   tablespace=new_tblspc
    Output :
    INFO: Dry run enabled, not executing repack
    INFO: repacking table "public.pgbench_accounts"
   ```

Use the following command to move just the table but not its indexes to a new tablespace:

```
$ pg_repack -d migops -t public.pgbench_accounts --
tablespace=new_tblspc
 Output :
 INFO: repacking table "public.pgbench_accounts"
```

Use the following command to move the table along with its indexes to the new tablespace:

```
$ pg_repack -d migops -t public.pgbench_accounts -S --
tablespace=new_tblspc
 Output :
 INFO: repacking table "public.pgbench_accounts"
```

2. Use the following commands to move an index online to another tablespace:

```
$ pg_repack --dry-run -d migops -i public.idx_1 --
tablespace=new_tblspc
 Output :
 INFO: Dry run enabled, not executing repack
 INFO: repacking index "public.idx_1"

$ pg_repack -d migops -i public.idx_1 --tablespace=new_tblspc
 Output :
 INFO: repacking index "public.idx_1"
```

How it works...

We could use the `--tablespace` flag or `-s` to specify the tablespace to which a table or an index has to move online. As seen in *Step 1*, upon performing a dry run, the table is moved to another tablespace online. However, the indexes of the table are not moved to the tablespace unless we specify the `-s` option to move the table along with its indexes to the new tablespace.

In the second step, we see that an index can be easily moved to another tablespace online by specifying the index name to `-i` and the tablespace name to `--tablespace`.

Warming up the cache using pg_prewarm

Upon the restart of a database cluster, it may take some time to load the whole of the cache into the PostgreSQL buffer cache or the OS buffer cache. Sometimes, we may wish to load certain tables into the cache on-demand before performing some special reporting tasks. To help cache a table or a specific set of pages to either the OS cache or the database buffer cache (shared buffers), there exists an extension called `pg_prewarm`.

`pg_prewarm` is a function that can take five arguments:

```
pg_prewarm(regclass, mode text default 'buffer', fork text default 'main',
  first_block int8 default null, last_block int8 default null) RETURNS int8
```

Let's discuss each of these arguments in detail:

- `regclass`: Fully qualified table name (`schemaname.tablename`).
- `mode`: You can choose any of the three prewarming methods:
    - `prefetch`: Asynchronous prefetch requests to the OS. Cached in the OS.
    - `read`: Synchronous prefetch. Cached in the OS.
    - `buffer`: Reads the pages into `shared_buffers`. Default.
- `fork`: The relation fork to be prewarmed. The default is `main`. Can take `main`, `fsm`, and `vm` as values.
- `first_block`: The number of the first block to prewarm. The default is `NULL`, which means the 0th block.
- `last_block`: The number of the last block prewarm. The default is `NULL`, which means the last block.

If the number of blocks being fetched does not fit in the desired cache, then blocks with lower numbers may be evicted.

In this recipe, we shall discuss how `pg_prewarm` can be used to warm up the cache in a PostgreSQL server.

Getting ready

`pg_prewarm` is an extension that is available with the `contrib` module. So, you require the `postgresql-contrib-13` package on Ubuntu or the `postgresql13-contrib` package on CentOS/Red Hat to install this extension.

How to do it...

Let's get started with the following steps:

1. Create the extension in the database that contains the table to be cached:

```
$ psql -d migops -c "CREATE EXTENSION pg_prewarm"
```

2. Prewarm the `public.pgbench_accounts` table using `pg_prewarm`:

```
$ psql -d migops -c "select pg_prewarm('public.pgbench_accounts')"
Output :
pg_prewarm
```

```
------------
16394
(1 row)
```

3. Upon a restart, if you wish to have the cache automatically warmed up to the same state at the time of shutdown, include `pg_prewarm` in `shared_preload_libraries`. Otherwise, proceed to *Step 2*:

```
$ psql -c "ALTER SYSTEM SET shared_preload_libraries TO pg_prewarm"

-- Changes to shared_preload_libraries requires a restart of the
PostgreSQL cluster
$ pg_ctl -D $PGDATA restart -mf
```

4. Check whether the `autoprewarm.blocks` file exists in the data directory when `pg_prewarm` is added to `shared_preload_libraries`. Now, `$PGDATA` should be replaced with the full path to the data directory if the `PGDATA` environment variable is not set:

```
$ ls -alrth $PGDATA/autoprewarm.blocks
-rw-------. 1 postgres postgres 5.2K Aug 24 03:08
/var/lib/pgsql/12/data/autoprewarm.blocks
```

A background worker is started to dump the contents of shared buffers to the `autoprewarm.blocks` file every `pg_prewarm.autoprewarm_interval` seconds:

```
migops=# select name, setting from pg_settings where name like
'pg_prewarm%';
name | setting
---------------------------------+---------
pg_prewarm.autoprewarm | on
pg_prewarm.autoprewarm_interval | 300
(2 rows)

$ ps -eaf | grep prewarm
 postgres 5637 5629 0 02:58 ? 00:00:00 postgres: autoprewarm master
```

How it works...

`pg_prewarm` can be used to manually warm up the cache or you can let it happen automatically. In the first two steps, we saw how the `pg_prewarm` extension can be created in the database and how a table can be cached manually. If we wish to let PostgreSQL dump the contents of the shared buffers to warm up the cache automatically upon a crash or a restart, we could load `pg_prewarm` to `shared_preload_libraries` as seen in *Step 3*. In this case, some background work, as seen in *Step 4's* output, is started to dump the contents of shared buffers to a file called `autoprewarm.blocks`. There are two parameters, as seen in *Step 4*, that can be used to modify the frequency and the behavior of `autoprewarm`.

How to tune a function or a stored procedure using plprofiler

`plprofiler` is an extension or a tool that can be extensively used to profile functions in PostgreSQL. When enabled as an extension, profile data can be collected for all the PL/pgSQL code being executed in a database (on-demand but not automatically). This profile data is stored within internal hash tables and it can be presented in an HTML report using an external tool.

There are two modes in which `plprofiler` can operate :

- **Session level**: During the migration of an Oracle database or a different database to PostgreSQL or while developing a new application functionality through a function, a developer may wish to see the time consumed for every line of code. This helps the developer to tune time-consuming queries or tune conditional logic that may be causing a delay in the function execution. For this reason, we can enable `plprofiler` at the session level and execute the function. This may also be referred to as `local-data`.
- **Global level**: If a developer or an admin wants to capture the profile data of every function being executed globally, then global-level profiling is needed. An HTML report can be generated to show the time consumed for every line of code for each of the functions executed globally within the monitored duration.

In this recipe, we shall see how `plprofiler` can be built from source code and how to use `plprofiler`.

Getting ready

PostgreSQL `devel` packages are needed to build this extension. `postgresql-server` and `contrib` modules are a must to proceed with installing `plprofiler`.

In order to install the pre-requisites on CentOS/Red Hat OSes, do the following:

```
$(root) yum install postgresql13-server postgresql13-devel postgresql13-
contrib -y
```

In order to install the pre-requisites on Ubuntu/Debian, we can do the following:

```
$ sudo apt install postgresql-13 postgresql-13-contrib postgresql-server-
dev-13 -y
```

How to do it...

This setup has been tested on CentOS 7.8. It should work for Ubuntu/Debian, with a few modifications:

1. Install the dependencies to enable the successful installation of `plprofiler`:

```
# yum install epel-release
# yum install centos-release-scl
# yum install llvm-toolset-7 llvm-toolset-7-llvm-devel.x86_64
```

2. Install all the dependencies required to compile `plprofiler`. As this is developed using Python, we shall also use `virtualenv`:

```
# yum install git make gcc unzip -y
# yum install python36 -y
# yum install python3-setuptools -y
# yum install python3-devel
# yum install python3-psycopg2
# yum install pip3 -y
# pip3 install virtualenv
```

3. Create a virtual environment to install `plprofiler` in the project-specific directory:

```
# mkdir -p /projects
# cd /projects
# virtualenv -p /usr/bin/python3.6 pg-tuning-packages
# source pg-tuning-packages/bin/activate
```

4. Download and compile `plprofiler`. Make sure to set the path for the Postgres binaries, for a successful installation:

```
# curl -LO https://github.com/bigsql/plprofiler/archive/master.zip
# unzip master.zip
# cd plprofiler-master/
# export PATH=$PATH:/usr/pgsql-13/bin
# make USE_PGXS=1
# make USE_PGXS=1 install
```

5. To use `plprofiler` as a tool along with the extension, run the following commands:

```
# su - postgres
# cd /projects/plprofiler-master/python-plprofiler
# python3.6 ./setup.py install
# deactivate
```

6. To use `plprofiler` with `virtualenv`, as the `postgres` user, run the following code:

```
# su - postgres
$ source /projects/pg-tuning-packages/bin/activate
$ plprofiler --help
```

7. To enabled global-level profiling, we can add `plprofiler` to `shared_preload_libraries`. Changes to `shared_preload_libraries` require a restart of the PostgreSQL cluster:

```
migops=# alter system set shared_preload_libraries = 'plprofiler';
 ALTER SYSTEM
$ pg_ctl -D /data01/planning/pgdata restart -mf
```

After the restart, verify that `shared_preload_libraries` reflects the change:

```
migops=# show shared_preload_libraries ;
 shared_preload_libraries
--------------------------
 plprofiler
(1 row)
```

8. Create the `plprofiler` extension in the database. Whether we want to enable global profiling or enable profiling at the session level, the extension must be created:

```
$ psql -d migops -c "create extension plprofiler"
 CREATE EXTENSION
```

9. Perform session-level profiling:

```
$ plprofiler run --command "SELECT tpcb(1, 2, 3, -42)" -d migops --
output tpcb-test1.html
 SELECT tpcb(1, 2, 3, -42)
 -- row1:
 tpcb: -42
 ----
 (1 rows)
 SELECT 1 (0.103 seconds)
```

10. Perform global level profiling.

To perform global-level profiling, we need to run `plprofiler` in monitoring mode for some amount of time using a command similar to the following:

```
$ plprofiler monitor --interval=10 --duration=60
 Output :
 monitoring for 60 seconds ...
 Done.
```

Upon monitoring for some duration, generate a report using the following command:

```
$ plprofiler report --from-shared --title=globalreport --
output=globalreport.html
```

Reset to clear the shared data:

```
$ plprofiler reset
```

How it works...

`plprofiler` can be compiled by downloading the source code. In *Step 1*, we see the commands to install all the dependencies required to download and install `python3`, `pip3`, and `llvm-toolset`. As `plprofiler` is coded using Python, we download `python3` and `virtualenv` using the commands seen in *Step 2*. We can then create a directory and activate it as a virtual environment for Python using the commands in *Step 3*. Once `virtualenv` has been activated, we can download `plprofiler` and install it using `make` as seen in *Step 4*.

Once `plprofiler` is installed, to use it as an external tool, it is required to set up the relevant binaries using the commands as seen in *Step 5*. To enable global-level profiling, we need to set `shared_preload_libraries` to `plprofiler` as seen in *Step 7*. To run `plprofiler` for session- or global-level profiling, we need to create this extension in the database in which the function(s) exist. To perform session-level profiling as seen in *Step 9*, we use `plprofiler run` and pass the SQL to call the function along with the parameters. This would execute the function and generate an HTML report using the profile data recorded in the hash table. A sample report can be found here: `https://wi3ck.info/plprofiler/doc/pgbench_pl-1.html`. To generate a global-level report as seen in *Step 10*, we should first run `plprofiler monitor` for a certain duration and then generate an HTML report from the profile data collected for all the functions executed during that duration. After generating the report, the shared data can be cleared using `plprofiler reset`.

Capturing statements that require tuning using pg_stat_statements

`pg_stat_statements` is an extension that enables us to see the history of SQL statements. It is part of the `contrib` module of PostgreSQL and is thus maintained by the community. In this recipe, we shall see how this extension can be installed and created to identify statements that require some tuning.

Getting ready

`pg_stat_statements` is an extension that is available with the `contrib` module. So, it requires the `postgresql-contrib-13` package on Ubuntu or the `postgresql13-contrib` package on CentOS/Red Hat to be installed.

How to do it...

The following steps should be taken:

1. Use the following command to create the extension in the database that needs tuning:

```
$ psql -d migops -c "CREATE EXTENSION pg_stat_statements"
```

2. Set the `share_preload_libraries` parameter to `pg_stat_statements` using the following command. Please note that a change to `shared_preload_libraries` requires a restart of the PostgreSQL cluster:

```
$ psql -c "ALTER SYSTEM set shared_preload_libraries TO
'pg_stat_statements'"
$ pg_ctl -D $PGDATA restart -mf
-- $PGDATA should be replaced with the appropriate data directory
location.
```

3. To see the queries that were executed at least 100 times, in descending order of execution time, we can use a query similar to the following:

```
postgres=# select calls, mean_exec_time, queryid, left(query, 40)
as query from pg_stat_statements
GROUP BY mean_exec_time,calls,queryid,query HAVING calls > 100
order by 2 desc limit 10;
 calls | mean_exec_time     | queryid               | query
-------+--------------------+-----------------------+-----------------
------
 15941 | 1.334794684398714  | -6224314747997477127  | UPDATE
pgbench_branch...
  6001 | 1.239037665222464  | -7909585113310871855  | UPDATE
pgbench_branch...
 15941 | 0.1672410964180416 | 4804212536274291778   | UPDATE
pgbench_teller...
  6001 | 0.15521646092317987| -296633118547193233   | UPDATE
pgbench_teller...
 15941 | 0.03303627369675681| 632451467550463882    | UPDATE
pgbench_accoun...
  6001 | 0.0316717338776871 | 1690858130455747536   | UPDATE
pgbench_accoun...
 15941 | 0.012144884511636691| -976283352041681943  | SELECT
abalance FROM ...
  6001 | 0.010474805532411263| -4769616705320674240 | SELECT
abalance FROM ...
 15941 | 0.009531014616397975| -6268184721328331922 | INSERT INTO
pgbench_h...
  6001 | 0.008393281786368952| -5761632574197284407 | INSERT INTO
pgbench_h...
(10 rows)
```

How it works...

`pg_stat_statements` is one of the most widely used extensions. This extension exposes information about the number of times a query was executed and the average of the total execution time of the query. In addition to that, it also gives the number of blocks hit in memory versus the number of blocks fetched from disk and the amount of temporarily blocked read and write by a specific query. Starting from PostgreSQL 13, we can also see the time spent preparing an execution plan and the actual execution time of a query. We can also see how many times an execution plan was created for a query. This helps in understanding the need for prepared statements to reduce the number of times a query execution plan gets created.

In order to install this extension, we can use the command seen in *Step 1*. To ensure that the information is visible, we need to set `shared_preload_libraries` as seen in *Step 2*. This is because this extension has to access the shared memory. Once the PostgreSQL server is restarted as seen in *Step 2*, we can see the query performance metrics as seen in *Step 3*.

Viewing the execution plans using EXPLAIN in PostgreSQL

EXPLAIN in PostgreSQL can be used to print the execution plan considered by the PostgreSQL optimizer for a given query. However, to see the actual cost and time consumed by SQL, we must use EXPLAIN ANALYZE. In this recipe, we will discuss how EXPLAIN can be used to identify an area where a query needs to be optimized.

Getting ready

In order to run EXPLAIN, we need to have a SQL statement that has its bind variables substituted with the actual values. Otherwise, EXPLAIN returns an error. In addition to that, while running EXPLAIN ANALYZE, we must always avoid running it on a SQL statement that is performing a DML or a DDL. This is because it executes the statement and prints the execution plan and actual cost information. In emergency situations, we may carefully open a transaction and run EXPLAIN ANALYZE on a statement and roll it back immediately.

How to do it...

EXPLAIN is available in PostgreSQL by default. The following are steps required to run EXPLAIN or EXPLAIN ANALYZE in PostgreSQL:

1. To generate the execution plan chosen by the optimizer, we must use EXPLAIN before the SQL statement as seen in the following command. We can see the output printed by the command:

```
migops=# EXPLAIN DELETE FROM t1 WHERE id IN (select dept from t2
where id between 1 and 100);
                              QUERY PLAN
-----------------------------------------------------------------------
------
 Delete on t1 (cost=20406.01..38437.02 rows=1 width=12)
   -> Hash Semi Join (cost=20406.01..38437.02 rows=1 width=12)
         Hash Cond: (t1.id = t2.dept)
         -> Seq Scan on t1 (cost=0.00..15406.00 rows=1000000
width=10)
         -> Hash (cost=20406.00..20406.00 rows=1 width=10)
               -> Seq Scan on t2 (cost=0.00..20406.00 rows=1
width=10)
                     Filter: ((id >= 1) AND (id <= 100))
```

2. The preceding command does not print the actual time consumed by the query in reality. For this reason, we may use EXPLAIN ANALYZE as seen in the following command:

```
migops=# BEGIN;
BEGIN
migops=*# EXPLAIN (ANALYZE, TIMING, COSTS, BUFFERS, VERBOSE) DELETE
FROM t1 WHERE id IN (select dept from t2 where id between 1 and
100);
                                                              QUERY
PLAN
-----------------------------------------------------------------------
---------
 Delete on public.t1 (cost=20406.01..38437.02 rows=1 width=12)
(actual time=1555.248..1555.257 rows=0 loops=1)
   Buffers: shared hit=11009 dirtied=95
   -> Hash Semi Join (cost=20406.01..38437.02 rows=1 width=12)
(actual time=70.796..1554.670 rows=100 loops=1)
         Output: t1.ctid, t2.ctid
         Hash Cond: (t1.id = t2.dept)
         Buffers: shared hit=10815
         -> Seq Scan on public.t1 (cost=0.00..15406.00 rows=1000000
width=10) (actual time=0.018..762.057 rows=1000000 loops=1
```

```
)
                        Output: t1.ctid, t1.id
                        Buffers: shared hit=5406
              -> Hash (cost=20406.00..20406.00 rows=1 width=10) (actual
time=65.417..65.420 rows=100 loops=1)
                        Output: t2.ctid, t2.dept
                        Buckets: 1024 Batches: 1 Memory Usage: 13kB
                        Buffers: shared hit=5406
                        -> Seq Scan on public.t2 (cost=0.00..20406.00 rows=1
width=10) (actual time=0.009..65.330 rows=100 loops=1)
                            Output: t2.ctid, t2.dept
                            Filter: ((t2.id >= 1) AND (t2.id <= 100))
                            Rows Removed by Filter: 999900
                            Buffers: shared hit=5406
 Planning Time: 0.123 ms
 Execution Time: 1555.292 ms
(20 rows)

migops=*# ROLLBACK ;
ROLLBACK
```

From the output of the preceding command, we can see that the query spends 0.123 ms preparing an execution plan and takes 1555.292 ms to actually execute the query. To make sure that we don't delete the records in reality, we can open a transaction block and roll it back after running EXPLAIN ANALYZE. This must be done carefully. Such an approach is never recommended in a production environment unless we are sure of what we are doing.

3. As seen in the following commands, we must either perform a re-write of the poorly performing SQL or optimize it with an index and validate it:

```
migops=# CREATE INDEX t1_idx ON t1 (id);
CREATE INDEX
migops=# CREATE INDEX t2_idx ON t2 (id);
CREATE INDEX

migops=# BEGIN ;
BEGIN
migops=*# EXPLAIN (ANALYZE, TIMING, COSTS, BUFFERS, VERBOSE) DELETE
FROM t1 WHERE id IN (select dept from t2 where id between 1 and
100);
QUERY PLAN
-------------------------------------------------------------
---------
 Delete on public.t1 (cost=11.21..891.35 rows=105 width=12) (actual
time=2.293..2.301 rows=0 loops=1)
    Buffers: shared hit=420 read=84
```

```
        -> Nested Loop (cost=11.21..891.35 rows=105 width=12) (actual
time=0.258..2.130 rows=100 loops=1)
          Output: t1.ctid, t2.ctid
          Buffers: shared hit=320 read=84
          -> HashAggregate (cost=10.79..11.84 rows=105 width=10)
(actual time=0.226..0.311 rows=100 loops=1)
              Output: t2.ctid, t2.dept
              Group Key: t2.dept
              Batches: 1 Memory Usage: 24kB
              Buffers: shared hit=4
              -> Index Scan using t2_idx on public.t2
(cost=0.42..10.53 rows=105 width=10) (actual time=0.016..0.098
rows=100
 loops=1)
                  Output: t2.ctid, t2.dept
                  Index Cond: ((t2.id >= 1) AND (t2.id <= 100))
                  Buffers: shared hit=4
          -> Index Scan using t1_idx on public.t1 (cost=0.42..8.37
rows=1 width=10) (actual time=0.014..0.015 rows=1 loops=100)
              Output: t1.ctid, t1.id
              Index Cond: (t1.id = t2.dept)
              Buffers: shared hit=316 read=84
  Planning:
    Buffers: shared hit=36 read=8
  Planning Time: 0.426 ms
  Execution Time: 2.360 ms
(22 rows)

migops=*# ROLLBACK ;
ROLLBACK
```

As we can see from the preceding output, after we created the two indexes on the appropriate columns, the query execution time decreased from 1555.292 ms to 2.360 ms.

How it works...

EXPLAIN in PostgreSQL is a very powerful tool. It helps in analyzing the plan node where the cost is high. If the output of EXPLAIN is not sufficient, we may generate the actuals using EXPLAIN ANALYZE. As seen in *Step 1*, we can use a simple EXPLAIN on a DML statement without too much thought. However, when we need to run EXPLAIN ANALYZE, we must use a transaction block so that the statement can be rolled back, as seen in *Step 2*. This must be done carefully. Once we find the node at which the query is spending more time, we may optimize it using a query rewrite or an index, similar to what we see in *Step 3*.

11
Upgrades and Patches

PostgreSQL is a database software that can be installed on various types of operating systems. The operating system and database software are further deployed on hardware such as a server, a virtual machine, or a user's computer.

There were days when PostgreSQL ran on old-school hard disks that were considered to be slow for random page fetches (index scans). Now, the assumption of an optimizer that index scans are costly may change if we are using SSDs for database servers. Additionally, an increase in the hardware capacity also gives a lot of room for new features and parallel processing in database software such as PostgreSQL. Any such modifications to the database software will be made available through new releases.

Over a period of time, upon the usage of several features that have been incorporated into a database software, users may discover new bugs or security vulnerabilities. Fixes to such bugs are incorporated as patches, which are released as part of immediate minor releases.

So, we need to perform upgrades or updates to a database software to do the following:

- Fix newly discovered security vulnerabilities in an operating system or database software.
- Apply patches to bugs identified by users.
- Incorporate new features to improve either performance or user experience.
- Implement missing features or ones commonly demanded by users.

One of the major challenges during an upgrade is downtime. While some methods enable faster database upgrades, those methods may not enable possibilities for cleaning up bloat/fragmentation while performing the upgrade.

Technical requirements

For this chapter, you must have a PostgreSQL server with at least two CPUs and 2 GB RAM and access to download RPMs over the internet from the PGDG repository and from GitHub.

Finding the difference between a major and minor release in PostgreSQL

It is very common to hear the term major or minor version upgrade in Postgres.

Up to the major PostgreSQL version 9.6, the first two digits of the version number are considered the major version. Starting from PostgreSQL 10, the first digit of the version number is termed as the major version. Similarly, the third digit of the version number is considered as the minor version until 9.6, while the second digit is considered as the minor version starting from PostgreSQL 10.

For example, if the PostgreSQL version is 9.6.5, 9.6 is the major version and 5 is the minor version number. If the version of PostgreSQL is 13.2, 13 is the major version and 2 is the minor version of major version 13. Thus, PostgreSQL 10.x, 11.x, 12.x, and 13.x are considered to be the major versions of PostgreSQL.

A minor release (or version) in PostgreSQL usually includes patches for bugs, fixes to security vulnerabilities, or improvements to the existing features. A major release may include new features that have never been implemented before or may include major enhancements to the already-existing features.

Performing a minor version upgrade would usually require a restart of the database or the server upon installing or updating the binaries. But a major version upgrade requires you to dump and restore the whole database to a different data directory that has been initialized using the binaries of the newer major version or by using `pg_upgrade`. This could require more downtime or man-hours than a minor version upgrade.

What is an obsolete version?

The PostgreSQL community continues to release minor versions that include bug fixes to the major version or the last minor version of a supported major version. A major version is supported by the PostgreSQL Global Development Group for just 5 years after its initial release, and then it is termed **EOL (end-of-life)**. While writing this book, the supported major versions of PostgreSQL for minor releases are 9.5 and later. So, PostgreSQL 9.4 and older are considered obsolete and are no longer supported by the community at this time. These details are available on the official PostgreSQL documentation at https://www.postgresql.org/support/versioning/.

Thus, it is always recommended to upgrade to the latest PostgreSQL major version upon performance and functional testing. However, upgrading major and minor releases may require some downtime. While minor version upgrades are straightforward, major upgrades may be challenging. In this chapter, we shall discuss some recipes that illustrate several methods available for performing major and minor version upgrades with huge as well as minimal downtime.

The following are the recipes discussed in this chapter:

- Major version upgrade to PostgreSQL 13 using pg_dumpall
- Major version upgrade to PostgreSQL 13 using pg_dump and pg_restore
- Major version upgrade to PostgreSQL 13 using pg_upgrade with downtime
- Major version upgrade to PostgreSQL 13 using pg_upgrade with hard links for seamless downtime
- Installing the pglogical extension to upgrade older versions to PostgreSQL 13
- Upgrading to PostgreSQL 13 using the pglogical extension to avoid downtime
- Upgrading to PostgreSQL 13 using logical replication and logical decoding
- Updating the minor version of PostgreSQL 13

Technical requirements

In order to follow along with the recipes discussed in this chapter, you should have one or two servers on CentOS (preferred) or an Ubuntu/Debian operating system that has internet connectivity to download packages from the PGDG repository. For testing purposes, the server configuration should be one CPU and 1 GB RAM with 20 GB available disk space.

Major version upgrade to PostgreSQL 13 using pg_dumpall

We discussed logical backups and the purpose of pg_dumpall in *Chapter 3, Backup and Recovery*. pg_dumpall is the only utility that can perform a logical backup of the whole cluster. This backup includes globals (such as users or tablespaces) and databases. The same pg_dumpall can be used to dump the whole cluster from an older version and restore it into PostgreSQL 13. In this recipe, we shall discuss the steps involved in performing an upgrade from PostgreSQL 9.3 to PostgreSQL 13 using pg_dumpall.

Getting ready

In order to perform a logical backup of a cluster, we need to have sufficient space on the server. If the upgrade is being performed within the same server, then we need to make sure that we have at least three times the space of the existing database cluster (excluding the space required by WAL segments and log files).

As an example, if we have a PostgreSQL 9.3 cluster with a size of 100 GB, we should have the following:

- 100 GB dedicated to the new PostgreSQL 13 cluster.
- An additional 100 GB for storing the backup dump generated using pg_dumpall.
- While performing the restore to PostgreSQL 13, we should see several WAL segments being generated in the server. If these need to be archived or used for replication, then we need to have sufficient space dedicated for the generated WAL segments considering the network lag for archiving and replication.

Never attempt to perform an upgrade in a production server without proper testing. It is important to test the disk usage and application functionality upon upgrade in a performance environment.

How to do it...

We shall consider upgrading PostgreSQL version 9.6 to 13 in this recipe. The same steps should work in the case of any version post 9.6 and most versions before 9.6. Additionally, we shall assume that the upgrade is happening locally on the same server. I will also explain what steps will change if the upgrade has to happen remotely. If a database of PostgreSQL version 9.6 exists on one server and the database has to be migrated to another server with PostgreSQL 13 on it, you may refer to it as an upgrade happening remotely.

The following steps have been performed on CentOS 7.8. These steps should remain similar for other distributions of Linux:

1. Get all the Postgres packages installed in an existing PostgreSQL server:

```
$ rpm -qa | grep postgres
postgresql96-libs-9.6.18-1PGDG.rhel7.x86_64
postgresql96-server-9.6.18-1PGDG.rhel7.x86_64
postgresql96-9.6.18-1PGDG.rhel7.x86_64
postgresql96-contrib-9.6.18-1PGDG.rhel7.x86_64
```

2. Install the target PostgreSQL version (PostgreSQL 13.1 here):

```
$ sudo yum install
https://yum.postgresql.org/13/redhat/rhel-7.8-x86_64/pgdg-redhat-re
po-latest.noarch.rpm
$ sudo yum install postgresql13-server postgresql13-contrib -y
```

3. Initialize the data directory for PostgreSQL 13:

```
$ /usr/pgsql-13/bin/initdb -D /var/lib/pgsql/13/data
```

4. Use a different port number for the new cluster, if the source and target server while upgrading are the same:

```
$ cd /var/lib/pgsql/13/data
$ echo "port = 5433" >> postgresql.auto.conf
$ /usr/pgsql-13/bin/pg_ctl -D /var/lib/pgsql/13/data start
```

5. Connect to each database in the older cluster and see the list of extensions installed:

```
$ /usr/pgsql-9.6/bin/psql -p 5432 -d percona -c "\dx"
```

This results in the following output:

```
$ /usr/pgsql-9.6/bin/psql -p 5432 -d percona -c "\dx"
 List of installed extensions
 Name | Version | Schema | Description
--------------------+---------+------------+-----------------------
-------------------------------------------
 pageinspect | 1.5 | public | inspect the contents of database
pages at a low level
 pg_repack | 1.4.5 | public | Reorganize tables in PostgreSQL
databases with minimal locks
 pg_stat_statements | 1.4 | public | track execution statistics of
all SQL statements executed
 pgstattuple | 1.4 | public | show tuple-level statistics
 plpgsql | 1.0 | pg_catalog | PL/pgSQL procedural language
(5 rows)
```

6. Install extensions for PostgreSQL 13 that are not part of `contrib`:

```
$ sudo yum install pg_repack13 -y
```

7. Fix the configuration parameter changes required for the new versions:

```
$ cd /var/lib/pgsql/13/data
$ sudo bash -c 'cat <<EOF >>postgresql.auto.conf
shared_preload_libraries = 'pg_stat_statements, pg_repack'
shared_buffers = '2GB'
EOF'
```

8. Use the `pg_dumpall` binary of the latest version to dump the cluster of the older version
(this could take a long time if the cluster is huge in size):

```
$ /usr/pgsql-13/bin/pg_dumpall > /backupdir/dumpall.sql
```

9. Use `psql` to restore the text format dump to the new cluster:

```
$ /usr/pgsql-13/bin/psql -p 5433 -f /backupdir/dumpall.sql
```

10. Shut down the old cluster and restart the new cluster with the desired port:

```
$ /usr/pgsql-9.6/bin/pg_ctl -D /var/lib/pgsql/9.6/data stop -mf
$ sed -i 's/5433/5432/' postgresql.auto.conf
$ /usr/pgsql-13/bin/pg_ctl -D /var/lib/pgsql/13/data restart -mf
```

11. Run a cluster-wide `ANALYZE` on the new cluster:

```
$ /usr/pgsql-13/bin/vacuumdb -a -z -j 4
```

The output looks like the following:

```
$ vacuumdb -a -z -j 4
vacuumdb: vacuuming database "percona"
vacuumdb: vacuuming database "postgres"
vacuumdb: vacuuming database "template1"
```

12. Remove the older version's data directory and PostgreSQL packages and extensions:

```
$ rm -rf /var/lib/pgsql/9.6/data
$ sudo yum remove postgresql96* pg_repack96 -y
```

How it works...

The desired target PostgreSQL version packages should be installed to proceed with the upgrade. But before proceeding with the install, we should look at the existing PostgreSQL packages. This way, we install similar packages for the target version. As seen in *step 1*, we can find the list of PostgreSQL 9.6 packages installed. Once we get the list, we can proceed to *step 2* to install the rpm repository and the packages for the latest release.

Once the installation is completed, we can proceed further with the initialization of the data directory using PostgreSQL 13 as seen in *step 3*. We can modify the data directory to any location as required. Before starting the database cluster using PostgreSQL 13, we should modify the port number if the upgrade is happening within the same server as PostgreSQL 9.6. If the older version is using port 5432, we may modify the port to 5433 or anything different, as seen in *step 4*, and then start the PostgreSQL server.

In order to avoid any dependency errors, we should look at all the extensions installed/used in the older version. This can be done using the shortcut seen in *step 5*. Most of the extensions that are part of contrib will be automatically created by the restore. But some of the extensions that are not part of the contrib module may throw errors during upgrade.

For example, if pg_repack is one of the extensions that are not part of the contrib module, the pg_repack binaries for PostgreSQL 13 must be installed before proceeding with the upgrade, if being used by the older version, as seen in *steps 5* and *6*.

Once all the dependencies have been fixed, we should incorporate all the required configuration parameter changes for the new version. *Step 7* gives an example of a couple of such parameters. We could do a `diff` between old and new versions and see what needs to be changed. At the same time, we need to make a note that every new version may add or remove one or more configuration parameters, so it is important to have an idea of what has changed in the new version before making such changes.

While performing the upgrade, it is important to note that the binaries used to back up and restore the cluster are of the latest version, as seen in *step 8*. Once the backup is completed, the dump can be restored to the new cluster using the new binaries as seen in step 9. As `pg_dumpall` generates a plain text format dumpfile, psql can be used to perform the restore.

Once the restore is completed, we can shut down the cluster that is running using the older version and start the new cluster on PostgreSQL 13 upon changing the port number, as seen in *step 10*. It is important to run an entire cluster-wise `ANALYZE` so that all the database statistics are updated, as seen in *step 11*.

The last step is to perform a cleanup by removing the data directory of the older cluster, removing the packages installed for PostgreSQL that belong to the older version and any extensions specifically installed to work on the older version. This can be done using the commands shown in *step 12*.

Major version upgrade to PostgreSQL 13 using pg_dump and pg_restore

In the previous recipe, we discussed how `pg_dumpall` can be used for performing a major version upgrade.
We noticed that the dump file generated by `pg_dumpall` is a plain test file and the process may be time-consuming as it cannot be done in parallel. In this recipe, we shall see how we can use `pg_dumpall` to copy the globals but use `pg_dump` and `pg_restore` for migrating databases to a new version.

Getting ready

In order to perform a logical backup of a cluster, we need to have sufficient space in the server. If the upgrade is being performed within the same server, then we need to make sure that we have at least three times the space of the existing database cluster (excluding the space required by WAL segments and log files).

As an example, if we have a PostgreSQL 9.3 cluster of size 100 GB, we should have the following:

- 100 GB dedicated to the new PostgreSQL 13 cluster.
- An additional 100 GB for storing the backup dump generated using `pg_dumpall`.
- While performing the restore to PostgreSQL 13, we should see several WAL segments being generated in the server. If these need to be archived or used for replication, then we need to have sufficient space dedicated for the generated WAL segments considering the network lag for archiving and replication.

Never attempt to perform an upgrade in a production server without proper testing. It is important to test the disk usage and application functionality upon upgrade in a performance environment.

How to do it...

The following are the steps to perform an upgrade using `pg_dump` and `pg_restore` with the `pg_dumpall` approach:

1. Get all the Postgres packages installed in the existing PostgreSQL server:

```
$ rpm -qa | grep postgres
postgresql96-libs-9.6.18-1PGDG.rhel7.x86_64
postgresql96-server-9.6.18-1PGDG.rhel7.x86_64
postgresql96-9.6.18-1PGDG.rhel7.x86_64
postgresql96-contrib-9.6.18-1PGDG.rhel7.x86_64
```

2. Install the target PostgreSQL version (PostgreSQL 13.1 here):

```
$ sudo yum install
https://yum.postgresql.org/13/redhat/rhel-7.8-x86_64/pgdg-redhat-re
po-latest.noarch.rpm
$ sudo yum install postgresql13-server postgresql13-contrib -y
```

3. Initialize the data directory for PostgreSQL 13:

```
$ /usr/pgsql-13/bin/initdb -D /var/lib/pgsql/13/data
```

4. Use a different port number for the new cluster, if the source and target server while upgrading are the same:

```
$ cd /var/lib/pgsql/13/data
$ echo "port = 5433" >> postgresql.auto.conf
$ /usr/pgsql-13/bin/pg_ctl -D /var/lib/pgsql/13/data start
```

5. Connect to each database in the older cluster and see the list of extensions installed:

```
$ /usr/pgsql-9.6/bin/psql -p 5432 -d percona -c "\dx"
```

This results in the following output:

```
$ /usr/pgsql-9.6/bin/psql -p 5432 -d percona -c "\dx"
 List of installed extensions
 Name | Version | Schema | Description
--------------------+----------+------------+-----------------------
------------------------------------------
 pageinspect | 1.5 | public | inspect the contents of database
pages at a low level
 pg_repack | 1.4.5 | public | Reorganize tables in PostgreSQL
databases with minimal locks
 pg_stat_statements | 1.4 | public | track execution statistics of
all SQL statements executed
 pgstattuple | 1.4 | public | show tuple-level statistics
 plpgsql | 1.0 | pg_catalog | PL/pgSQL procedural language
(5 rows)
```

6. Install extensions for PostgreSQL 13 that are not part of `contrib`:

```
$ sudo yum install pg_repack13 -y
```

7. Fix the configuration parameter changes required for the new versions:

```
$ cd /var/lib/pgsql/13/data
$ sudo bash -c 'cat <<EOF >>postgresql.auto.conf
shared_preload_libraries = 'pg_stat_statements, pg_repack'
shared_buffers = '2GB'
EOF'
```

8. Use the `pg_dumpall` binary of the latest version to dump the globals from the older cluster:

    ```
    $ /usr/pgsql-13/bin/pg_dumpall -g > /backupdir/globals.sql
    ```

9. Use `psql` to restore the text format dump to the new cluster:

    ```
    $ /usr/pgsql-13/bin/psql -p 5433 -f /backupdir/globals.sql
    ```

10. Take a schema-only dump of the database to be migrated and restore it to the new cluster. Create the target database(s) on the new cluster before performing the schema-only restore:

    ```
    $ /usr/pgsql-13/bin/psql -h localhost -p 5433 -c "CREATE DATABASE
    percona"
    $ /usr/pgsql-13/bin/pg_dump -s -d percona -p 5432 | psql -h
    localhost -p 5433 -U postgres -d percona
    ```

11. To perform a data-only dump, either use a single process or multiple parallel processes to speed up the restore.

    The following command is for a single-process dump and restores using a pipe. This may take more time:

    ```
    $ /usr/pgsql-13/bin/pg_dump -a -d percona -p 5432 | psql -h
    localhost -p 5433 -U postgres -d percona
    ```

    The following commands are for parallel dump and parallel restore. This may take less time:

    ```
    $ /usr/pgsql-13/bin/pg_dump -Fd -j 4 -a -d percona -p 5432 -f
    /backupdir/
    $ /usr/pgsql-13/bin/pg_restore -h localhost -p 5433 -U postgres -Fd
    -j 4 -d percona /tmp/backupdir
    ```

    Repeat the preceding step for all the databases.

12. Shut down the old cluster and restart the new cluster with the desired port:

    ```
    $ /usr/pgsql-9.6/bin/pg_ctl -D /var/lib/pgsql/9.6/data stop -mf
    $ sed -i 's/5433/5432/' postgresql.auto.conf
    $ /usr/pgsql-13/bin/pg_ctl -D /var/lib/pgsql/13/data restart -mf
    ```

13. Run a cluster-wide `ANALYZE` on the new cluster:

    ```
    $ /usr/pgsql-13/bin/vacuumdb -a -z -j 4
    ```

This results in the following output:

```
$ vacuumdb -a -z -j 4
vacuumdb: vacuuming database "percona"
vacuumdb: vacuuming database "postgres"
vacuumdb: vacuuming database "template1"
```

14. Remove the older version's data directory and PostgreSQL packages and extensions:

```
$ rm -rf /var/lib/pgsql/9.6/data
$ sudo yum remove postgresql96* pg_repack96 -y
```

How it works...

The desired target PostgreSQL version packages should be installed to proceed with the upgrade. But before proceeding with the install, we should look at the existing PostgreSQL packages. This way, we install similar packages for the target version. As seen in *step 1*, we can find the list of PostgreSQL 9.6 packages installed. Once we get the list, we can proceed to *step 2* to install the rpm repository and the packages for the latest release.

Once the installation is completed, we can proceed further with the initialization of the data directory using PostgreSQL 13 as seen in *step 3*. We can modify the data directory to any location as required. Before starting the database cluster using PostgreSQL 13, we should modify the port number if the upgrade is happening within the same server as PostgreSQL 9.6. If the older version is using port 5432, we may modify the port to 5433 or anything different, as seen in *step 4*, and then start the PostgreSQL server.

In order to avoid any dependency errors, we should look at all the extensions installed/used in the older version. This can be done using the shortcut seen in *step 5*. Most of the extensions that are part of contrib will be automatically created by the restore. But some of the extensions that are not part of the contrib module may throw errors during upgrade, for example, pg_repack. pg_repack binaries for PostgreSQL 13 must be installed before proceeding with the upgrade, if being used by the older version, as seen in *steps 5* and *6*.

Once all the dependencies have been fixed, we should incorporate all the required configuration parameter changes for the new version. *Step 7* gives an example of a couple of such parameters. We could do a diff between old and new versions and see what needs to be changed. At the same time, we need to make a note that every new version may add or remove one or more configuration parameters, so it is important to have an idea of what has changed in the new version before making such changes.

While performing the upgrade, it is important to note that the binaries used to back up and restore the globals are of the latest version, as seen in *step 8*. Once the backup is completed, the globals can be restored to the new cluster using the new binaries, as seen in *step 9*. The globals contain users, roles, and tablespaces.

As we are using `pg_dumpall` only for the globals; the databases can be dumped and restored using `pg_dump` and `pg_restore`. To take the advantage of parallel dump and restore, we can use *step 10* to perform a schema-only dump/restore, and then proceed to a single or a parallel process dump and restore using the commands specified in *step 11*.

Once the restore is completed, we can shut down the cluster that is running using the older version and start the new cluster on PostgreSQL 13 upon changing the port number, as seen in *step 12*. It is important to run an entire cluster-wise `ANALYZE` so that all the database statistics are updated, as seen in *step 13*.

The last step is to perform a cleanup by removing the data directory of the older cluster, removing the packages installed for PostgreSQL that belong to the older version and any extensions specifically installed to work on the older version. This can be done using the commands shown in *step 14*.

Major version upgrade to PostgreSQL 13 using pg_upgrade with downtime

In order to simplify the database upgrades, there is a utility that is built into the community PostgreSQL software: `pg_upgrade`. We can avoid performing a globals dump or database dump and directly run the upgrade using a single command when using `pg_upgrade`. In this recipe, we shall see how this utility can be used to perform simple database upgrades.

Getting ready

In order to perform an upgrade using `pg_upgrade`, we need to have sufficient space in the server. If the upgrade is being performed within the same server, then we need to make sure that we have at least three times the space of the existing database cluster (excluding the space required by WAL segments and log files).

As an example, if we have a PostgreSQL 9.3 cluster of size 100 GB, we should have the following:

- 100 GB dedicated to the new PostgreSQL 13 cluster.
- An additional 100 GB for storing the backup dump generated using `pg_dumpall`.
- While performing the restore to PostgreSQL 13, we should see several WAL segments being generated in the server. If these need to be archived or used for replication, then we need to have sufficient space dedicated for the generated WAL segments considering the network lag for archiving and replication.

Never attempt to perform an upgrade in a production server without proper testing. It is important to test the disk usage and application functionality upon upgrade in a performance environment.

How to do it...

We will do this using the following steps:

1. Get all the `postgres` packages installed in the existing PostgreSQL server:

   ```
   $ rpm -qa | grep postgres
   postgresql96-libs-9.6.18-1PGDG.rhel7.x86_64
   postgresql96-server-9.6.18-1PGDG.rhel7.x86_64
   postgresql96-9.6.18-1PGDG.rhel7.x86_64
   postgresql96-contrib-9.6.18-1PGDG.rhel7.x86_64
   ```

2. Install the target PostgreSQL version (PostgreSQL 13.1 here):

   ```
   $ sudo yum install
   https://yum.postgresql.org/13/redhat/rhel-7.8-x86_64/pgdg-redhat-re
   po-latest.noarch.rpm
   $ sudo yum install postgresql13-server postgresql13-contrib -y
   ```

3. Initialize the data directory for PostgreSQL 13:

   ```
   $ /usr/pgsql-13/bin/initdb -D /var/lib/pgsql/13/data
   ```

4. Use a different port number for the new cluster, if the source and target server while upgrading are the same:

   ```
   $ cd /var/lib/pgsql/13/data
   $ echo "port = 5433" >> postgresql.auto.conf
   $ /usr/pgsql-13/bin/pg_ctl -D /var/lib/pgsql/13/data start
   ```

5. Connect to each database in the older cluster and see the list of extensions installed:

```
$ /usr/pgsql-9.6/bin/psql -p 5432 -d percona -c "\dx"
```

This results in the following output:

```
$ /usr/pgsql-9.6/bin/psql -p 5432 -d percona -c "\dx"
 List of installed extensions
 Name | Version | Schema | Description
 --------------------+---------+------------+---------------------
 ----------------------------------------
 pageinspect | 1.5 | public | inspect the contents of database
 pages at a low level
 pg_repack | 1.4.5 | public | Reorganize tables in PostgreSQL
 databases with minimal locks
 pg_stat_statements | 1.4 | public | track execution statistics of
 all SQL statements executed
 pgstattuple | 1.4 | public | show tuple-level statistics
 plpgsql | 1.0 | pg_catalog | PL/pgSQL procedural language
 (5 rows)
```

6. Install extensions for PostgreSQL 12 that are not part of `contrib`:

```
$ sudo yum install pg_repack13 -y
```

7. Fix the configuration parameter changes required for the new versions:

```
$ cd /var/lib/pgsql/13/data
$ sudo bash -c 'cat <<EOF >>postgresql.auto.conf
shared_preload_libraries = 'pg_stat_statements, pg_repack'
shared_buffers = '2GB'
EOF'
```

8. Perform consistency checks between the old and new clusters. The new cluster on PostgreSQL 13 must be down during this check:

```
$ /usr/pgsql-13/bin/pg_ctl -D /var/lib/pgsql/13/data stop -mf
$ /usr/pgsql-13/bin/pg_upgrade -b /usr/pgsql-9.6/bin -B
/usr/pgsql-13/bin -d /var/lib/pgsql/9.6/data -D
/var/lib/pgsql/13/data -c
```

The output from the preceding command may look like the following:

```
$ /usr/pgsql-13/bin/pg_upgrade -b /usr/pgsql-9.6/bin -B
/usr/pgsql-13/bin -d /var/lib/pgsql/9.6/data -D
/var/lib/pgsql/13/data -c
 Performing Consistency Checks on Old Live Server
```

```
--------------------------------------------------
Checking cluster versions ok
Checking database user is the install user ok
Checking database connection settings ok
Checking for prepared transactions ok
Checking for reg* data types in user tables ok
Checking for contrib/isn with bigint-passing mismatch ok
Checking for tables WITH OIDS ok
Checking for invalid "sql_identifier" user columns ok
Checking for invalid "unknown" user columns ok
Checking for hash indexes ok
Checking for presence of required libraries fatal

Your installation references loadable libraries that are missing
from the
new installation. You can add these libraries to the new
installation,
or remove the functions using them from the old installation. A
list of
problem libraries is in the file:
loadable_libraries.txt

Failure, exiting

$ cat loadable_libraries.txt
could not load library "$libdir/pg_repack": ERROR: could not
access file  "$libdir/pg_repack": No such file or directory
Database: percona
```

9. Resolve errors observed during consistency checks and re-run the check using the previous step:

```
$ sudo yum install pg_repack13 -y

$ /usr/pgsql-13/bin/pg_upgrade -b /usr/pgsql-9.6/bin -B
/usr/pgsql-13/bin -d /var/lib/pgsql/9.6/data -D
/var/lib/pgsql/13/data -c
Performing Consistency Checks on Old Live Server
--------------------------------------------------
Checking cluster versions ok
Checking database user is the install user ok
Checking database connection settings ok
Checking for prepared transactions ok
Checking for reg* data types in user tables ok
Checking for contrib/isn with bigint-passing mismatch ok
Checking for tables WITH OIDS ok
Checking for invalid "sql_identifier" user columns ok
Checking for invalid "unknown" user columns ok
```

```
Checking for hash indexes ok
Checking for presence of required libraries ok
Checking database user is the install user ok
Checking for prepared transactions ok

*Clusters are compatible*
```

10. **Shut down both old and new clusters and perform the upgrade:**

```
$ /usr/pgsql-9.6/bin/pg_ctl -D /var/lib/pgsql/9.6/data stop -mf
$ /usr/pgsql-13/bin/pg_ctl -D /var/lib/pgsql/13/data stop -mf
$ /usr/pgsql-13/bin/pg_upgrade -b /usr/pgsql-9.6/bin -B
/usr/pgsql-13/bin -d /var/lib/pgsql/9.6/data -D
/var/lib/pgsql/13/data
```

Output log :
```
$ /usr/pgsql-13/bin/pg_upgrade -b /usr/pgsql-9.6/bin -B
/usr/pgsql-13/bin -d /var/lib/pgsql/9.6/data -D
/var/lib/pgsql/13/data
Performing Consistency Checks
-----------------------------
Checking cluster versions ok
Checking database user is the install user ok
Checking database connection settings ok
Checking for prepared transactions ok
Checking for reg* data types in user tables ok
Checking for contrib/isn with bigint-passing mismatch ok
Checking for tables WITH OIDS ok
Checking for invalid "sql_identifier" user columns ok
Checking for invalid "unknown" user columns ok
Creating dump of global objects ok
Creating dump of database schemas
ok
Checking for presence of required libraries ok
Checking database user is the install user ok
Checking for prepared transactions ok

If pg_upgrade fails after this point, you must re-initdb the
new cluster before continuing.

Performing Upgrade
------------------
Analyzing all rows in the new cluster ok
Freezing all rows in the new cluster ok
Deleting files from new pg_xact ok
Copying old pg_clog to new server ok
Setting next transaction ID and epoch for new cluster ok
Deleting files from new pg_multixact/offsets ok
```

```
Copying old pg_multixact/offsets to new server ok
Deleting files from new pg_multixact/members ok
Copying old pg_multixact/members to new server ok
Setting next multixact ID and offset for new cluster ok
Resetting WAL archives ok
Setting frozenxid and minmxid counters in new cluster ok
Restoring global objects in the new cluster ok
Restoring database schemas in the new cluster
ok
Copying user relation files
ok
Setting next OID for new cluster ok
Sync data directory to disk ok
Creating script to analyze new cluster ok
Creating script to delete old cluster ok
Checking for hash indexes ok

Upgrade Complete
----------------
Optimizer statistics are not transferred by pg_upgrade so,
once you start the new server, consider running:
./analyze_new_cluster.sh

Running this script will delete the old cluster's data files:
./delete_old_cluster.sh
```

11. Start the new cluster and run a cluster-wide ANALYZE on the new cluster:

```
$ /usr/pgsql-13/bin/pg_ctl -D /var/lib/pgsql/13/data start
$ /usr/pgsql-13/bin/vacuumdb -a -z -j 4
```

This results in the following output:

```
$ vacuumdb -a -z -j 4
vacuumdb: vacuuming database "percona"
vacuumdb: vacuuming database "postgres"
vacuumdb: vacuuming database "template1"
```

12. Remove the older version's data directory and PostgreSQL packages and extensions:

```
$ rm -rf /var/lib/pgsql/9.6/data
$ sudo yum remove postgresql96* pg_repack96 -y
```

How it works...

The desired target PostgreSQL version packages should be installed to proceed with the upgrade. But before proceeding with the install, we should look at the existing PostgreSQL packages. This way, we install similar packages for the target version. As seen in *step 1*, we can find a list of the PostgreSQL 9.6 packages installed. Once we get the list, we can proceed to *step 2* to install the rpm repository and the packages for the latest release.

Once the installation is completed, we can proceed further with the initialization of the data directory using PostgreSQL 13 as seen in *step 3*. We can modify the data directory to any location as required. Before starting the database cluster using PostgreSQL 12, we should modify the port number if the upgrade is happening within the same server as PostgreSQL 9.6. If the older version is using port 5432, we may modify the port to 5433 or anything different, as seen in *step 4*, and then start the PostgreSQL server.

In order to avoid any dependency errors, we should look at all the extensions installed/used in the older version. This can be done using the shortcut seen in *step 5*. Most of the extensions that are part of contrib will be automatically created by the restore. But some of the extensions that are not part of the contrib module may throw errors during upgrade, for example, pg_repack. pg_repack binaries for PostgreSQL 13 must be installed before proceeding with the upgrade, if being used by the older version, as seen in *steps 5* and *6*.

Once all the dependencies have been fixed, we should incorporate all the required configuration parameter changes for the new version. *Step 7* gives an example of a couple of such parameters. We could do a diff between the old and new versions and see what needs to be changed. At the same time, we need to make a note that every new version may add or remove one or more configuration parameters, so it is important to have an idea of what has changed in the new version before making such changes.

Now, we can use pg_upgrade to look for consistency checks between the old and new clusters, as seen in *step 8*. In the following command that has been used for consistency checks, we see several arguments and one of them is -c. -c is used to perform the consistency check:

```
$ /usr/pgsql-13/bin/pg_upgrade -b /usr/pgsql-9.6/bin -B /usr/pgsql-13/bin -
d /var/lib/pgsql/9.6/data -D /var/lib/pgsql/13/data -c
```

The following parameters are present here:

- `-b`: The location of the binaries of the old cluster
- `-B`: The location of the binaries of the new cluster
- `-d`: The location of the data directory of the old cluster
- `-D`: The location of the data directory of the new cluster

A very specific error is printed when there is a failure, as seen in *step 8*. Upon resolving the error, as seen in *step 9*, we can proceed to *step 10*. In this step, we shall make sure that both the clusters and down and remove `-c` from the command used for consistency checks. This will perform the upgrade by copying the entire cluster from the old data directory to the new data directory. It may take a long time to perform this type of upgrade but it is not a complicated procedure as it just involves a couple of steps.

Once the upgrade is completed, we should start the new cluster on PostgreSQL 13, as seen in *step 11*, and then run an entire cluster-wise `ANALYZE` so that all the database statistics are updated.

The last step is to perform a cleanup by removing the data directory of the older cluster, removing the packages installed for PostgreSQL that belong to the older version and any extensions specifically installed to work on the older version. This can be done using the commands shown in *step 12*.

Major version upgrade to PostgreSQL 13 using pg_upgrade with hard links for seamless downtime

In the previous recipe, we saw how `pg_upgrade` can be used to perform a major version in simple steps. However, it does take a long time to perform the upgrade this way when the database cluster is of several GBs or TBs in size. For this reason, we have an option in `pg_upgrade` to use hard links to make the upgrades finish in a few seconds.

When the hard links option is used, the data files are not copied from one cluster to another cluster. Instead, the files and directories created in the new cluster are linked to the files and directories in the old cluster. So, only the files and directories are created but the data copy is avoided when hard links are used. This only works when the upgrade is happening within the same filesystem. The only difference between the previous recipe and this recipe is that the upgrade using hard links is done by adding a `-k` argument to the `pg_upgrade` command used in the previous recipe.

In this recipe, we shall see how hard links can be used to perform a faster upgrade using `pg_upgrade`.

Getting ready

This approach works while upgrading not only from currently supported older versions to PostgreSQL 13 but also from several obsolete versions of PostgreSQL. However, the hard links can only be used when the upgrade is happening within the same server and the data directory of the new cluster is also on the same filesystem.

How to do it...

We will do this using the following steps:

1. Get all the Postgres packages installed in the existing PostgreSQL server:

```
$ rpm -qa | grep postgres
 postgresql96-libs-9.6.18-1PGDG.rhel7.x86_64
 postgresql96-server-9.6.18-1PGDG.rhel7.x86_64
 postgresql96-9.6.18-1PGDG.rhel7.x86_64
 postgresql96-contrib-9.6.18-1PGDG.rhel7.x86_64
```

2. Install the target PostgreSQL version (PostgreSQL 13.1 here):

```
$ sudo yum install
https://yum.postgresql.org/13/redhat/rhel-7.8-x86_64/pgdg-redhat-re
po-latest.noarch.rpm
$ sudo yum install postgresql13-server postgresql13-contrib -y
```

3. Initialize the data directory for PostgreSQL 13:

```
$ /usr/pgsql-13/bin/initdb -D /var/lib/pgsql/13/data
```

4. Use a different port number for the new cluster, if the source and target server while upgrading are the same:

```
$ cd /var/lib/pgsql/13/data
$ echo "port = 5433" >> postgresql.auto.conf
$ /usr/pgsql-13/bin/pg_ctl -D /var/lib/pgsql/13/data start
```

5. Connect to each database in the older cluster and see the list of extensions installed:

```
$ /usr/pgsql-9.6/bin/psql -p 5432 -d percona -c "\dx"
```

This results in the following output:

```
$ /usr/pgsql-9.6/bin/psql -p 5432 -d percona -c "\dx"
 List of installed extensions
 Name | Version | Schema | Description
--------------------+---------+------------+-----------------------
-----------------------------------------------
 pageinspect | 1.5 | public | inspect the contents of database
pages at a low level
 pg_repack | 1.4.5 | public | Reorganize tables in PostgreSQL
databases with minimal locks
 pg_stat_statements | 1.4 | public | track execution statistics of
all SQL statements executed
 pgstattuple | 1.4 | public | show tuple-level statistics
 plpgsql | 1.0 | pg_catalog | PL/pgSQL procedural language
(5 rows)
```

6. Install extensions for PostgreSQL 13 that are not part of `contrib`:

```
$ sudo yum install pg_repack13 -y
```

7. Fix configuration parameter changes required for the new versions:

```
$ cd /var/lib/pgsql/13/data
$ sudo bash -c 'cat <<EOF >>postgresql.auto.conf
shared_preload_libraries = 'pg_stat_statements, pg_repack'
shared_buffers = '2GB'
EOF'
```

8. Perform consistency checks between the old and new clusters. The new cluster on PostgreSQL 12 must be down during this check:

```
$ /usr/pgsql-13/bin/pg_ctl -D /var/lib/pgsql/13/data stop -mf
 $ /usr/pgsql-13/bin/pg_upgrade -b /usr/pgsql-9.6/bin -B
/usr/pgsql-13/bin -d /var/lib/pgsql/9.6/data -D
/var/lib/pgsql/13/data -c
```

The following is an example output of the preceding command:

```
$ /usr/pgsql-13/bin/pg_upgrade -b /usr/pgsql-9.6/bin -B
/usr/pgsql-13/bin -d /var/lib/pgsql/9.6/data -D
/var/lib/pgsql/13/data -c
 Performing Consistency Checks on Old Live Server
 ------------------------------------------------
 Checking cluster versions ok
 Checking database user is the install user ok
 Checking database connection settings ok
 Checking for prepared transactions ok
 Checking for reg* data types in user tables ok
 Checking for contrib/isn with bigint-passing mismatch ok
 Checking for tables WITH OIDS ok
 Checking for invalid "sql_identifier" user columns ok
 Checking for invalid "unknown" user columns ok
 Checking for hash indexes ok
 Checking for presence of required libraries fatal

 Your installation references loadable libraries that are missing
from the
 new installation. You can add these libraries to the new
installation,
 or remove the functions using them from the old installation. A
list of
 problem libraries is in the file:
 loadable_libraries.txt

 Failure, exiting

 $ cat loadable_libraries.txt
 could not load library "$libdir/pg_repack": ERROR: could not
access file "$libdir/pg_repack": No such file or directory
 Database: percona
```

9. Resolve errors observed during consistency checks and re-run the check using
   the previous step:

```
$ sudo yum install pg_repack13 -y

$ /usr/pgsql-13/bin/pg_upgrade -b /usr/pgsql-9.6/bin -B
/usr/pgsql-13/bin -d /var/lib/pgsql/9.6/data -D
/var/lib/pgsql/13/data -c

 Performing Consistency Checks on Old Live Server
 ------------------------------------------------
 Checking cluster versions ok
 Checking database user is the install user ok
```

```
Checking database connection settings ok
Checking for prepared transactions ok
Checking for reg* data types in user tables ok
Checking for contrib/isn with bigint-passing mismatch ok
Checking for tables WITH OIDS ok
Checking for invalid "sql_identifier" user columns ok
Checking for invalid "unknown" user columns ok
Checking for hash indexes ok
Checking for presence of required libraries ok
Checking database user is the install user ok
Checking for prepared transactions ok

*Clusters are compatible*
```

10. Shut down both the old and new clusters and perform the upgrade using hard links:

```
$ /usr/pgsql-9.6/bin/pg_ctl -D /var/lib/pgsql/9.6/data stop -mf
$ /usr/pgsql-13/bin/pg_ctl -D /var/lib/pgsql/13/data stop -mf
$ /usr/pgsql-13/bin/pg_upgrade -b /usr/pgsql-9.6/bin -B
/usr/pgsql-13/bin -d /var/lib/pgsql/9.6/data -D
/var/lib/pgsql/13/data -k
```

The following is an example output of the preceding command:

```
$ /usr/pgsql-13/bin/pg_upgrade -b /usr/pgsql-9.6/bin -B
/usr/pgsql-13/bin -d /var/lib/pgsql/9.6/data -D
/var/lib/pgsql/13/data -k
Performing Consistency Checks
-----------------------------
Checking cluster versions ok
Checking database user is the install user ok
Checking database connection settings ok
Checking for prepared transactions ok
Checking for reg* data types in user tables ok
Checking for contrib/isn with bigint-passing mismatch ok
Checking for tables WITH OIDS ok
Checking for invalid "sql_identifier" user columns ok
Checking for invalid "unknown" user columns ok
Creating dump of global objects ok
Creating dump of database schemas
ok
Checking for presence of required libraries ok
Checking database user is the install user ok
Checking for prepared transactions ok

If pg_upgrade fails after this point, you must re-initdb the
new cluster before continuing.
```

```
Performing Upgrade
------------------
Analyzing all rows in the new cluster ok
Freezing all rows in the new cluster ok
Deleting files from new pg_xact ok
Copying old pg_clog to new server ok
Setting next transaction ID and epoch for new cluster ok
Deleting files from new pg_multixact/offsets ok
Copying old pg_multixact/offsets to new server ok
Deleting files from new pg_multixact/members ok
Copying old pg_multixact/members to new server ok
Setting next multixact ID and offset for new cluster ok
Resetting WAL archives ok
Setting frozenxid and minmxid counters in new cluster ok
Restoring global objects in the new cluster ok
Restoring database schemas in the new cluster
ok
Adding ".old" suffix to old global/pg_control ok

If you want to start the old cluster, you will need to remove
the ".old" suffix from
/var/lib/pgsql/9.6/data/global/pg_control.old.
Because "link" mode was used, the old cluster cannot be safely
started once the new cluster has been started.

Linking user relation files
ok
Setting next OID for new cluster ok
Sync data directory to disk ok
Creating script to analyze new cluster ok
Creating script to delete old cluster ok
Checking for hash indexes ok

Upgrade Complete
----------------
Optimizer statistics are not transferred by pg_upgrade so,
once you start the new server, consider running:
./analyze_new_cluster.sh

Running this script will delete the old cluster's data files:
./delete_old_cluster.sh
```

11. Start the new cluster and run a cluster-wide ANALYZE on the new cluster:

```
$ /usr/pgsql-13/bin/pg_ctl -D /var/lib/pgsql/13/data start
$ /usr/pgsql-13/bin/vacuumdb -a -z -j 4
```

This results in the following output:

```
$ vacuumdb -a -z -j 4
 vacuumdb: vacuuming database "percona"
 vacuumdb: vacuuming database "postgres"
 vacuumdb: vacuuming database "template1"
```

12. Remove the older version's data directory and PostgreSQL packages and extensions:

```
$ rm -rf /var/lib/pgsql/9.6/data
$ sudo yum remove postgresql96* pg_repack96 -y
```

How it works...

The desired target PostgreSQL version packages should be installed to proceed with the upgrade. But before proceeding with the install, we should look at the existing PostgreSQL packages. This way, we install similar packages for the target version. As seen in *step 1*, we can find a list of the PostgreSQL 9.6 packages installed. Once we get the list, we can proceed to *step 2* to install the rpm repository and the packages for the latest release.

Once the installation is completed, we can proceed further with the initialization of the data directory using PostgreSQL 13 as seen in *step 3*. We can modify the data directory to any location as required. Before starting the database cluster using PostgreSQL 13, we should modify the port number if the upgrade is happening within the same server as PostgreSQL 9.6. If the older version is using port 5432, we may modify the port to 5433 or anything different, as seen in *step 4*, and then start the PostgreSQL server.

In order to avoid any dependency errors, we should look at all the extensions installed/used in the older version. This can be done using the shortcut seen in *step 5*. Most of the extensions that are part of contrib will be automatically created by the restore. But some of the extensions that are not part of the contrib module may throw errors during upgrade. For example, pg_repack. pg_repack binaries for PostgreSQL 13 must be installed before proceeding with the upgrade, if being used by the older version, as seen in *steps 5* and *6*.

Once all the dependencies have been fixed, we should incorporate all the required configuration parameter changes for the new version. *Step 7* gives an example of a couple of such parameters. We could do a diff between the old and new versions and see what needs to be changed. At the same time, we need to make a note that every new version may add or remove one or more configuration parameters, so it is important to have an idea of what has changed in the new version before making such changes.

Now use pg_upgrade to look for consistency checks between the old and new clusters as seen in *step 8*. In the following command that has been used for consistency checks, we see several arguments and one of them is -c. -c is used to perform the consistency check:

```
$ /usr/pgsql-13/bin/pg_upgrade -b /usr/pgsql-9.6/bin -B /usr/pgsql-13/bin -
d /var/lib/pgsql/9.6/data -D /var/lib/pgsql/13/data -c
```

The following parameters are used here:

- -b: The location of the binaries of the old cluster
- -B: The location of the binaries of the new cluster
- -d: The location of the data directory of the old cluster
- -D: The location of the data directory of the new cluster

A very specific error is printed when there is any failure, as seen in *step 8*. Upon resolving the error, as seen in *step 9*, we can proceed to *step 10*. In this step, we shall make sure that both the clusters are down, and then remove -c and add -k to the command used for consistency checks. This would perform the upgrade in place of using hard links. It may take a few seconds to perform this type of upgrade but it is not a complicated procedure as it just involves a couple of steps.

Once the upgrade is completed, we should start the new cluster on PostgreSQL 13, as seen in *step 11*, and then run an entire cluster-wise ANALYZE so that all the database statistics are updated.

The last step is to perform a cleanup by removing the data directory of the older cluster, removing the packages installed for the PostgreSQL that belong to the older version and any extensions specifically installed to work on the older version. This can be done using the commands shown in *step 12*.

Installing the pglogical extension to upgrade older versions to PostgreSQL 13

PostgreSQL supports logical replication and logical decoding built into the source starting from PostgreSQL 10. For versions prior to PostgreSQL 10, there is an extension called `pglogical`. This extension can be used to configure replication between PostgreSQL 9.6 to PostgreSQL 13 so that the downtime can be minimized. In this recipe, we shall see how `pglogical` can be installed in the PostgreSQL 9.6 and PostgreSQL 13 versions.

Note: The older-version PostgreSQL cluster may be called the provider or the publisher and the newer-version node may be called the subscriber.

Getting ready

The `pglogical` extension replicates tables that have a primary key only. It works for replicating PostgreSQL versions starting from PostgreSQL 9.4.x to any version higher than 9.4. So, if the Postgres version is 9.3 or older, `pglogical` would not serve the purpose.

How to do it...

We will do this using the following steps:

1. Set up the appropriate package manager or repo based on the operating systems of the database servers:

```
$ sudo yum install
https://yum.postgresql.org/13/redhat/rhel-7.8-x86_64/pgdg-redhat-re
po-latest.noarch.rpm
```

2. Install the `pglogical` extension on the old and new clusters.

Run the following command on the PostgreSQL 9.6 server:

```
$ sudo yum install pglogical_96 -y
```

Run the following command on the PostgreSQL 13 server:

```
$ sudo yum install pglogical_13 -y
```

3. Set `wal_level` to `logical` and `shared_preload_libraries` to use `pglogical` and create the extension in the database being replicated to the new Postgres version.

On the old cluster, run the following commands:

```
$ /usr/pgsql-9.6/bin/psql -c "ALTER SYSTEM SET wal_level TO
'logical'"
$ /usr/pgsql-9.6/bin/psql -c "ALTER SYSTEM SET
shared_preload_libraries TO pglogical"
$ /usr/pgsql-9.6/bin/psql -d percona -c "CREATE EXTENSION
pglogical"
```

On the new cluster with PostgreSQL 13, run the following commands:

```
$ /usr/pgsql-13/bin/psql -c "ALTER SYSTEM SET wal_level TO
'logical'"
$ /usr/pgsql-13/bin/psql -c "ALTER SYSTEM SET
shared_preload_libraries TO pglogical"
```

Create the empty databases on the new cluster:

```
$ /usr/pgsql-13/bin/psql -c "CREATE DATABASE percona"
```

Create the extension on the new database:

```
$ /usr/pgsql-13/bin/psql -d percona -c "CREATE EXTENSION pglogical"
```

How it works...

Make sure you have access to the PGDG repository by either adding the latest `yum` repository or the `apt` repository to your database server. Once the repository has been set up, install the `pglogical` extension on both the old and new version clusters as seen in *step 2*. Once `pglogical` is installed, we need to modify two mandatory parameters on both clusters, as seen in *step 3*. The first of them is `wal_level`. In order to enable logical replication, `wal_level` must be set to `logical` on both the provider and subscriber nodes. Additionally, `pglogical` should also be added to `shared_preload_libraries` to perform logical replication.

On the new cluster, if the databases are not created yet, create the empty databases and create the extension in each of the databases being enabled for logical replication as seen in *step 3*.

Upgrading to PostgreSQL 13 using the pglogical extension

In the previous recipe, we saw how the `pglogical` extension can be installed to perform logical replication between two PostgreSQL servers. Streaming replication does not allow replication between two different Postgres major versions. For this reason, we can use logical replication to perform replication between two different PostgreSQL versions to perform a migration without huge downtime. As an example, we could configure logical replication between the PostgreSQL 9.6 and 12 versions using the `pglogical` extension. As long as all the tables have primary keys, this procedure should work. In this recipe, we shall discuss the steps involved in performing a logical replication between multiple PostgreSQL versions using the `pglogical` extension.

Getting ready

In order to proceed with this approach, we need to have the `pglogical` extension installed in both the old and the new version of the PostgreSQL servers. We can use `pglogical` to copy the pre-existing data from the old to the new cluster or we can use a parallel `pg_dump` and `pg_restore` to configure the replication faster. Once the already-existing data is copied, `pglogical` should be automatically able to catch up with replication using the WAL segments.

How to do it...

We will do this using the following steps:

1. Create a provider node using the `pglogical.create_node` function on the old cluster:

```
$ /usr/pgsql-9.6/bin/psql -d percona -c "SELECT
pglogical.create_node(node_name := 'providernode', dsn :=
'host=localhost port=5432 dbname=percona user=postgres
password=secret')"
```

This results in the following output:

```
percona=# SELECT pglogical.create_node(node_name := 'providernode',
dsn := 'host=localhost port=5432 dbname=percona user=postgres
password=secret');
 create_node
```

```
-------------
206982618
(1 row)
```

2. Copy the schema (DDL) of the database from the old cluster to the new cluster. Run the following command from either the old or the new cluster:

```
$ /usr/pgsql-13/bin/pg_dump -h <old_cluster_ip> -p 5432 -d percona
-Fc -s -U postgres | /usr/pgsql-13/bin/pg_restore -d percona -h
<new_cluster_ip> -p 5432 -U postgres
```

3. Add tables to the replication set. A subscriber node (on PostgreSQL 13) could replicate these tables from the provider node (on PostgreSQL 9.6). Substitute all the schema names that contain the tables that need to be replicated to the new cluster:

```
$ /usr/pgsql-9.6/bin/psql -d percona -c "SELECT
pglogical.replication_set_add_all_tables('default',ARRAY['public','
scott','tiger'])"
```

We will see errors for all the tables that do not contain primary keys:

```
$ /usr/pgsql-9.6/bin/psql -d percona -c "SELECT
pglogical.replication_set_add_all_tables('default',ARRAY['scott']);
"

 ERROR: table bar cannot be added to replication set default
 DETAIL: table does not have PRIMARY KEY and given replication set
is configured to replicate UPDATEs and/or DELETEs
 HINT: Add a PRIMARY KEY to the table
```

4. Validate the provider node creation and the list of tables added to the replication set:

```
$ /usr/pgsql-9.6/bin/psql -d percona -c "select * from
pglogical.node"
$ /usr/pgsql-9.6/bin/psql -d percona -c "select * from
pglogical.replication_set_table"
```

This results in the following output:

```
$ /usr/pgsql-9.6/bin/psql -d percona -c "select * from
pglogical.node"
 node_id | node_name
-----------+--------------
 206982618 | providernode
 (1 row)
```

```
$ /usr/pgsql-9.6/bin/psql -d percona -c "select * from
pglogical.replication_set_table"
 set_id | set_reloid | set_att_list | set_row_filter
------------+------------+--------------+----------------
 1142164937 | scott.emp | |
 1142164937 | tiger.emp | |
(2 rows)
```

5. Create the subscriber node using the `pglogical.create_node` function on the new cluster:

```
$ /usr/pgsql-13/bin/psql -d percona -c "SELECT
pglogical.create_node(node_name := 'subscriber1',dsn :=
'host=localhost port=5432 dbname=percona user=postgres
password=secret')"
```

6. Enable replication along with the copy of the existing data by creating the subscription:

```
$ /usr/pgsql-13/bin/psql -d percona -c "SELECT
pglogical.create_subscription(subscription_name :=
'subscription1',provider_dsn := 'host=old_cluster_IP port=5432
dbname=percona user=postgres password=secret'
,synchronize_structure:= true)"
```

How it works...

Assuming that the `pglogical` extension has been installed and created using the previous recipe, we shall continue creating a provider node using the commands shown in *step 1*. We can replace the database name, username, and password appropriately in the DSN. Before proceeding to the next steps to enable replication, ensure that the schema of the database(s) on the old cluster exists on the new cluster. This is can be done by performing a schema-only dump and restore using `pg_dump/pg_restore` as seen in *step 2*. The next step is to add all the tables or selected tables to the replication set using the command specified in *step 2*. We could pass multiple schemas in a single command and all the tables that have primary keys will be automatically added to the replication set. In order to see the list of tables that have been added to the replication set, we could use the commands seen in *step 4*.

To add a single table or remove a single table from the replication set, the following commands can be used:

```
select pglogical.replication_set_remove_table('default','scott.emp');
select
pglogical.replication_set_add_table('default','scott.emp'::regclass::oid);
```

After adding tables to the replication set, we could create the subscriber node by running the command seen in *step 5* on the new cluster. Once the subscriber node is created, we can use the command seen in *step 6* to create a subscription. In this step, we could see `synchronize_structure` set to `true`. This means that the existing data in PostgreSQL 9.6 (or the old cluster) should be copied sequentially (table by table). Then the replication continues for the changes that have happened since the data copy. So technically, this is very simple as `pglogical` will take care of copying the data and also continue replication from where it has to start automatically.

In order to speed up this process, we may stop writes to the old cluster and start a parallel `pg_dump` job. Once the restore is completed in parallel, we could create the subscription and start the writes so that the replication can continue from the time the subscription was created. But this time, we should set `synchronize_structure` to `false` as the pre-existing data of the old cluster has already been copied through `pg_dump` and `pg_restore`.

Once the replication is intact, we can shut down the application connecting to the old cluster and switch the connections to the new cluster. This way, we have finished the upgrade with a minimalistic downtime.

Upgrading to PostgreSQL 13 using logical replication and logical decoding

Starting from PostgreSQL 10, we have logical replication built into the PostgreSQL source. This way, we can perform replication between PostgreSQL 10 and later using built-in logical replication and do not need to rely on the `pglogical` extension. In this recipe, we shall see the steps involved in configuring logical replication between PostgreSQL 10 and PostgreSQL 13 so that the upgrade can happen with less downtime.

Getting ready

In order to use built-in logical replication to replicate to PostgreSQL 13, the old cluster should be using PostgreSQL 10 or 11. This type of replication can be used to replicate all the tables. However, we need to set the replica identity for those tables that do not contain any primary keys.

If there is no primary key, use either a unique index that has *no null values* or the entire row:

```
ALTER TABLE sales REPLICA IDENTITY USING INDEX unique_index_name;
ALTER TABLE sales REPLICA IDENTITY FULL;
```

How to do it...

We will do this using the following steps:

1. Set `wal_level` to `logical` on both the old and new clusters. This requires a restart of the database cluster.

   Run the following commands on the old cluster with PostgreSQL 10 or later:

   ```
   $ psql -c "ALTER SYSTEM SET wal_level TO 'logical'"
   $ pg_ctl -D /var/lib/pgsql/10/data restart -mf
   ```

   Run the following commands on the new cluster with PostgreSQL 13:

   ```
   $ psql -c "ALTER SYSTEM SET wal_level TO 'logical'"
   $ pg_ctl -D /var/lib/pgsql/13/data restart -mf
   ```

2. Create a publication for the tables that need to be replicated from the old to the new cluster.

   The following commands need to be performed on the old cluster running on PostgreSQL 10:

   ```
   $ /usr/pgsql-10/bin/psql -d percona -c "CREATE PUBLICATION percpub
   FOR ALL TABLES"
   ```

   For adding selected tables in the database, use the following command:

   ```
   $ /usr/pgsql-10/bin/psql -d percona -c "CREATE PUBLICATION percpub
   FOR TABLE scott.employee scott.departments"
   ```

3. Copy the schema (DDL) of the database from the old cluster to the new cluster. Run the following command from either the old or the new cluster:

```
$ /usr/pgsql-13/bin/pg_dump -h <old_cluster_ip> -p 5432 -d percona
-Fc -s -U postgres | /usr/pgsql-13/bin/pg_restore -d percona -h
<new_cluster_ip> -p 5432 -U postgres
```

4. Create a subscription on the database of the new cluster so that the logical replication can be enabled from the old to the new cluster using the publication specified:

```
$ /usr/pgsql-13/bin/psql -d percona -c "CREATE SUBSCRIPTION percsub
CONNECTION 'host=publisher_server_ip dbname=percona user=postgres
password=secret port=5432' PUBLICATION percpub"
```

Here, the publisher server is the old cluster. The subscriber is the new cluster.

The preceding command also copies the pre-existing data from the tables. If the copy of the pre-existing data must be disabled, the following syntax can be used. It will only start copying the changes to the publisher since the time the command started:

```
$ /usr/pgsql-13/bin/psql -d percona -c "CREATE SUBSCRIPTION percsub
CONNECTION 'host=publisher_server_ip dbname=percona user=postgres
password=oracle port=5432' PUBLICATION percpub WITH (copy_data =
false)"
```

5. Monitor the replication lag using the following command on the publishing node:

```
$ /usr/pgsql-13/bin/psql
\x
select * from pg_stat_replication;
```

How it works...

In order to enable logical replication, `wal_level` must be set to logical on both the old and new clusters. This requires a restart of the database cluster as seen in *step 1*. The only step that needs to be performed on the old cluster is the command seen in *step 2*. Here, we are creating a publication to which all the tables in the database are being added to the publication. We could also add a list of selected tables but not all, as seen in *step 2*, but that may be rare for the purpose of database upgrades.

Once the publication is created, we should copy the schema (DDL) of the database in the old cluster to the new cluster. This can be done using `pg_dump` and `pg_restore`, as seen in *step 3*. After the schema dump/restore is completed, we need to create a subscription on the new cluster that is given the details of the old cluster (or the publisher node) and the publication name, as seen in *step 4*.

In the command to create a subscription, `copy_data` is set to `true` by default. This means that the already-existing data should be copied first and the replication should continue once the data copy is completed. In order to speed up this process, we may stop writes to the old cluster and start a parallel `pg_dump` job. Once the restore is completed in parallel, we could create the subscription and start the writes so that the replication can continue from the time the subscription has been created. But this time, we should set `copy_data` to `false` as the pre-existing data of the old cluster has already been copied through `pg_dump` and `pg_restore`.

The replication status will be visible through the `pg_stat_replication` view. We could run the command, as seen in *step 5*, to validate the replication status between the old and new clusters. Once the replication is intact, we could shut down the application connecting to the old cluster and switch the connections to the new cluster. This way, we have finished the upgrade with minimal downtime.

Updating the minor version of PostgreSQL 13

Every 3 months, the PostgreSQL community releases minor version updates that are available for all the supported PostgreSQL versions. Let's say that we are using PostgreSQL 13.1 but a new minor version, PostgreSQL 13.2, has been released. In this recipe, we shall see how a minor version upgrade can be performed when using PostgreSQL 13.

Getting ready

In order to perform a minor version PostgreSQL 13 update, we should have a database server with an already-running PostgreSQL 13 cluster. To use `yum` or `apt`, we should have the `yum` or `apt` repository configured.

How to do it...

We will do this using the following steps:

1. Shut down the PostgreSQL cluster:

    ```
    $ /usr/pgsql-13/bin/pg_ctl -D /var/lib/pgsql/13/data stop -mf
    ```

2. Get all the Postgres packages installed in the existing PostgreSQL server:

    ```
    $ rpm -qa | grep postgres
    postgresql13-13.1-3PGDG.rhel7.x86_64
    postgresql13-server-13.1-3PGDG.rhel7.x86_64
    postgresql13-libs-13.1-3PGDG.rhel7.x86_64
    postgresql13-contrib-13.1-3PGDG.rhel7.x86_64
    ```

3. Install the latest minor version using yum or apt for all the packages installed.

    For CentOS/Red Hat, use the following:

    ```
    $ sudo yum install postgresql13-server postgresql13-contrib
    ```

    For Ubuntu/Debian, use the following:

    ```
    $ sudo apt-get update postgresql13-server postgresql13-contrib
    ```

4. Start the PostgreSQL cluster:

    ```
    $ /usr/pgsql-13/bin/pg_ctl -D /var/lib/pgsql/13/data stop -mf
    ```

5. Validate the minor version update:

    ```
    $ /usr/pgsql-13/bin/psql -c "select version()"
    ```

    This results in the following output:

    ```
    $ /usr/pgsql-13/bin/psql -c "select version()"
     version
    ----------------------------------------------------------------
    ---------------------------------------------
     PostgreSQL 13.1 on x86_64-pc-linux-gnu, compiled by gcc (GCC)
    4.8.5 20150623 (Red Hat 4.8.5-39), 64-bit
     (1 row)
    ```

How it works...

Updating a PostgreSQL minor version is a very simple procedure. The first step is to shut down the PostgreSQL cluster running on the database servers, as seen in *step 1*. Once the database is down, we need to look at the packages that are installed and use `yum` or `apt` to get a list of the latest PostgreSQL packages, as seen in *step 2*. After installing the latest packages, we can start the Postgres cluster and notice that the version has been updated successfully, as seen in *steps 3* and *4*. The application can restart the connectivity to the databases once *step 4* is completed successfully.

Packt.com

Subscribe to our online digital library for full access to over 7,000 books and videos, as well as industry leading tools to help you plan your personal development and advance your career. For more information, please visit our website.

Why subscribe?

- Spend less time learning and more time coding with practical eBooks and Videos from over 4,000 industry professionals

- Improve your learning with Skill Plans built especially for you

- Get a free eBook or video every month

- Fully searchable for easy access to vital information

- Copy and paste, print, and bookmark content

Did you know that Packt offers eBook versions of every book published, with PDF and ePub files available? You can upgrade to the eBook version at www.packt.com and as a print book customer, you are entitled to a discount on the eBook copy. Get in touch with us at customercare@packtpub.com for more details.

At www.packt.com, you can also read a collection of free technical articles, sign up for a range of free newsletters, and receive exclusive discounts and offers on Packt books and eBooks.

Other Books You May Enjoy

If you enjoyed this book, you may be interested in these other books by Packt:

Learn PostgreSQL
Luca Ferrari , Enrico Pirozzi

ISBN: 978-1-83898-528-8

- Interact with transaction boundaries using server-side programming
- Identify bottlenecks to maintain your database efficiently
- Create and manage extensions to add new functionalities to your cluster
- Choose the best index type for each situation
- Use online tools to set up a memory configuration that will suit most databases
- Explore how Postgres can be used in multi-instance environments to provide high-availability, redundancy, and scalability

Mastering PostgreSQL 13 - Fourth Edition

Hans-Jürgen Schönig

ISBN: 978-1-80056-749-8

- Get well versed with advanced SQL functions in PostgreSQL 13
- Get to grips with administrative tasks such as log file management and monitoring
- Work with stored procedures and manage backup and recovery
- Employ replication and failover techniques to reduce data loss
- Perform database migration from Oracle to PostgreSQL with ease
- Replicate PostgreSQL database systems to create backups and scale your database
- Manage and improve server security to protect your data
- Troubleshoot your PostgreSQL instance to find solutions to common and not-so-common problems

Packt is searching for authors like you

If you're interested in becoming an author for Packt, please visit `authors.packtpub.com` and apply today. We have worked with thousands of developers and tech professionals, just like you, to help them share their insight with the global tech community. You can make a general application, apply for a specific hot topic that we are recruiting an author for, or submit your own idea.

Leave a review - let other readers know what you think

Please share your thoughts on this book with others by leaving a review on the site that you bought it from. If you purchased the book from Amazon, please leave us an honest review on this book's Amazon page. This is vital so that other potential readers can see and use your unbiased opinion to make purchasing decisions, we can understand what our customers think about our products, and our authors can see your feedback on the title that they have worked with Packt to create. It will only take a few minutes of your time, but is valuable to other potential customers, our authors, and Packt. Thank you!

Index